The Five]
Six Na
1970–2009
A Complete Record

IAN BRONDERSON

PARKBENCH PUBLICATIONS

Copyright © 2009 by Ian Bronderson

Published in Great Britain by Parkbench Publications,
PO Box 1081, Belfast BT1 9EP

A CIP catalogue record for this title is available from the British Library

ISBN 978-0-9562725-1-5

Designed and typeset by Bookcraft Ltd,
Stroud, Gloucestershire

Printed and bound in Great Britain by
CPI Antony Rowe, Chippenham and Eastbourne

1970

SCOTLAND 9 FRANCE 11; at Murrayfield; 10th of January 1970

15	Smith [TRY]	15	Villepreux
14	Biggar	14	Bourgarel
13	Frame	13	Marot
12	Rea	12	Lux [TRY]
11	Hinshelwood	11	Sillieres
10	Robertson	10	Paries [DG, CON]
9	Connell	9	Sutra
8	Telfer (c)	8	Dauga [TRY]
7	Arneil	7	Carrere (c)
6	Lauder	6	Viard
5	Brown [2 PENs]	5	Cester
4	Stagg	4	Bastiat
3	Carmichael	3	Iracabal
2	Laidlaw	2	Benesis
1	McLauchlan	1	Azarete

Comments: The away team failed to score in the second half but their 11-6 interval lead was not overturned by the Scots.

FRANCE 8 IRELAND 0; at Stade Colombes; 24th of January 1970

15	Villepreux	15	Kiernan (c)
14	Bourgarel	14	Duggan
13	Marot	13	Bresnihan
12	Lux	12	Gibson
11	Sillieres [TRY]	11	Brown
10	Paries [DG, CON]	10	McGann
9	Sutra	9	Young
8	Dauga	8	Goodall
7	Carrere (c)	7	Slattery
6	Biemouret	6	Lamont
5	Cester	5	McBride
4	Bastiat	4	Molloy
3	Iracabal	3	O'Callaghan
2	Benesis	2	Kennedy
1	Azarete	1	Millar

Comments: This close encounter was decided by a Jean Sillieres try whilst Lucien Paries kicked a conversion and a drop goal against a toothless Ireland.

WALES 18 SCOTLAND 9; at Cardiff; 7th of February 1970

15	Williams. J		15	Smith. I
14	Daniel [TRY, CON]		14	Smith. M
13	Dawes [TRY]		13	Frame
12	Bennett		12	Rea
11	Hall		11	Hinshelwood
10	John		10	Robertson [TRY, DG]
9	Edwards (c) [2 CONs]		9	Young
8	Davies		8	Telfer (c)
7	Hughes		7	Arneil
6	Morris [TRY]		6	Lauder [PEN]
5	Thomas		5	Brown
4	Evans		4	Stagg
3	Llewelyn [TRY]		3	Carmichael
2	Perrins		2	Laidlaw
1	Williams. D		1	McLauchlan

Comments: Scotland actually led 9-6 at half-time. Mike Smith, Robert Young and Laurie Daniel made their debut. Daniel scored a try and never played again.

ENGLAND 9 IRELAND 3; at Twickenham; 14th of February 1970

15	Hiller (c) [2 DGs]		15	Kiernan (c) [PEN]
14	Fielding		14	Duggan
13	Spencer		13	Bresnihan
12	Duckham		12	Gibson
11	Hale		11	O'Reilly
10	Shackleton [TRY]		10	McGann
9	Starmer-Smith		9	Young
8	Taylor		8	Goodall
7	Bucknall		7	Slattery
6	West		6	Lamont
5	Larter		5	McBride
4	Davis		4	Molloy
3	Fairbrother		3	O'Callaghan
2	Pullin		2	Kennedy
1	Stevens		1	Millar

Comments: Tom Kiernan's penalty was the only score of the first half. Roger Shackleton sealed a home win with a late try.

ENGLAND 13 WALES 17; at Twickenham; 28th of February 1970

15	Hiller (c) [PEN, 2 CONs]	15	Williams. J [TRY, CON]
14	Novak [TRY]	14	Watkins
13	Spencer	13	Dawes
12	Duckham [TRY]	12	Raybould
11	Hale	11	Hall
10	Shackleton	10	John [TRY, DG]
9	Starmer-Smith	9	Edwards (c)
8	Taylor	8	Davies [TRY]
7	Bucknall	7	Hughes
6	West	6	Morris
5	Larter	5	Thomas
4	Davis	4	Evans
3	Fairbrother	3	Llewelyn
2	Pullin	2	Young
1	Stevens	1	Williams. D

Comments: England actually led 13-3 at the interval. Michael Novak and Ray Hopkins both scored debut tries. The latter replaced Edwards to win his only cap.

IRELAND 16 SCOTLAND 11; at Lansdowne Road; 28th of February 1970

15	Kiernan (c) [2 CONs]	15	Smith. I [CON]
14	Duggan	14	Smith. M [TRY]
13	Bresnihan	13	Frame
12	Gibson [TRY]	12	Rea
11	Brown [TRY]	11	Biggar
10	McGann	10	Robertson [DG]
9	Young	9	Paterson
8	Goodall [TRY]	8	Telfer (c)
7	Slattery	7	Arneil
6	Lamont	6	Lauder [TRY]
5	McBride	5	Brown
4	Molloy [TRY]	4	Stagg
3	O'Callaghan	3	Carmichael
2	Kennedy	2	Laidlaw
1	Millar	1	Suddon

Comments: The men in green crossed the try-line twice in each half. The 5 points thin margin is explained by the low value of 3 points for a try in those times.

IRELAND 14 WALES 0; at Lansdowne Road; 14th of March 1970

15	Kiernan (c) [PEN, CON]		15	Williams. J
14	Duggan [TRY]		14	Watkins
13	Bresnihan		13	Dawes
12	Gibson		12	Raybould
11	Brown		11	Hughes. K
10	McGann [DG]		10	John
9	Young		9	Edwards (c)
8	Goodall [TRY]		8	Davies
7	Slattery		7	Hughes. D
6	Lamont		6	Morris
5	McBride		5	Thomas
4	Molloy		4	Evans
3	O'Callaghan		3	Llewelyn
2	Kennedy		2	Young
1	Millar		1	Williams. D

Comments: Wales's Triple Crown bid was well and truly dashed as Keith Hughes made his debut for the visitors.

SCOTLAND 14 ENGLAND 5; at Murrayfield; 21st of March 1970

15	Smith. I		15	Hiller (c) [CON]
14	Smith. M		14	Novak
13	Frame		13	Spencer [TRY]
12	Turner [TRY]		12	Duckham
11	Biggar [TRY]		11	Bulpitt
10	Robertson		10	Shackleton
9	Paterson		9	Starmer-Smith
8	Brown. P [2 PENs, CON]		8	Taylor
7	Arneil		7	Bucknall
6	Elliot		6	West
5	Brown. G		5	Larter
4	Stagg		4	Davis
3	Carmichael		3	Fairbrother
2	Laidlaw (c)		2	Pullin
1	Suddon		1	Stevens

Comments: Scotland led 6-0 at half-time. Mike Bulpitt won his only England cap while Barry Jackson came on as a replacement to win his first England cap.

WALES 11 FRANCE 6; at Cardiff; 4th of April 1970

15	Williams [2 PENs, CON]	15	Villepreux
14	Mathias	14	Cantoni [TRY]
13	Dawes (c)	13	Marot
12	Lewis	12	Lux
11	Shanklin	11	Bonal [TRY]
10	Bennett	10	Paries
9	Edwards	9	Puget
8	Davies	8	Dauga
7	Taylor	7	Carrere (c)
6	Morris [TRY]	6	Biemouret
5	Thomas	5	Cester
4	Gallacher	4	Bastiat
3	Llewelyn	3	Iracabal
2	Young	2	Benesis
1	Lloyd	1	Azarete

Comments: First caps were awarded to Gallacher and the backs Lewis, Mathias, Shanklin, and Cantoni. The latter scored a try, but there would be no Grand Slam.

FRANCE 35 ENGLAND 13; at Stade Colombes; 18th of April 1970

15	Villepreux [PEN, 4 CONs, DG]	15	Jorden [PEN, 2 CONs]
14	Bourgarel [TRY]	14	Fielding
13	Trillo [TRY]	13	Spencer [TRY]
12	Lux [TRY]	12	Duckham
11	Bonal [TRY]	11	Novak
10	Berot [TRY, DG]	10	Finlan
9	Pebeyre	9	Starmer-Smith
8	Dauga [TRY]	8	Redmond
7	Carrere (c)	7	Bucknall
6	Biemouret	6	Taylor (c) [TRY]
5	Cester	5	Larter
4	le Droff	4	Leadbetter
3	Iracabal	3	Fairbrother
2	Benesis	2	Pullin
1	Lasserre	1	Jackson

Comments: France were already 14-0 ahead at the interval. Jorden, Leadbetter, Redmond, and Pebeyre all made their debut in this annihilation.

1970 FINAL TABLE

		Points For	Points Against	Total Points
1ST	FRANCE	60	33	6
1ST	WALES	46	42	6
3RD	IRELAND	33	28	4
4TH	SCOTLAND	43	50	2
4TH	ENGLAND	40	69	2

Comments: France who shared the honours with Wales played 2 fixtures in January followed peculiarly by the next 2 in April.

THE INTERNATIONAL RUGBY HALL OF FAME

The following 23 players inducted into the Hall of Fame played at various times in the Five Nations/Six Nations since 1970:

Serge Blanco (France); inducted in 1997
Gareth Edwards (Wales); inducted in 1997
Mike Gibson (Ireland); inducted in 1997
Barry John (Wales); inducted in 1997
Willie-John McBride (Ireland); inducted in 1997
Jean-Pierre Rives (France); inducted in 1997
JPR Williams (Wales); inducted in 1997
Gerald Davies (Wales); inducted in 1999
Andy Irvine (Scotland); inducted in 1999
Philippe Sella (France); inducted in 1999
Gordon Brown (Scotland); inducted in 2001
Mervyn Davies (Wales); inducted in 2001
Bill Beaumont (England); inducted in 2003
Gavin Hastings (Scotland); inducted in 2003
Jo Maso (France); inducted in 2003
Phil Bennett (Wales); inducted in 2005
Martin Johnson (England); inducted in 2005
Ian McGeechan (Scotland); inducted in 2005
Keith Wood (Ireland); inducted in 2005
Ieuan Evans (Wales); inducted in 2007
Tom Kiernan (Ireland); inducted in 2007
Jason Leonard (England); inducted in 2007
Fergus Slattery (Ireland); inducted in 2007

1971

FRANCE 13 SCOTLAND 8; at Stade Colombes; 16th of January 1971

15	Villepreux [TRY, PEN, 2 CONs]	15	Smith [PEN]
14	Sillieres [TRY]	14	Steele [TRY]
13	Trillo	13	Frame
12	Lux	12	Rea
11	Cantoni	11	Biggar
10	Berot	10	Turner
9	Barrau	9	Paterson
8	Dauga (c)	8	Brown. P (c) [CON]
7	Viard	7	Arneil
6	Dubois	6	MacEwan
5	le Droff	5	Brown. G
4	Bastiat	4	McHarg
3	Etcheverry	3	Carmichael
2	Benesis	2	Laidlaw
1	Azarete	1	McLauchlan

Comments: First caps were awarded to Barrau, Dubois, Etcheverry, and MacEwan. This contest had been deadlocked at 3-3 at the halfway stage.

WALES 22 ENGLAND 6; at Cardiff; 16th of January 1971

15	Williams. J [PEN]	15	Rossborough [PEN]
14	Davies. G [2 TRIES]	14	Janion
13	Dawes (c)	13	Wardlow
12	Lewis	12	Spencer
11	Bevan [TRY]	11	Duckham
10	John [2 DGs]	10	Wright
9	Edwards	9	Page
8	Davies. M	8	Hannaford [TRY]
7	Taylor [2 CONs]	7	Neary
6	Morris	6	Bucknall (c)
5	Thomas	5	Ninnes
4	Roberts	4	Larter
3	Llewelyn	3	Fairbrother
2	Young	2	Pullin
1	Williams. D	1	Powell

Comments: First caps were awarded to Bevan and Roberts, while England had 7 debutants: Hannaford, Janion, Neary, Ninnes, Page, Rossborough, and Wright!

IRELAND 9 FRANCE 9; at Lansdowne Road; 30th of January 1971

15	Kiernan (c)	15	Villepreux [2 PENs]
14	Duggan	14	Sillieres
13	Bresnihan	13	Lux
12	Gibson	12	Trillo
11	Grant [TRY]	11	Cantoni
10	McGann	10	Berot [DG]
9	Young	9	Pebeyre
8	Hickie	8	Dauga (c)
7	Slattery	7	Viard
6	Hipwell	6	Quilis
5	Molloy	5	le Droff
4	McBride	4	Bastiat
3	Lynch	3	Etcheverry
2	Kennedy	2	Benesis
1	McLoughlin	1	Azarete

Comments: Two penalties from the substitute Barry O'Driscoll and a try from another debutant Edwin Grant ensured a draw. France had led 3-0 at half-time.

SCOTLAND 18 WALES 19; at Murrayfield; 6th of February 1971

15	Smith	15	Williams. J
14	Steele	14	Davies. G [TRY]
13	Frame	13	Dawes (c)
12	Rea [TRY]	12	Hall
11	Biggar	11	Bevan
10	Turner	10	John [TRY, PEN, CON]
9	Paterson	9	Edwards [TRY]
8	Brown. P (c) [4 PENs]	8	Davies. M
7	Arneil	7	Taylor [TRY, CON]
6	MacEwan	6	Morris
5	Brown. G	5	Thomas
4	McHarg	4	Roberts
3	Carmichael [TRY]	3	Llewelyn
2	Laidlaw	2	Young
1	McLauchlan	1	Williams. D

Comments: Gerald Davies scored a last-gasp try. However it all rested on John Taylor who proceeded to slot home 'the greatest conversion since St. Paul'.

IRELAND 6 ENGLAND 9; at Lansdowne Road; 13th of February 1971

15	O'Driscoll		15	Hiller [3 PENs]
14	Duggan [TRY]		14	Janion
13	Bresnihan		13	Spencer (c)
12	Gibson (c)		12	Wardlow
11	Grant [TRY]		11	Duckham
10	McGann		10	Wright
9	Young		9	Page
8	Hickie		8	Hannaford
7	Slattery		7	Neary
6	Hipwell		6	Bucknall
5	Molloy		5	Larter
4	McBride		4	Horton
3	Lynch		3	Fairbrother
2	Kennedy		2	Pullin
1	McLoughlin		1	Powell

Comments: Bob Hiller's three first-half penalties ensured victory, but nowadays in these 'enlightened times', Ireland's 2 tries would have yielded them victory.

ENGLAND 14 FRANCE 14; at Twickenham; 27th of February 1971

15	Hiller (c) [TRY, 3 PENs, CON]		15	Villepreux [PEN, CON]
14	Janion		14	Sillieres
13	Wardlow		13	Bertranne [TRY]
12	Duckham		12	Lux
11	Glover		11	Cantoni [TRY]
10	Wright		10	Berot [DG]
9	Page		9	Barrau
8	Hannaford		8	Dauga
7	Neary		7	Carrere (c)
6	Bucknall		6	Yachvili
5	Larter		5	Spanghero. C
4	Horton		4	Spanghero. W
3	Fairbrother		3	Lasserre
2	Pullin		2	Benesis
1	Powell		1	Azarete

Comments: Hiller scored all of England's points again, but a second-half French revival denied England both points. Roland Bertranne scored a try on his debut.

SCOTLAND 5 IRELAND 17; at Murrayfield; 27th of February 1971

15	Smith		15	O'Driscoll
14	Steele		14	Duggan [2 TRIES]
13	Frame [TRY]		13	Bresnihan
12	Biggar		12	Gibson (c) [2 PENs, CON]
11	Hannah		11	Grant [TRY]
10	Turner		10	McGann
9	Paterson		9	Young
8	Brown. P (c) [CON]		8	Hickie
7	Arneil		7	Slattery
6	MacEwan		6	Hipwell
5	Brown. G		5	Molloy
4	McHarg		4	McBride
3	Carmichael		3	Lynch
2	Laidlaw		2	Kennedy
1	McLauchlan		1	McLoughlin

Comments: Ronald Hannah made his only Scotland appearance as his team were well beaten in this 'battle of the celts'.

WALES 23 IRELAND 9; at Cardiff; 13th of March 1971

15	Williams. J		15	O'Driscoll
14	Davies. G [2 TRIES]		14	Duggan
13	Dawes (c)		13	Bresnihan
12	Lewis		12	Gibson (c) [3 PENs]
11	Bevan		11	Grant
10	John [2 PENs, DG, CON]		10	McGann
9	Edwards [2 TRIES]		9	Young
8	Davies. M		8	Hickie
7	Taylor		7	Slattery
6	Morris		6	Hipwell
5	Thomas		5	Molloy
4	Roberts		4	McBride
3	Llewelyn		3	Lynch
2	Young		2	Kennedy
1	Williams. D		1	McLoughlin

Comments: The elusive Gerald Davies was among the try scorers again as Wales emphatically helped themselves to another Triple Crown.

ENGLAND 15 SCOTLAND 16; at Twickenham; 20th of March 1971

15	Hiller [TRY, 3 PENs]	15	Brown. A
14	Janion	14	Steele
13	Wardlow	13	Frame
12	Spencer (c)	12	Rea [TRY]
11	Duckham	11	Biggar
10	Cowman	10	Turner
9	Page	9	Paterson [TRY, DG]
8	Taylor	8	Brown. P (c) [TRY, 2 CONs]
7	Neary [TRY]	7	Arneil
6	Bucknall	6	MacEwan
5	Horton	5	Brown. G
4	Larter	4	McHarg
3	Cotton	3	Carmichael
2	Pullin	2	Dunlop
1	Powell	1	McLauchlan

Comments: Brown, Cotton, Cowman, Dunlop, and the Scotland substitute Turk all made debut appearances as the Scots squeezed home in this Calcutta Cup encounter.

FRANCE 5 WALES 9; at Stade Colombes; 27th of March 1971

15	Villepreux [CON]	15	Williams. J
14	Bourgarel	14	Davies. G
13	Bertranne	13	Dawes (c)
12	Lux	12	Lewis
11	Cantoni	11	Bevan
10	Berot	10	John [TRY, PEN]
9	Barrau	9	Edwards [TRY]
8	Dauga [TRY]	8	Davies. M
7	Carrere (c)	7	Taylor
6	Biemouret	6	Morris
5	Spanghero. C	5	Thomas
4	Spanghero. W	4	Roberts
3	Lasserre	3	Llewelyn
2	Benesis	2	Young
1	Iracabal	1	Williams. D

Comments: The ace half-backs of Barry John and Gareth Edwards were the heroes as Wales came from 5-3 behind at the interval to claim the coveted Grand Slam.

1971 FINAL TABLE

		Points For	Points Against	Total Points
1ST	WALES	73	38	8
2ND	FRANCE	41	40	4
3RD	IRELAND	41	46	3
3RD	ENGLAND	44	58	3
5TH	SCOTLAND	47	64	2

Comments: This was Wales's first clean sweep since 1952 and their sixth in total.

THE BRITISH AND IRISH LIONS, 1970 TO 1989

WON 9-3 v New Zealand; in Dunedin; 26th of June 1971
LOST 22-12 v New Zealand; in Christchurch; 10th of July 1971
WON 13-3 v New Zealand; in Wellington; 31st of July 1971
DREW 14-14 v New Zealand; in Auckland; 14th of August 1971
WON 12-3 v South Africa; in Cape Town; 8th of June 1974
WON 28-9 v South Africa; in Pretoria; 22nd of June 1974
WON 26-9 v South Africa; in Port Elizabeth; 13th of July 1974
DREW 13-13 v South Africa; in Johannesburg; 27th of July 1974
LOST 16-12 v New Zealand; in Wellington; 18th of June 1977
WON 13-9 v New Zealand; in Christchurch; 9th of July 1977
LOST 19-7 v New Zealand; in Dunedin; 30th of July 1977
LOST 10-9 v New Zealand; in Auckland; 13th of August 1977
LOST 26-22 v South Africa; in Cape Town; 31st of May 1980
LOST 26-19 v South Africa; in Bloemfontein; 14th of June 1980
LOST 12-10 v South Africa; in Port Elizabeth; 28th of June 1980
WON 17-13 v South Africa; in Pretoria; 12th of July 1980
LOST 16-12 v New Zealand; in Christchurch; 4th of June 1983
LOST 9-0 v New Zealand; in Wellington; 18th of June 1983
LOST 15-8 v New Zealand; in Dunedin; 2nd of July 1983
LOST 38-6 v New Zealand; in Auckland; 16th of July 1983
LOST 30-12 v Australia; in Sydney; 1st of July 1989
WON 19-12 v Australia; in Brisbane; 8th of July 1989
WON 19-18 v Australia; in Sydney; 15th of July 1989

1972

SCOTLAND 20 FRANCE 9; at Murrayfield; 15th of January 1972

15	Brown. A	15	Villepreux [PEN, CON]
14	Steele	14	Bertranne
13	Frame [TRY]	13	Trillo
12	Renwick [TRY]	12	Lux
11	Biggar	11	Cantoni
10	Telfer [TRY, DG]	10	Berot
9	McCrae	9	Aguirre
8	Brown. P (c) [PEN, CON]	8	Spanghero
7	Arneil	7	Saisset
6	MacEwan	6	Boffelli
5	Brown. G	5	Dauga (c) [TRY]
4	McHarg	4	Bastiat
3	Carmichael	3	Martin
2	Clark	2	Benesis
1	McLauchlan	1	Vaquerin

Comments: Robert Clark and substitute scrum-half Alan Lawson won their first caps, while Jim Renwick scored a try on his debut in this comfortable home win.

ENGLAND 3 WALES 12; at Twickenham; 15th of January 1972

15	Hiller (c) [PEN]	15	Williams [TRY]
14	Janion	14	Davies. G
13	Beese	13	Bergiers
12	Duckham	12	Lewis
11	Fielding	11	Bevan
10	Old	10	John [2 PENs, CON]
9	Webster	9	Edwards
8	Ripley	8	Davies. M
7	Neary	7	Taylor
6	Dixon	6	Morris
5	Ralston	5	Evans
4	Brinn	4	Thomas
3	Burton	3	Llewelyn
2	Pullin	2	Young
1	Stevens	1	Lloyd (c)

Comments: Roy Bergiers made his debut for Wales while the hosts paraded six more new recruits, namely Beese, Brinn, Burton, Old, Ripley, and Webster.

FRANCE 9 IRELAND 14; at Stade Colombes; 29th of January 1972

15	Villepreux [PEN, CON]		15	Kiernan (c) [2 PENs]
14	Bertranne		14	Grace
13	Dourthe		13	Gibson
12	Lux [TRY]		12	Flynn
11	Cantoni		11	McMaster
10	Berot		10	McGann
9	Astre		9	Moloney [TRY]
8	Buonomo		8	Hickie
7	Saisset		7	Slattery
6	Boffelli		6	McKinney
5	Dauga (c)		5	Feighery
4	Esteve		4	McBride
3	Martin		3	Lynch
2	Benesis		2	Kennedy
1	Vaquerin		1	McLoughlin [TRY]

Comments: Feighery, Grace, McKinney, and McMaster all won their first caps, while another debutant Moloney scored a try in this rare and historic win in Paris.

WALES 35 SCOTLAND 12; at Cardiff; 5th of February 1972

15	Williams		15	Brown. A
14	Davies. G [TRY]		14	Steele
13	Bergiers [TRY]		13	Frame
12	Lewis		12	Renwick [PEN]
11	Bevan		11	Biggar
10	John [3 PENs, 3 CONs]		10	Telfer
9	Edwards [2 TRIES]		9	Paterson
8	Davies. M		8	Brown. P (c) [PEN, CON]
7	Taylor [TRY]		7	Arneil
6	Morris		6	MacEwan
5	Evans		5	Brown. G
4	Thomas		4	Barnes
3	Llewelyn		3	Carmichael
2	Young		2	Clark [TRY]
1	Lloyd (c)		1	McLauchlan

Comments: Ian Barnes and the replacement Lewis Dick collected first caps for Scotland, but their team was trounced by the mighty dragon, courtesy of five tries.

ENGLAND 12 IRELAND 16; at Twickenham; 12th of February 1972

15 Hiller (c) [2 PENs, CON]	15 Kiernan (c) [PEN, CON]
14 Fielding	14 Grace [TRY]
13 Beese	13 Gibson
12 Duckham	12 Flynn [TRY]
11 Webb	11 McMaster
10 Old	10 McGann [DG]
9 Webster	9 Moloney
8 Ripley	8 Hickie
7 Neary	7 Slattery
6 Dixon	6 McKinney
5 Ralston [TRY]	5 Feighery
4 Brinn	4 McBride
3 Burton	3 Lynch
2 Pullin	2 Kennedy
1 Stevens	1 McLoughlin

Comments: Second-half tries from Tom Grace and the veteran Michael Flynn helped overturn England's lead. However, this would be Ireland's last outing in 1972.

FRANCE 37 ENGLAND 12; at Stade Colombes; 26th of February 1972

15 Villepreux [PEN, 5 CONs]	15 Knight
14 Duprat [2 TRIES]	14 Fielding
13 Maso	13 Beese [TRY]
12 Lux [TRY]	12 Duckham
11 Sillieres [TRY]	11 Webb
10 Berot	10 Old [2 PENs, CON]
9 Barrau	9 Weston
8 Spanghero. W (c)	8 Ripley
7 Skrela	7 Neary
6 Biemouret [TRY]	6 Dixon (c)
5 Spanghero. C [TRY]	5 Ralston
4 Esteve	4 Barton
3 Iracabal	3 Burton
2 Benesis	2 Pullin
1 Azarete	1 Stevens

Comments: Hapless England were put to the sword in an unhappy debut for Lionel Weston and Peter Knight. Nicholas Martin came off the bench for his only cap.

SCOTLAND 23 ENGLAND 9; at Murrayfield; 18th of March 1972

15	Brown. A [PEN]	15	Knight
14	Steele	14	Fielding
13	Frame	13	Janion
12	Renwick	12	Evans
11	Dick	11	Duckham
10	Telfer [DG]	10	Old [3 PENs]
9	Lawson	9	Weston
8	Brown. P (c) [TRY, 3 PENs]	8	Ripley
7	Arneil	7	Neary
6	MacEwan [TRY]	6	Dixon (c)
5	Brown. G	5	Ralston
4	McHarg	4	Brinn
3	Carmichael	3	Burton
2	Clark	2	Pullin
1	McLauchlan	1	Stevens

Comments: Geoff Evans made his debut for the visitors but England suffered another rout with Nairn MacEwan scoring his only Scotland try in this tartan triumph.

WALES 20 FRANCE 6; at Cardiff; 25th of March 1972

15	Williams	15	Villepreux (c) [2 PENs]
14	Davies. G [TRY]	14	Duprat
13	Bergiers	13	Maso
12	Lewis	12	Lux
11	Bevan [TRY]	11	Sillieres
10	John [4 PENs]	10	Berot
9	Edwards	9	Barrau
8	Davies. M	8	Dauga
7	Taylor	7	Skrela
6	Morris	6	Biemouret
5	Evans	5	Spanghero
4	Thomas	4	Esteve
3	Llewelyn	3	Iracabal
2	Young	2	Benesis
1	Lloyd (c)	1	Azarete

Comments: Second-half tries from the Welsh wingers would have set up a Grand Slam showdown, but the 'fearless' Welsh refused to travel to strife-torn Ireland.

1972 FINAL TABLE

		Points For	Points Against	Total Points
1ST	WALES	67	21	6
2ND	IRELAND	30	21	4
2ND	SCOTLAND	55	53	4
4TH	FRANCE	61	66	2
5TH	ENGLAND	36	88	0

COMMENTS: Wales and Scotland refused to play in Ireland due to the violence there, so the Five Nations remained incomplete.

DID YOU KNOW?

Ireland's victory at the Stade Colombes was their last triumph on French soil in the Five Nations tournament. By the time that they won again in France 28 long years later, it was now the Six Nations championship. Furthermore, the win in 2000 was at the Stade de France. In the intervening period, the men in green paid twelve Five Nations visits to the Parc des Princes and left empty-handed on each occasion.

1973

FRANCE 16 SCOTLAND 13; at Parc des Princes; 13th of January 1973

15	Cantoni		15	Irvine
14	Trillo		14	Steele
13	Dourthe [TRY]		13	Forsyth
12	Lux		12	Renwick
11	Bourgarel		11	Shedden
10	Romeu [3 PENs, DG]		10	McGeechan [DG]
9	Barrau		9	Lawson [TRY]
8	Spanghero (c)		8	Brown (c) [2 PENs]
7	Biemouret		7	Lauder
6	Saisset		6	MacEwan
5	Esteve		5	Wright
4	Cester		4	McHarg
3	Iracabal		3	Carmichael
2	Lubrano		2	Clark
1	Vaquerin		1	McLauchlan

Comments: Ronald Wright made his only Scotland appearance in this narrow defeat. Claude Dourthe scored the only try for the hosts.

WALES 25 ENGLAND 9; at Cardiff; 20th of January 1973

15	Williams		15	Doble [2 PENs]
14	Davies. G [TRY]		14	Morley
13	Bergiers		13	Warfield
12	Lewis (c) [TRY]		12	Preece
11	Bevan [2 TRIES]		11	Duckham
10	Bennett [CON]		10	Cowman [DG]
9	Edwards [TRY]		9	Webster
8	Davies. M		8	Ripley
7	Taylor [PEN]		7	Neary
6	Morris		6	Watkins
5	Quinnell		5	Ralston
4	Thomas		4	Larter
3	Lloyd		3	Cotton
2	Young		2	Pullin (c)
1	Shaw		1	Stevens

Comments: John Bevan crossed the try-line twice in this five-try demolition of the next-door neighbours as Wales's mastery of England continued unrelentlessly.

SCOTLAND 10 WALES 9; at Murrayfield; 3rd of February 1973

15	Irvine	15	Williams
14	Steele [TRY]	14	Davies. G
13	McGeechan	13	Bergiers
12	Forsyth	12	Lewis (c)
11	Shedden	11	Bevan
10	Telfer [TRY]	10	Bennett [2 PENs]
9	Morgan [CON]	9	Edwards
8	Strachan	8	Davies. M
7	Millican	7	Taylor [PEN]
6	MacEwan	6	Morris
5	Brown	5	Quinnell
4	McHarg	4	Thomas
3	Carmichael	3	Lloyd
2	Clark	2	Young
1	McLauchlan (c)	1	Shaw

Comments: John Millican and Doug Morgan won their first caps as the Welsh this time succumbed to a slender defeat. All Scotland's points came in the first half.

IRELAND 18 ENGLAND 9; at Lansdowne Road; 10th of February 1973

15	Kiernan (c)	15	Jorden [PEN, CON]
14	Grace [TRY]	14	Morley
13	Milliken [TRY]	13	Warfield
12	Gibson	12	Preese
11	McMaster	11	Duckham
10	McGann [PEN, DG, 2 CONs]	10	Cowman
9	Moloney	9	Smith
8	Moore	8	Ripley
7	Slattery	7	Neary [TRY]
6	Buckley	6	Dixon
5	Mays	5	Ralston
4	McBride	4	Uttley
3	Lynch	3	Cotton
2	Kennedy	2	Pullin (c)
1	McLoughlin	1	Stevens

Comments: Milliken scored a try on his debut and not even a Neary second-half try could save the visitors. Buckley, Smith and Uttley also won their first caps.

ENGLAND 14 FRANCE 6; at Twickenham; 24th of February 1973

15	Jorden [2 PENs]		15	Droitecourt
14	Squires		14	Bertranne [TRY]
13	Evans		13	Dourthe
12	Preece		12	Trillo
11	Duckham [2 TRIES]		11	Lux
10	Cooper		10	Romeu [CON]
9	Smith		9	Barrau
8	Ripley		8	Spanghero (c)
7	Neary		7	Biemouret
6	Dixon		6	Saisset
5	Ralston		5	Esteve
4	Uttley		4	Bastiat
3	Cotton		3	Iracabal
2	Pullin (c)		2	Benesis
1	Stevens		1	Darrieussecq

Comments: David Duckham recorded a try in each half and Tony Jorden converted a penalty in each half as England rediscovered the art of winning.

SCOTLAND 19 IRELAND 14; at Murrayfield; 24th of February 1973

15	Irvine		15	Kiernan (c) [TRY]
14	Steele		14	Grace
13	McGeechan [DG]		13	Milliken
12	Forsyth [TRY]		12	Gibson
11	Shedden		11	McMaster [TRY]
10	Telfer		10	McGann [2 PENs]
9	Morgan [2 PENs, 2 DGs]		9	Moloney
8	Strachan		8	Moore
7	Millican		7	Slattery
6	MacEwan		6	Buckley
5	Brown		5	Mays
4	McHarg		4	McBride
3	Carmichael		3	Lynch
2	Clark		2	Kennedy
1	McLauchlan (c)		1	McLoughlin

Comments: Hamish Bryce won his only cap as a replacement as Scotland came from behind to earn another narrow home win, helped by Forsyth's second-half try.

WALES 16 IRELAND 12; at Cardiff; 10th of March 1973

15	Williams		15	Ensor
14	Davies. G		14	Grace
13	Bergiers		13	Milliken
12	Lewis (c)		12	Gibson [TRY]
11	Shanklin [TRY]		11	McMaster
10	Bennett [2 PENs, CON]		10	McGann [2 PENs, CON]
9	Edwards [TRY]		9	Moloney
8	Davies. M		8	Moore
7	Taylor		7	Slattery
6	Morris		6	McKinney
5	Roberts		5	Mays
4	Thomas		4	McBride (c)
3	Lloyd		3	Lynch
2	Young		2	Kennedy
1	Shaw		1	McLoughlin

Comments: Phil Llewellyn and Tony Ensor won their first caps as Wales carved out a slender victory. Gibson's second-half try proved to be in vain for the Irish.

ENGLAND 20 SCOTLAND 13; at Twickenham; 17th of March 1973

15	Jorden [2 CONs]		15	Irvine [CON]
14	Squires [TRY]		14	Steele [2 TRIES]
13	Evans [TRY]		13	McGeechan
12	Preece		12	Forsyth
11	Duckham		11	Shedden
10	Cooper		10	Telfer
9	Smith		9	Morgan [PEN]
8	Ripley		8	Strachan
7	Neary		7	Millican
6	Dixon [2 TRIES]		6	MacEwan
5	Ralston		5	Brown
4	Uttley		4	McHarg
3	Cotton		3	Carmichael
2	Pullin (c)		2	Clark
1	Stevens		1	McLauchlan (c)

Comments: Dixon crossed the try-line twice to foil Scotland's Triple Crown quest. Steele bagged a pair of consolation tries after the interval for the Scots.

FRANCE 12 WALES 3; at Parc des Princes; 24th of March 1973

15	Aguirre	15	Williams
14	Phliponeau	14	Davies. G
13	Badin	13	Bergiers
12	Maso	12	Lewis
11	Cantoni	11	Shanklin
10	Romeu [3 PENs, DG]	10	Bennett [DG]
9	Pebeyre	9	Edwards (c)
8	Saisset	8	Davies. M
7	Biemouret	7	David
6	Skrela	6	Taylor
5	Spanghero (c)	5	Roberts
4	Cester	4	Thomas
3	Iracabal	3	Llewellyn
2	Benesis	2	Young
1	Azarete	1	Shaw

Comments: Jean-Pierre Romeu's trio of penalties were the decisive difference between the two teams as Wales lost again on their travels.

IRELAND 6 FRANCE 4; at Lansdowne Road; 14th of April 1973

15	Ensor [PEN]	15	Aguirre
14	Dennison	14	Phliponeau [TRY]
13	Milliken	13	Badin
12	Gibson [PEN]	12	Maso
11	McMaster	11	Cantoni
10	Quinn	10	Romeu
9	Moloney	9	Barrau
8	Moore	8	Spanghero (c)
7	Slattery	7	Biemouret
6	McKinney	6	Saisset
5	Molloy	5	Esteve
4	McBride (c)	4	Cester
3	Clegg	3	Iracabal
2	Kennedy	2	Benesis
1	McLoughlin	1	Azarete

Comments: Phliponeau's only try for his country after the break was not sufficient to land the Five Nations title, as Ireland held on to ensure a five-way tie.

1973 FINAL TABLE

		Points For	Points Against	Total Points
1ST	WALES	53	43	4
1ST	IRELAND	50	48	4
1ST	FRANCE	38	36	4
1ST	SCOTLAND	55	59	4
1ST	ENGLAND	52	62	4

Comments: Only 1 match had a winning margin of more than 9 points as every team won twice in the closest Five Nations ever.

DID YOU KNOW?

Between 1973 and 1997 inclusive, France played 50 Five Nations matches at Parc des Princes, winning forty-two times, drawing once, and losing only seven times. Scotland belatedly managed only won win there in 1995, while Wales could only muster one win at the venue in 1975, albeit a convincing one. Ireland had no success at this stadium while England in the 1980s and the 1990s amassed an impressive haul of five successful trips to the Parc Des Princes.

1974

FRANCE 9 IRELAND 6; at Parc des Princes; 19th of January 1974

15	Aguirre [CON]	15	Ensor [2 PENs]
14	Bertranne	14	Becker
13	Dourthe	13	Gibson
12	Lux	12	Milliken
11	Dubertrand	11	McMaster
10	Berot [PEN]	10	Quinn
9	Barrau (c)	9	Moloney
8	Spanghero	8	Moore
7	Boffelli [TRY]	7	Slattery
6	Saisset	6	McKinney
5	Cester	5	Keane
4	Esteve	4	McBride (c)
3	Iracabal	3	Lynch
2	Benesis	2	Kennedy
1	Azarete	1	McLoughlin

Comments: Victor Bofelli's second-half try was enough to see France claim two points. Becker and Keane won their first Irish caps, as did the substitute Agnew.

WALES 6 SCOTLAND 0; at Cardiff; 19th of January 1974

15	Williams. JP	15	Irvine
14	Davies. G	14	Gill
13	Hughes	13	Renwick
12	Hall	12	McGeechan
11	Williams. JJ	11	Dick
10	Bennett [CON]	10	Telfer
9	Edwards (c)	9	Lawson
8	Davies. M	8	Watson
7	Cobner [TRY]	7	Lauder
6	Morris	6	MacEwan
5	Quinnell	5	McHarg
4	Martin	4	Brown
3	Llewellyn	3	Carmichael
2	Windsor	2	Madsen
1	Shaw	1	McLauchlan (c)

Comments: Failing to score may be embarrassing, but this was a big improvement on Scotland's last trip to the Arms Park. Terry Cobner scored a try on his debut.

IRELAND 9 WALES 9; at Lansdowne Road; 2nd of February 1974

15	Ensor [3 PENs]	15	Williams. JP
14	Becker	14	Rees
13	Gibson	13	Hall
12	Milliken	12	Finlayson
11	Lavery	11	Williams. JJ [TRY]
10	Quinn	10	Bennett [PEN, CON]
9	Moloney	9	Edwards (c)
8	Moore	8	Davies
7	Slattery	7	Cobner
6	Deering	6	Morris
5	Keane	5	Wheel
4	McBride (c)	4	Martin
3	McLoughlin	3	Shaw
2	Kennedy	2	Windsor
1	Lynch	1	Williams. W

Comments: This match was level at half-time and full-time as 6 players collected their first caps, namely Deering, Finlayson, Lavery, Rees, Wheel, and Williams.

SCOTLAND 16 ENGLAND 14; at Murrayfield; 2nd of February 1974

15	Irvine [TRY, 2 PENs, CON]	15	Rossborough [DG]
14	Gill	14	Squires
13	Renwick	13	Roughley
12	McGeechan	12	Evans
11	Dick	11	Duckham
10	Telfer	10	Old [PEN]
9	Lawson	9	Webster
8	Watson	8	Ripley
7	Lauder [TRY]	7	Neary [TRY]
6	MacEwan	6	Dixon
5	McHarg	5	Ralston
4	Brown	4	Horton
3	Carmichael	3	Cotton [TRY]
2	Madsen	2	Pullin (c)
1	McLauchlan (c)	1	Stevens

Comments: Both teams scored a try in each half, but regrettably for England, their failure to land a conversion was the difference between the two protagonists.

ENGLAND 21 IRELAND 26; at Twickenham; 16th of February 1974

15	Rossborough	15	Ensor [PEN]
14	Squires [TRY]	14	Grace
13	Roughley	13	Gibson [2 TRIES, 2 CONs]
12	Evans	12	Milliken
11	Duckham	11	McMaster
10	Old [5 PENs, CON]	10	Quinn [DG]
9	Smith	9	Moloney [TRY]
8	Ripley	8	Moore [TRY]
7	Neary	7	Slattery
6	Dixon	6	McKinney
5	Ralston	5	Keane
4	Uttley	4	McBride (c)
3	Cotton	3	Lynch
2	Pullin (c)	2	Kennedy
1	Stevens	1	McLoughlin

Comments: 31 points were scored after half-time as England failed against celtic opposition again. The gifted Mike Gibson was the hero with a brace of tries.

WALES 16 FRANCE 16; at Cardiff; 16th of February 1974

15	Williams. JP	15	Aguirre
14	Davies. G	14	Bertranne
13	Hall	13	Pecune
12	Finlayson	12	Lux [TRY]
11	Williams. JJ [TRY]	11	Dubertrand
10	Bennett [3 PENs]	10	Romeu [3 PENS, DG]
9	Edwards (c) [DG]	9	Fouroux
8	Davies. M	8	Spanghero
7	Cobner	7	Boffelli
6	Morris	6	Skrela
5	Quinnell	5	Cester (c)
4	Robinson	4	Esteve
3	Shaw	3	Iracabal
2	Windsor	2	Benesis
1	Williams. W	1	Vaquerin

Comments: Pecune and Robinson made their first international appearances as Wales found themselves deadlocked at half-time and full-time for the second time.

FRANCE 12 ENGLAND 12; at Parc des Princes; 2nd of March 1974

	France			England
15	Droitecourt		15	Jorden
14	Bertranne		14	Squires
13	Pecune		13	Smith. K
12	Lux		12	Evans [DG]
11	Dubertrand		11	Duckham [TRY]
10	Romeu [TRY, PEN, DG, CON]		10	Old [PEN, CON]
9	Fouroux		9	Smith. S
8	Spanghero		8	Ripley
7	Boffelli		7	Neary
6	Skrela		6	Dixon
5	Cester (c)		5	Ralston
4	Esteve		4	Uttley
3	Iracabal		3	Burton
2	Benesis		2	Pullin (c)
1	Vaquerin		1	Stevens

Comments: In the second half David Duckham crossed the try line and Geoff Evans converted a drop goal as France were forced to settle for another single point.

IRELAND 9 SCOTLAND 6; at Lansdowne Road; 2nd of March 1974

	Ireland			Scotland
15	Ensor		15	Irvine [2 PENs]
14	Grace		14	Gill
13	Gibson [CON]		13	Renwick
12	Milliken [TRY]		12	McGeechan
11	McMaster		11	Dick
10	Quinn		10	Telfer
9	Moloney		9	Morgan
8	Moore		8	Watson
7	Slattery		7	Lauder
6	McKinney [PEN]		6	MacEwan
5	Keane		5	McHarg
4	McBride (c)		4	Brown
3	Lynch		3	Carmichael
2	Kennedy		2	Madsen
1	McLoughlin		1	McLauchlan (c)

Comments: Scotland were scoreless at half-time and yet they too nearly earned a draw, but Dick Milliken's first-half try proved to be decisive.

ENGLAND 16 WALES 12; at Twickenham; 16th of March 1974

15	Hare	15	Blyth
14	Squires	14	Davies. G [TRY]
13	Smith	13	Bergiers
12	Evans	12	Finlayson
11	Duckham [TRY]	11	Williams
10	Old [2 PENs, CON]	10	Bennett [2 PENs, CON]
9	Webster	9	Edwards (c)
8	Ripley [TRY]	8	Davies. M
7	Neary	7	Cobner
6	Dixon	6	Morris
5	Ralston	5	Thomas
4	Uttley	4	Robinson
3	Burton	3	Llewellyn
2	Pullin (c)	2	Windsor
1	Stevens	1	Shaw

Comments: Both full backs, Dusty Hare and Roger Blyth, were making their debut, as England finally overcame the Welsh in another close encounter.

SCOTLAND 19 FRANCE 6; at Murrayfield; 16th of March 1974

15	Irvine [2 PENs, CON]	15	Droitecourt
14	Gill	14	Gourdon
13	Renwick	13	Pecune
12	Hunter	12	Lux
11	Dick [TRY]	11	Bertranne
10	McGeechan	10	Romeu [PEN, DG]
9	Morgan [PEN]	9	Barrau
8	Watson	8	Spanghero
7	Lauder	7	Boffelli
6	MacEwan	6	Skrela
5	McHarg [TRY]	5	Cester (c)
4	Brown	4	Esteve
3	Carmichael	3	Iracabal
2	Madsen	2	Benesis
1	McLauchlan (c)	1	Vaquerin

Comments: Michael Hunter made his only appearance for Scotland in what proved to be the only match in the competition which witnessed a comfortable victory.

1974 FINAL TABLE

		Points For	Points Against	Total Points
1ST	IRELAND	50	45	5
2ND	SCOTLAND	41	35	4
2ND	WALES	43	41	4
2ND	FRANCE	43	53	4
5TH	ENGLAND	63	66	3

Comments: For the 4th time in 5 seasons, England conceded most points. Ireland won another desperately close Five Nations.

DID YOU KNOW?

In cricketing parlance, a hapless batsman who fails to score any runs is sometimes diplomatically referred to as someone who didn't trouble the scorer. There have been some occasions since 1970 when various teams in the Five Nations didn't trouble the scorer:

France 8 Ireland 0 (1970)
Ireland 14 Wales 0 (1970)
Wales 6 Scotland 0 (1974)
Ireland 0 England 4 (1977)
Scotland 0 England 15 (1978)
Ireland 17 England 0 (1987)
England 11 France 0 (1989)
England 23 Ireland 0 (1990)
Scotland 21 France 0 (1990)
England 24 Wales 0 (1992)
Scotland 20 Wales 0 (1993)
Wales 0 France 51 (1998)
France 25 Italy 0 (2004)
Scotland 0 France 31 (2004)

1975

FRANCE 10 WALES 25; at Parc des Princes; 18th of January 1975

15	Taffary [2 PENs]		15	Williams. JP
14	Gourdon [TRY]		14	Davies. G [TRY]
13	Dourthe		13	Fenwick [TRY, PEN, CON]
12	Bertranne		12	Gravell
11	Lux		11	Williams. JJ
10	Romeu		10	Bevan
9	Fouroux (c)		9	Edwards [TRY]
8	Bastiat		8	Davies. M (c)
7	Boffelli		7	Evans
6	Saisset		6	Cobner [TRY]
5	Esteve		5	Wheel
4	Senal		4	Martin
3	Azarete		3	Price [TRY]
2	Paco		2	Windsor
1	Vaquerin		1	Faulkner

Comments: The visitors paraded six new recruits, and two of them, Graham Price and Steve Fenwick were amongst the try-scorers in this Parisian demolition job.

IRELAND 12 ENGLAND 9; at Lansdowne Road; 18th of January 1975

15	Ensor		15	Rossborough
14	Grace		14	Squires
13	Milliken		13	Warfield
12	Gibson [TRY]		12	Preece
11	Dennison		11	Duckham
10	McCombe [TRY, 2 CONs]		10	Old [DG, CON]
9	Moloney		9	Webster
8	Duggan		8	Ripley
7	Slattery		7	Neary
6	McKinney		6	Cotton
5	Keane		5	Ralston
4	McBride (c)		4	Beaumont
3	Clegg		3	Cotton (c)
2	Whelan		2	Pullin
1	McLoughlin		1	Stevens [TRY]

Comments: Bill Beaumont, Willie Duggan, and Pat Whelan won their first caps as England lost to Ireland for the fourth successive time.

ENGLAND 20 FRANCE 27; at Twickenham; 1st of February 1975

15	Rossborough [TRY, 4 PENs]	15	Taffary
14	Squires	14	Gourdon [TRY]
13	Warfield	13	Dourthe (c)
12	Preece	12	Etchenique [TRY]
11	Duckham [TRY]	11	Bertranne
10	Cooper	10	Paries [PEN, 4 CONs]
9	Webster	9	Astre
8	Ripley	8	Spanghero [TRY]
7	Neary	7	Skrela
6	Watkins	6	Rives
5	Ralston	5	Guilbert [TRY]
4	Uttley	4	Esteve
3	Cotton (c)	3	Cholley
2	Wheeler	2	Paco
1	Stevens	1	Vaquerin

Comments: The away team scored two tries in each half to earn both points. Amongst the try-scorers was the debutant Alain Guilbert.

SCOTLAND 20 IRELAND 13; at Murrayfield; 1st of February 1975

15	Irvine [2 PENs]	15	Ensor
14	Steele [TRY]	14	Grace [TRY]
13	Renwick [TRY]	13	Milliken
12	Bell	12	Gibson
11	Dick	11	Dennison [TRY]
10	McGeechan [DG]	10	McCombe [PEN, CON]
9	Morgan [DG]	9	Moloney
8	Leslie	8	Duggan
7	Lauder	7	Slattery
6	Biggar	6	McKinney
5	Brown	5	Keane
4	McHarg	4	McBride (c)
3	Carmichael	3	Clegg
2	Madsen	2	Whelan
1	McLauchlan (c)	1	McLoughlin

Comments: First-half tries from Jim Renwick and Billy Steele ensured a happy first cap for their team-mates David Bell, Mike Biggar, and David Leslie.

FRANCE 10 SCOTLAND 9; at Parc des Princes; 15th of February 1975

15	Taffary		15	Irvine [3 PENs]
14	Gourdon		14	Steele
13	Dourthe (c) [TRY]		13	Renwick
12	Bertranne		12	Bell
11	Averous		11	Dick
10	Paries [PEN]		10	McGeechan
9	Astre [DG]		9	Morgan
8	Boffelli		8	Leslie
7	Skrela		7	Lauder
6	Rives		6	Biggar
5	Spanghero		5	Brown
4	Guilbert		4	McHarg
3	Cholley		3	Carmichael
2	Ugartemendia		2	Madsen
1	Vaquerin		1	McLauchlan (c)

Comments: Claude Dourthe, France's captain, scored the match's only try in the second half as his team held on for victory by the thinnest possible margin.

WALES 20 ENGLAND 4; at Cardiff; 15th of February 1975

15	Williams. JP [TRY]		15	Jorden
14	Davies. G [TRY]		14	Squires
13	Fenwick [TRY]		13	Smith
12	Gravell		12	Preece
11	Williams. JJ		11	Duckham
10	Bevan		10	Cooper
9	Edwards		9	Webster
8	Davies. M (c)		8	Uttley
7	Evans		7	Neary
6	Cobner		6	Watkins
5	Wheel		5	Ralston
4	Martin [2 PENs, CON]		4	Horton [TRY]
3	Price		3	Cotton (c)
2	Windsor		2	Wheeler
1	Faulkner		1	Stevens

Comments: Nigel Horton's second-half try was merely a consolation as the rampant Welsh were already 16 points ahead at the interval.

IRELAND 25 FRANCE 6; at Lansdowne Road; 1st of March 1975

15	Ensor [TRY]	15	Taffary
14	Grace [TRY]	14	Gourdon
13	Milliken	13	Sangalli
12	Gibson	12	Bertranne
11	McMaster	11	Averous
10	McCombe [PEN, 2 DGs, 2 CONs]	10	Paries [PEN, DG]
9	Moloney	9	Astre (c)
8	Duggan	8	Boffelli
7	Slattery	7	Skrela
6	Sherry	6	Rives
5	Keane	5	Spanghero
4	McBride (c) [TRY]	4	Guilbert
3	Clegg	3	Cholley
2	Kennedy	2	Ugartemendia
1	McLoughlin	1	Vaquerin

Comments: Francois Sangalli and Michael Sherry made their first international appearances for each team, as Ireland dished out a second-half thrashing.

SCOTLAND 12 WALES 10; at Murrayfield; 1st of March 1975

15	Irvine	15	Williams. JP
14	Steele	14	Davies. G
13	Renwick	13	Fenwick [2 PENs]
12	Bell	12	Gravell
11	Dick	11	Williams. JJ
10	McGeechan [DG]	10	Bevan
9	Morgan [3 PENs]	9	Edwards
8	Leslie	8	Davies. M (c)
7	MacEwan	7	Evans [TRY]
6	Biggar	6	Cobner
5	Brown	5	Roberts
4	McHarg	4	Martin
3	Carmichael	3	Price
2	Madsen	2	Windsor
1	McLauchlan (c)	1	Faulkner

Comments: Morgan's penalties foiled Wales on St. David's Day in front of a crowd of 100,000. Wales would have earned a draw if Evans's try had been converted.

ENGLAND 7 SCOTLAND 6; at Twickenham; 15th of March 1975

15	Jorden	15	Irvine
14	Squires	14	Steele
13	Warfield	13	Renwick
12	Smith	12	Bell
11	Morley [TRY]	11	Dick
10	Bennett [PEN]	10	McGeechan
9	Page	9	Morgan [2 PENs]
8	Ripley	8	Leslie
7	Neary (c)	7	MacEwan
6	Rollitt	6	Biggar
5	Ralston	5	Brown
4	Uttley	4	McHarg
3	Burton	3	Carmichael
2	Pullin	2	Madsen
1	Stevens	1	McLauchlan (c)

Comments: A second-half try from Alan Morley ruined Scotland's Triple Crown hopes. Before the interval Neil Bennett slotted home a penalty on his debut.

WALES 32 IRELAND 4; at Cardiff; 15th of March 1975

15	Williams. JP	15	Ensor
14	Davies. G [TRY]	14	Grace
13	Bergiers [TRY]	13	Milliken
12	Gravell	12	Gibson
11	Williams. JJ [TRY]	11	McMaster
10	Bennett [2 PENs, 3 CONs]	10	McCombe
9	Edwards [TRY]	9	Moloney
8	Davies. M (c)	8	Duggan [TRY]
7	Evans	7	Slattery
6	Cobner	6	Sherry
5	Wheel	5	Keane
4	Martin	4	McBride (c)
3	Price	3	Clegg
2	Windsor	2	Kennedy
1	Faulkner [TRY]	1	McLoughlin

Comments: The home team scored 25 points after the interval, including 4 tries. Willie Duggan's try was the only crumb of comfort for the annihilated visitors.

		Points For	Points Against	Total Points
1ST	WALES	87	30	6
2ND	SCOTLAND	47	40	4
2ND	IRELAND	54	67	4
2ND	FRANCE	53	79	4
5TH	ENGLAND	40	65	2

Comments: This was a 'poor season' for Wales. They 'only' managed three wins and merely accumulated a total of 87 points!

DID YOU KNOW?

In 1975 Gareth Edwards was awarded an MBE. There is simply no means of determining who was the best rugby player of all time, but in any such imaginary poll, the Welsh scrum-half maestro would be a frontrunner. Edwards first played for Wales on April Fools' Day 1967 when his team lost to France. Fittingly, his last international was a Grand Slam victory over France in 1978. Scorer of a memorable solo try against Scotland when he emerged from the ground, caked in mud, Edwards played in every single Five Nations encounter from April 1967 to 1978. This astonishing record is rendered all the more remarkable by the quality of the Welsh teams in this era. Edwards was a key player in an outstanding team and his run of fifty-three successive caps speaks loudly for itself.

1976

SCOTLAND 6 FRANCE 13; at Murrayfield; 10th of January 1976

15	Hay		15	Droitecourt
14	Irvine		14	Gourdon
13	Renwick [PEN]		13	Bertranne
12	McGeechan		12	Sangalli
11	Dick		11	Dubertrand [TRY]
10	Telfer		10	Romeu [3 PENs]
9	Morgan [DG]		9	Fouroux (c)
8	Mackie		8	Bastiat
7	Leslie		7	Skrela
6	Lauder		6	Rives
5	Brown		5	Palmie
4	McHarg		4	Haget
3	Carmichael		3	Paparemborde
2	Madsen		2	Paco
1	McLauchlan (c)		1	Cholley

Comments: Andre Dubertrand registered the match's only try in the first half as France made the best possible start to the new Five Nations campaign.

ENGLAND 9 WALES 21; at Twickenham; 17th of January 1976

15	Hignell [3 PENs]		15	Williams. JP [2 TRIES]
14	Squires		14	Davies. G
13	Maxwell		13	Gravell
12	Cooke		12	Fenwick [3 CONs]
11	Duckham		11	Williams. JJ
10	Cooper		10	Bennett
9	Lampkowski		9	Edwards [TRY]
8	Ripley		8	Davies. M (c)
7	Neary (c)		7	Evans
6	Keyworth		6	Cobner
5	Wilkinson		5	Wheel
4	Beaumont		4	Martin [PEN]
3	Cotton		3	Price
2	Wheeler		2	Windsor
1	Burton		1	Faulkner

Comments: David Cooke made an unhappy debut as Wales ran out comfortable winners, scoring the match's three tries.

FRANCE 26 IRELAND 3; at Parc des Princes; 7th of February 1976

15	Droitecourt	15	Ensor
14	Gourdon	14	Grace
13	Bertranne	13	McIlrath
12	Pecune [TRY]	12	Gibson (c)
11	Averous	11	McMaster
10	Romeu [PEN, CON]	10	McGann
9	Fouroux (c) [TRY]	9	Robbie [PEN]
8	Bastiat [PEN, CON]	8	Duggan
7	Skrela	7	Deering
6	Rives [TRY]	6	McKinney
5	Palmie	5	Foley
4	Imbernon	4	Keane
3	Paparemborde	3	O'Callaghan
2	Paco	2	Cantrell
1	Cholley [TRY]	1	Orr

Comments: The hosts accumulated 20 points in the second half as they emphatically avenged their defeat in Dublin the previous year.

WALES 28 SCOTLAND 6; at Cardiff; 7th of February 1976

15	Williams. JP	15	Irvine [TRY]
14	Davies. G	14	Steele
13	Gravell	13	Renwick
12	Fenwick [DG]	12	Cranston
11	Williams. JJ [TRY]	11	Shedden
10	Bennett [3 PENS, 2 CONs]	10	McGeechan
9	Edwards [TRY]	9	Morgan [CON]
8	Davies. M (c)	8	Mackie
7	Evans [TRY]	7	Leslie
6	Cobner	6	Biggar
5	Wheel	5	Brown
4	Martin	4	McHarg
3	Price	3	Carmichael
2	Windsor	2	Fisher
1	Faulkner	1	McLauchlan (c)

Comments: Alastair Cranston had a baptism of fire as Wales made light work of Scotland, and now a possible Triple Crown loomed on the horizon.

IRELAND 9 WALES 34; at Lansdowne Road; 21st of February 1976

15	Ensor	15	Williams. JP
14	Grace (c)	14	Davies. G [2 TRIES]
13	Lavery	13	Gravell
12	Gibson	12	Fenwick
11	McMaster	11	Williams. JJ
10	McGann [3 PENs]	10	Bennett [TRY, 3 PENs, 3 CONs]
9	Canniffe	9	Edwards [TRY]
8	Duggan	8	Davies. M (c)
7	Deering	7	Evans
6	McKinney	6	David
5	Hakin	5	Wheel
4	Keane	4	Martin [PEN]
3	O'Callaghan	3	Price
2	Cantrell	2	Windsor
1	Orr	1	Faulkner

Comments: Wales only led 10-9 at the interval, but then proceeded to run riot. Phil Bennett helped himself to 19 points as the Welsh landed the Triple Crown.

SCOTLAND 22 ENGLAND 12; at Murrayfield; 21st of February 1976

15	Irvine [2 PENs, 2 CONs]	15	Hignell
14	Steele	14	Plummer
13	Cranston	13	Maxwell [TRY]
12	McGeechan	12	Cooke
11	Shedden	11	Duckham
10	Wilson	10	Old [2 PENs, CON]
9	Lawson [2 TRIES]	9	Lampkowski
8	McHarg	8	Ripley
7	Leslie [TRY]	7	Neary (c)
6	Biggar	6	Keyworth
5	Brown	5	Wilkinson
4	Tomes	4	Beaumont
3	Carmichael	3	Cotton
2	Fisher	2	Wheeler
1	McLauchlan (c)	1	Burton

Comments: England actually led 12-9 at half-time, but they were thwarted mainly by Alan Lawson's pair of tries as Scotland re-claimed the Calcutta Cup.

ENGLAND 12 IRELAND 13; at Twickenham; 6th of March 1976

15	Hignell		15	Ensor
14	Plummer		14	Grace (c) [TRY]
13	Maxwell		13	Brady
12	Cooke		12	Gibson
11	Slemen		11	Blake-Knox
10	Old [4 PENs]		10	McGann [2 PENs, DG]
9	Lampkowski		9	Canniffe
8	Adey		8	Steele
7	Neary (c)		7	Deering
6	Keyworth		6	McKinney
5	Wilkinson		5	Foley
4	Beaumont		4	Keane
3	Cotton		3	O'Callaghan
2	Wheeler		2	Whelan
1	Burton		1	Orr

Comments: The only scores in the first half were three Alan Old penalties, and yet the Irish snatched another victory over England, thanks to a try from Tom Grace.

WALES 19 FRANCE 13; at Cardiff; 6th of March 1976

15	Williams. JP		15	Droitecourt
14	Davies. M		14	Gourdon [TRY]
13	Gravell		13	Bertranne
12	Fenwick [2 PENs]		12	Pecune
11	Williams. JJ [TRY]		11	Averous [TRY]
10	Bennett [2 PENs]		10	Romeu [PEN, CON]
9	Edwards		9	Fouroux (c)
8	Davies. M (c)		8	Bastiat
7	Evans		7	Skrela
6	David		6	Rives
5	Wheel		5	Palmie
4	Martin [PEN]		4	Imbernon
3	Price		3	Paparemborde
2	Windsor		2	Paco
1	Faulkner		1	Cholley

Comments: Phil Bennett, Steve Fenwick, and Alan Martin shared five penalties between them as Wales nailed down their second Grand Slam of the decade.

FRANCE 30 ENGLAND 9; at Parc des Princes; 20th of March 1976

15	Aguirre	15	Butler [PEN, CON]
14	Gourdon [TRY]	14	Plummer
13	Bertranne	13	Maxwell
12	Pecune	12	Cooke
11	Averous	11	Slemen
10	Romeu [TRY, 3 CONs]	10	Williams
9	Fouroux (c) [TRY]	9	Smith
8	Bastiat [TRY]	8	Adey
7	Skrela	7	Neary (c)
6	Rives	6	Dixon [TRY]
5	Palmie	5	Wilkinson
4	Imbernon	4	Beaumont
3	Paparemborde [2 TRIES]	3	Cotton
2	Paco	2	Pullin
1	Cholley	1	Burton

Comments: Poor Christoper Williams never got beyond this first cap as Les Bleus stormed to a six-try victory and secured a second-place finish in the Five Nations.

IRELAND 6 SCOTLAND 15; at Lansdowne Road; 20th of March 1976

15	Moloney	15	Irvine [4 PENs]
14	Grace (c)	14	Steele
13	Brady	13	Cranston
12	Gibson	12	McGeechan
11	Blake-Knox	11	Shedden
10	McGann [2 PENs]	10	Wilson [DG]
9	Canniffe	9	Lawson
8	Duggan	8	McHarg
7	Deering	7	Leslie
6	McKinney	6	Biggar
5	Hakin	5	Brown
4	Keane	4	Tomes
3	O'Callaghan	3	Carmichael
2	Cantrell	2	Fisher
1	Orr	1	McLauchlan (c)

Comments: Christopher McKibbin came on as a substitute for his only Irish cap, but his team were well beaten by the Scots. Andy Irvine's 4 penalties proved crucial.

1976 FINAL TABLE

		Points For	Points Against	Total Points
1ST	WALES	102	37	8
2ND	FRANCE	82	37	6
3RD	SCOTLAND	49	59	4
4TH	IRELAND	31	87	2
5TH	ENGLAND	42	86	0

Comments: The all-conquering Welsh posted more than 100 points in their Grand Slam journey. Woeful England were whitewashed.

DID YOU KNOW?

In the Five Nations and Six Nations 'hall of shame' lurk the following teams who suffered the embarrassment of a whitewash season in which they failed to earn a single point from any of their fixtures:

1976: England
1977: Ireland
1978: Scotland
1981: Ireland
1984: Ireland
1985: Scotland
1986: Ireland
1990: Wales
1992: Ireland
1995: Wales
1998: Ireland
2001: Italy
2002: Italy
2003: Wales
2004: Scotland
2005: Italy
2009: Italy

FRANCE have not suffered a whitewash season since 1957.

1977

ENGLAND 26 SCOTLAND 6; at Twickenham; 15th of January 1977

15	Hignell [2 PENs, 2 CONs]	15	Irvine [2 PENs]
14	Squires	14	Steele
13	Corless	13	McGeechan (c)
12	Kent [TRY]	12	Cranston
11	Slemen [TRY]	11	Dick
10	Cooper	10	Wilson
9	Young [TRY]	9	Lawson
8	Uttley (c) [TRY]	8	MacDonald
7	Rafter	7	Brewster
6	Dixon	6	Lauder
5	Horton	5	McHarg
4	Beaumont	4	Tomes
3	Cotton	3	Carmichael
2	Wheeler	2	Madsen
1	Cowling	1	Aitkin

Comments: There were seven debutants in this contest. Amongst them were Charles Kent and Malcolm Young who scored their only England tries in this triumph.

WALES 25 IRELAND 9; at Cardiff; 15th of January 1977

15	Williams. JP	15	Wilson
14	Davies [TRY]	14	Grace (c)
13	Fenwick [DG]	13	McKibbin
12	Burcher	12	McIlrath
11	Williams. JJ [TRY]	11	Bowen
10	Bennett (c) [2 PENs, 2 CONs]	10	Gibson [3 PENs]
9	Edwards	9	McGrath
8	Squire	8	Duggan [SENT OFF]
7	Burgess [TRY]	7	Deering
6	Evans	6	McKinney
5	Wheel [SENT OFF]	5	Hakin
4	Martin	4	Keane
3	Price	3	Feighery
2	Windsor	2	Whelan
1	Shaw	1	Orr

Comments: The visitors actually led 6-0 at half time. However, with both teams reduced to 14 men, Wales then executed a three-try demolition of the away team.

FRANCE 16 WALES 9; at Parc des Princes; 5th of February 1977

15	Aguirre		15	Williams. JP
14	Harize [TRY]		14	Davies
13	Bertranne		13	Fenwick [3 PENs]
12	Sangalli		12	Burcher
11	Averous		11	Williams. JJ
10	Romeu [2 PENs, CON]		10	Bennett (c)
9	Fouroux (c)		9	Edwards
8	Bastiat		8	Squire
7	Skrela [TRY]		7	Burgess
6	Rives		6	Cobner
5	Palmie		5	Quinnell
4	Imbernon		4	Martin
3	Paparemborde		3	Price
2	Paco		2	Windsor
1	Cholley		1	Shaw

Comments: Two second-half tries from Dominique Harize and Jean-Claude Skrela helped France to their first win against Wales since 1973.

IRELAND 0 ENGLAND 4; at Lansdowne Road; 5th of February 1977

15	Wilson		15	Hignell
14	Grace (c)		14	Squires
13	McKibbin		13	Corless
12	McIlrath		12	Kent
11	Bowen		11	Slemen
10	Gibson		10	Cooper [TRY]
9	McGrath		9	Young
8	Duggan		8	Uttley (c)
7	Deering		7	Neary
6	McKinney		6	Dixon
5	Hakin		5	Horton
4	Keane		4	Beaumont
3	Feighery		3	Cotton
2	Whelan		2	Wheeler
1	Orr		1	Cowling

Comments: Martin Cooper scored his only try for England and the only points in this match, which was ruined by the weather, not that England were complaining.

ENGLAND 3 FRANCE 4; at Twickenham; 19th of February 1977

15	Hignell [PEN]	15	Aguirre
14	Squires	14	Harize
13	Corless	13	Bertranne
12	Kent	12	Sangalli [TRY]
11	Slemen	11	Averous
10	Cooper	10	Romeu
9	Young	9	Fouroux (c)
8	Uttley (c)	8	Bastiat
7	Rafter	7	Skrela
6	Neary	6	Rives
5	Horton	5	Palmie
4	Beaumont	4	Imbernon
3	Cotton	3	Paparemborde
2	Wheeler	2	Paco
1	Cowling	1	Cholley

Comments: This time England lost a peculiarly low-scoring contest. Francois Sangalli's only try for France was barely adequate to achieve two precious points.

SCOTLAND 21 IRELAND 18; at Murrayfield; 19th of February 1977

15	Irvine [2 PENs]	15	Wilson
14	Gammell [2 TRIES]	14	Grace (c)
13	McGeechan (c)	13	McKibbin
12	Renwick	12	Gibson [TRY, 2 PENs, CON]
11	Shedden	11	Bowen
10	Wilson	10	Quinn [PEN, DG]
9	Morgan [DG]	9	Robbie
8	MacDonald	8	Duggan
7	Watson	7	Slattery
6	Biggar	6	McKinney
5	McHarg	5	Murtagh
4	Barnes	4	Keane
3	Pender	3	Byrne
2	Madsen [TRY]	2	Whelan
1	Aitkin	1	Orr

Comments: Bill Gammell crossed the try-line twice on his debut as Scotland inflicted a third consecutive defeat on the Irish, after having trailed 9-7 at half-time.

FRANCE 23 SCOTLAND 3; at Parc des Princes; 5th of March 1977

15	Aguirre	15	Irvine [PEN]
14	Harize [TRY]	14	Gammell
13	Bertranne [TRY]	13	McGeechan (c)
12	Sangalli	12	Renwick
11	Averous	11	Shedden
10	Romeu [PEN, 2 CONs]	10	Wilson
9	Fouroux (c)	9	Morgan
8	Bastiat	8	MacDonald
7	Skrela	7	Watson
6	Rives	6	Biggar
5	Palmie	5	McHarg
4	Imbernon	4	Barnes
3	Paparemborde [TRY]	3	Carmichael
2	Paco [TRY]	2	Madsen
1	Cholley	1	Aitkin

Comments: France made light work of the Scots with two tries from their backs and two tries from their front row forwards. The Grand Slam was now on the horizon.

WALES 14 ENGLAND 9; at Cardiff; 5th of March 1977

15	Williams. JP [TRY]	15	Hignell [3 PENs]
14	Davies	14	Squires
13	Fenwick [2 PENs]	13	Corless
12	Burcher	12	Kent
11	Williams. JJ	11	Slemen
10	Bennett (c) [TRY]	10	Cooper
9	Edwards	9	Young
8	Quinnell	8	Uttley (c)
7	Burgess	7	Rafter
6	Cobner	6	Dixon
5	Wheel	5	Horton
4	Martin	4	Beaumont
3	Price	3	Cotton
2	Windsor	2	Wheeler
1	Williams. C	1	Cowling

Comments: Clive Williams made his debut as Wales moved a step towards securing yet another Triple Crown.

IRELAND 6 FRANCE 15; at Lansdowne Road; 19th of March 1977

15	Ensor		15	Aguirre [2 PENs, CON]
14	Grace (c)		14	Harize
13	Finn		13	Bertranne
12	Gibson [PEN]		12	Sangalli
12	McLennan		11	Averous
10	Quinn [PEN]		10	Romeu [PEN]
9	Robbie		9	Fouroux (c)
8	Duggan		8	Bastiat [TRY]
7	Slattery		7	Skrela
6	Steele		6	Rives
5	Hakin		5	Palmie
4	Keane		4	Imbernon
3	Byrne		3	Paparemborde
2	Whelan		2	Paco
1	Orr		1	Cholley

Comments: The French came from behind to grab the coveted Grand Slam, courtesy of a try from Jean-Pierre Bastiat. Ireland had to make do with the wooden spoon.

SCOTLAND 9 WALES 18; at Murrayfield; 19th of March 1977

15	Irvine [TRY, CON]		15	Williams. JP
14	Gammell		14	Davies
13	Renwick		13	Fenwick
12	Cranston		12	Burcher
11	Shedden		11	Williams. JJ [TRY]
10	McGeechan (c) [DG]		10	Bennett (c) [TRY, 2 PENs, 2 CONs]
9	Morgan		9	Edwards
8	MacDonald		8	Quinnell
7	Watson		7	Burgess
6	Biggar		6	Cobner
5	McHarg		5	Wheel
4	Barnes		4	Martin
3	Carmichael		3	Price
2	Madsen		2	Windsor
1	McLauchlan		1	Williams. C

Comments: Deadlocked 3-3 at the interval, Wales then crossed the try-line twice to land another Triple Crown. Bennett finished off an excellent counter-attack.

1977 FINAL TABLE

		Points For	Points Against	Total Points
1ST	FRANCE	58	21	8
2ND	WALES	66	43	6
3RD	ENGLAND	42	24	4
4TH	SCOTLAND	39	85	2
5TH	IRELAND	33	65	0

Comments: The all-conquering French kept the same fifteen in all 4 matches. Remarkably, nobody scored a try against them.

DID YOU KNOW?

Italy need not be discouraged about their slow progress in the Six Nations thus far. If one looks at the story of France's progress in the Five Nations, it took Les Bleus from their arrival in 1908 until 1959 before they won the tournament outright, and it wasn't until 1968 that they recorded their first Grand Chelem. Since then, the formidable French have stamped their considerable presence upon rugby union's answer to the Eurovision Song Contest with a total of eight slams, averaging out at an impressive one every five years since 1968.

1978

FRANCE 15 ENGLAND 6;at Parc des Princes; 21st of January 1978

15	Aguirre [PEN, 2 CONs]	15	Hare
14	Gourdon	14	Squires
13	Bertranne	13	Corless
12	Belascain	12	Maxwell
11	Averous [TRY]	11	Slemen
10	Vivies	10	Old [2 DGs]
9	Gallion [TRY]	9	Young
8	Bastiat (c)	8	Scott
7	Skrela	7	Rafter
6	Rives	6	Dixon
5	Palmie	5	Horton
4	Imbernon	4	Beaumont (c)
3	Paparemborde	3	Burton
2	Paco	2	Wheeler
1	Cholley	1	Cowling

Comments: The home team actually trailed 6-3 at half-time but were rescued by tries from Jean-Luc Averous and the debutant, Jerome Gallion.

IRELAND 12 SCOTLAND 9; at Lansdowne Road; 21st of January 1978

15	Ensor	15	Hay
14	Grace	14	Irvine
13	McKibbin	13	Renwick
12	McNaughton	12	McGeechan
11	McLennan	11	Shedden
10	Ward [2 PENs, CON]	10	Wilson
9	Moloney (c)	9	Morgan (c) [3 PENs]
8	Duggan	8	MacDonald
7	Slattery	7	Hegarty
6	O'Driscoll	6	Biggar
5	Spring	5	McHarg
4	Keane	4	Tomes
3	Fitzpatrick	3	Carmichael
2	Whelan	2	Madsen
1	Orr	1	McLauchlan

Comments: Stewart McKinney came on as a first-half replacement and scored the only try. 5 Irishmen won their first caps as well as Hegarty of Scotland.

ENGLAND 6 WALES 9; at Twickenham; 4th of February 1978

	England			Wales
15	Hignell [2 PENs]		15	Williams. JP
14	Squires		14	Davies
13	Corless		13	Gravell
12	Dodge		12	Fenwick
11	Slemen		11	Williams. JJ
10	Horton		10	Bennett (c) [3 PENs]
9	Young		9	Edwards
8	Scott		8	Quinnell
7	Rafter		7	Cobner
6	Mordell		6	Squire
5	Horton		5	Wheel
4	Beaumont (c)		4	Martin
3	Burton		3	Price
2	Wheeler		2	Windsor
1	Nelmes		1	Faulkner

Comments: Wales sneaked home courtesy of two second-half penalties from Phil Bennett. Paul Dodge, John Horton, and Bob Mordell all won their first caps.

SCOTLAND 16 FRANCE 19; at Murrayfield; 4th of February 1978

	Scotland			France
15	Irvine [TRY]		15	Aguirre [3 PENs, CON]
14	Hay		14	Gourdon
13	Renwick		13	Bertranne
12	McGeechan		12	Belascain
11	Shedden [TRY]		11	Averous
10	Wilson		10	Vivies
9	Morgan (c) [PEN, DG, CON]		9	Gallion [TRY]
8	Mackie		8	Bastiat (c)
7	Hegarty		7	Skrela
6	Biggar		6	Rives
5	McHarg		5	Haget [TRY]
4	Tomes		4	Palmie
3	Pender		3	Paparemborde
2	Deans		2	Paco
1	McLauchlan		1	Cholley

Comments: It was deja-vu as France overturned another interval deficit, as Gallion crossed the try-line again. Colin Deans made his first start for Scotland.

FRANCE 10 IRELAND 9; at Parc des Princes; 18th of February 1978

15	Aguirre [2 PENs]		15	Ensor
14	Bilbao		14	Gibson
13	Bertranne		13	McKibbin
12	Belascain		12	McNaughton
11	Averous		11	McLennan
10	Vivies		10	Ward [3 PENs]
9	Gallion [TRY]		9	Moloney (c)
8	Bastiat (c)		8	Duggan
7	Skrela		7	Slattery
6	Rives		6	McKinney
5	Haget		5	Steele
4	Palmie		4	Keane
3	Paparemborde		3	Byrne
2	Paco		2	Whelan
1	Cholley		1	Orr

Comments: Jerome Gallion scored a try for the third consecutive match. The only score in the second half was a Ward penalty, but France held on for both points.

WALES 22 SCOTLAND 14; at Cardiff; 18th of February 1978

15	Williams. JP		15	Hay
14	Davies		14	Gammell
13	Gravell [TRY]		13	Renwick [TRY]
12	Fenwick [TRY]		12	Cranston
11	Williams. JJ		11	Shedden
10	Bennett (c) [PEN, DG]		10	McGeechan
9	Edwards [TRY]		9	Morgan (c) [2 PENs]
8	Quinnell [TRY]		8	MacDonald
7	Squire		7	Hegarty
6	Cobner		6	Biggar
5	Wheel		5	Tomes [TRY]
4	Martin		4	McHarg
3	Price		3	Pender
2	Windsor		2	Deans
1	Faulkner		1	McLauchlan

Comments: Wales recorded two tries in each half and Scotland managed one in each half as the home team moved towards a third consecutive Triple Crown.

IRELAND 16 WALES 20; at Lansdowne Road; 4th of March 1978

15	Ensor		15	Williams. JP
14	Gibson		14	Davies
13	McKibbin		13	Gravell
12	McNaughton		12	Fenwick [TRY, 4 PENs]
11	McLennan		11	Williams. JJ [TRY]
10	Ward [3 PENs, DG]		10	Bennett (c)
9	Moloney (c) [TRY]		9	Edwards
8	Duggan		8	Quinnell
7	Slattery		7	Cobner
6	McKinney		6	Squire
5	Steele		5	Wheel
4	Keane		4	Martin
3	Byrne		3	Price
2	Whelan		2	Windsor
1	Orr		1	Faulkner

Comments: Fenwick accumulated 16 points as Wales completed another clean sweep of the home unions. They now faced France in a Grand Slam decider.

SCOTLAND 0 ENGLAND 15; at Murrayfield; 4th of March 1978

15	Irvine		15	Caplan
14	Gammell		14	Squires [TRY]
13	Renwick		13	Corless
12	Cranston		12	Dodge [PEN]
11	Hay		11	Slemen
10	Breakey		10	Horton
9	Morgan (c)		9	Young [2 CONs]
8	MacDonald		8	Scott
7	Hegarty		7	Rafter
6	Biggar		6	Dixon
5	Gray		5	Colclough
4	Tomes		4	Beaumont (c)
3	Pender		3	Cotton
2	Deans		2	Wheeler
1	McLauchlan		1	Nelmes [TRY]

Comments: England scored a try in each half as Scotland endured a whitewash season. First caps were awarded to Caplan, Colclough, and Gray.

ENGLAND 15 IRELAND 9; at Twickenham; 18th of March 1978

15	Caplan		15	Ensor
14	Squires		14	Gibson
13	Corless		13	McKibbin
12	Dodge		12	McNaughton
11	Slemen [TRY]		11	McLennan
10	Horton		10	Ward [2 PENs, DG]
9	Young [PEN, 2 CONs]		9	Moloney (c)
8	Scott		8	Duggan
7	Rafter		7	Slattery
6	Dixon [TRY]		6	McKinney
5	Colclough		5	Steele
4	Beaumont (c)		4	Keane
3	Cotton		3	Byrne
2	Wheeler		2	Whelan
1	Nelmes		1	Orr

Comments: The home team crosed the try-line in each half to record their first Twickenham win against Ireland since 1970.

WALES 16 FRANCE 7; at Cardiff; 18th of March 1978

15	Williams. JP		15	Aguirre
14	Williams. JJ		14	Bustaffa
13	Gravell		13	Bertranne
12	Fenwick [DG]		12	Belascain
11	Evans		11	Noves
10	Bennett (c) [2 TRIES, CON]		10	Vivies [DG]
9	Edwards [DG]		9	Gallion
8	Quinnell		8	Bastiat (c)
7	Cobner		7	Skrela [TRY]
6	Squire		6	Rives
5	Wheel		5	Palmie
4	Martin		4	Haget
3	Price		3	Paparemborde
2	Windsor		2	Paco
1	Faulkner		1	Cholley

Comments: Two first-half tries from Phil Bennett saw the home team over the finishing line as Wales secured their third Grand Slam of the 1970s.

1978 FINAL TABLE

		Points For	Points Against	Total Points
1ST	WALES	67	43	8
2ND	FRANCE	51	47	6
3RD	ENGLAND	42	33	4
4TH	IRELAND	46	54	2
5TH	SCOTLAND	39	68	0

Comments: England finished with the same amount of points scored as in 1977. They also conceded the least number of points.

DID YOU KNOW?

It is a commonly-held belief that the most successful teams in rugby union (and indeed any sport) tend to comprise a blend of both youth and experience. In view of this, the England selectors appeared to take this concern a bit too literally when they appointed their half-backs for the opening match of the 1978 Five Nations season. Taking the field in Paris against the reigning champions were Young and Old.

1979

IRELAND 9 FRANCE 9; at Lansdowne Road; 20th of January 1979

15	Spring		15	Aguirre [PEN, CON]
14	Kennedy		14	Bilbao
13	McKibbin		13	Bertranne
12	McNaughton		12	Belascain
11	McLennan		11	Noves
10	Ward [3 PENS]		10	Caussade [TRY]
9	Patterson		9	Gallion
8	Gibson		8	Guilbert
7	Slattery (c)		7	Joinel
6	Tucker		6	Rives (c)
5	Steele		5	Imbernon
4	Keane		4	Haget
3	McLoughlin		3	Paparemborde
2	Whelan		2	Paco
1	Orr		1	Cholley

Comments: Alain Caussade rescued the away team with a second-half try. Ireland would have won if Tony Ward had not allowed a drop goal to be charged down.

SCOTLAND 13 WALES 19; at Murrayfield; 20th of January 1979

15	Irvine [TRY, 3 PENs]		15	Williams. JP (c)
14	Robertson		14	Rees [TRY]
13	Renwick		13	Gravell
12	McGeechan (c)		12	Fenwick [3 PENs, CON]
11	Hay		11	Williams. JJ
10	Rutherford		10	Davies
9	Lawson		9	Holmes [TRY]
8	Lambie		8	Quinnell
7	Dickson		7	Squire
6	Biggar		6	Ringer
5	McHarg		5	Wheel
4	Tomes		4	Martin
3	Cunningham		3	Price
2	Deans		2	Windsor
1	McLauchlan		1	Faulkner

Comments: Andy Irvine scored 13 points in the first half but ended up on the losing team as the visitors also replied with 13 points in the second half.

ENGLAND 7 SCOTLAND 7; at Twickenham; 3rd of February 1979

15	Hignell	15	Irvine [PEN]
14	Squires	14	Robertson
13	Bond	13	Renwick
12	Dodge	12	McGeechan (c)
11	Slemen [TRY]	11	Hay
10	Bennett [PEN]	10	Rutherford [TRY]
9	Young	9	Lawson
8	Uttley (c)	8	Lambie
7	Rafter	7	Dickson
6	Neary	6	Biggar
5	Horton	5	McHarg
4	Beaumont	4	Tomes
3	Pearce	3	Cunningham
2	Wheeler	2	Deans
1	Cowling	1	McLauchlan

Comments: Gary Pearce made his debut as both teams shared the Calcutta Cup. John Rutherford scored a first-half try in his second international outing.

WALES 24 IRELAND 21; at Cardiff; 3rd of February 1979

15	Williams. JP (c)	15	Spring
14	Rees	14	Kennedy
13	Gravell	13	McKibbin
12	Fenwick [4 PENs, 2 CONs]	12	McNaughton
11	Williams. JJ	11	McLennan [TRY]
10	Davies	10	Ward [3 PENs, 2 CONs]
9	Holmes	9	Patterson [TRY]
8	Quinnell	8	Gibson
7	Squire	7	Slattery (c)
6	Ringer [TRY]	6	Tucker
5	Wheel	5	Steele
4	Martin [TRY]	4	Keane
3	Price	3	McLoughlin
2	Windsor	2	Whelan
1	Faulkner	1	Orr

Comments: Ireland came back from 24-9 behind with 2 tries, but it was in vain. Ireland's full back, Dick Spring, later became his country's Foreign Minister.

FRANCE 14 WALES 13; at Parc des Princes; 17th of February 1979

15	Aguirre [2 PENs]	15	Williams. JP (c)
14	Gourdon [2 TRIES]	14	Rees
13	Bertranne	13	Richards
12	Belascain	12	Fenwick [3 PENs]
11	Noves	11	Williams. JJ
10	Caussade	10	Davies
9	Gallion	9	Holmes [TRY]
8	Guilbert	8	Quinnell
7	Joinel	7	Squire
6	Rives (c)	6	Ringer
5	Maleig	5	Clegg
4	Haget	4	Martin
3	Paparemborde	3	Price
2	Paco	2	Windsor
1	Vaquerin	1	Faulkner

Comments: Jean-Francois Gourdon crossed the try-line in each half to deny Wales another Grand Slam. The match had been poised at 7-7 at half-time.

IRELAND 12 ENGLAND 7; at Lansdowne Road; 17th of February 1979

15	Spring	15	Hignell
14	Finn	14	Squires
13	McKibbin	13	Bond
12	McNaughton	12	Dodge
11	McLennan [TRY]	11	Slemen
10	Ward [PEN, DG, CON]	10	Bennett [TRY, PEN]
9	Patterson	9	Kingston
8	Gibson	8	Scott
7	Slattery (c)	7	Rafter
6	Duggan	6	Neary
5	Steele	5	Horton
4	Keane	4	Beaumont (c)
3	McLoughlin	3	Pearce
2	Whelan	2	Wheeler
1	Orr	1	Cowling

Comments: Moss Finn made his debut, but Ireland's try scorer was his wing partner, Freddie McLennan. Neil Bennett scored all of England's points.

ENGLAND 7 FRANCE 6; at Twickenham; 3rd of March 1979

15	Hignell		15	Aguirre [CON]
14	Squires		14	Gourdon
13	Cardus		13	Bertranne
12	Dodge		12	Belascain
11	Slemen		11	Costes [TRY]
10	Bennett [TRY, PEN]		10	Caussade
9	Kingston		9	Gallion
8	Scott		8	Guilbert
7	Rafter		7	Joinel
6	Neary		6	Rives (c)
5	Horton		5	Maleig
4	Beaumont (c)		4	Haget
3	Pearce		3	Paparemborde
2	Wheeler		2	Paco
1	Smart		1	Vaquerin

Comments: England could only muster 7 points for the third consecutive match, but Bennett's second-half try was just about enough to achieve a victory.

SCOTLAND 11 IRELAND 11; at Murrayfield; 3rd of March 1979

15	Irvine [TRY, PEN]		15	Elliott
14	Robertson [TRY]		14	Gibson
13	Renwick		13	McKibbin
12	McGeechan (c)		12	McNaughton
11	Hay		11	McLennan
10	Rutherford		10	Ward [PEN]
9	Lawson		9	Patterson [2 TRIES]
8	Watson		8	Gibson
7	Dickson		7	Slattery (c)
6	Biggar		6	Duggan
5	Gray		5	Spring
4	Tomes		4	Keane
3	Milne		3	McLoughlin
2	Deans		2	Whelan
1	McLauchlan		1	Orr

Comments: Ron Elliott won his only Ireland cap as his fellow Ulsterman Colin Patterson grabbed two opportunist tries. Iain Milne also made his debut.

FRANCE 21 SCOTLAND 17; at Parc des Princes; 17th of March 1979

15	Aguirre [PEN]	15	Irvine [TRY, PEN, CON]
14	Gourdon	14	Robertson [TRY]
13	Bertranne	13	Renwick
12	Belascain [TRY]	12	McGeechan (c)
11	Costes	11	Hay
10	Aguerre [PEN, DG]	10	Rutherford
9	Gallion	9	Lawson
8	Malquier [2 TRIES]	8	Watson
7	Joinel	7	Dickson [TRY]
6	Rives (c)	6	Biggar
5	Marchal	5	Gray
4	Haget	4	Tomes
3	Paparemborde	3	Milne
2	Paco	2	Deans
1	Cholley	1	McLauchlan

Comments: Yves Malquier scored 2 tries on his debut and never played for France again! Scotland shared the try count with 3 tries and were unlucky to lose.

WALES 27 ENGLAND 3; at Cardiff; 17th of March 1979

15	Williams. JP (c) [TRY]	15	Hignell
14	Rees [TRY]	14	Squires
13	Richards [TRY]	13	Cardus
12	Fenwick [CON]	12	Dodge
11	Williams. JJ	11	Slemen
10	Davies [DG]	10	Bennett [PEN]
9	Holmes	9	Kingston
8	Quinnell	8	Scott
7	Squire	7	Rafter
6	Ringer [TRY]	6	Neary
5	Roberts [TRY]	5	Horton
4	Martin [CON]	4	Beaumont (c)
3	Price	3	Pearce
2	Phillips	2	Wheeler
1	Richardson	1	Smart

Comments: Wales clocked out of the 1970s in style with this 5-try Triple Crown triumph. England licked their wounds and responded emphatically in 1980.

1979 FINAL TABLE

		Points For	Points Against	Total Points
1ST	WALES	83	51	6
2ND	FRANCE	50	46	5
3RD	IRELAND	53	51	4
4TH	ENGLAND	24	52	3
5TH	SCOTLAND	48	58	2

Comments: England only averaged 6 points per match. The great JPR Williams had played in 38 matches out of 39 in the 1970s.

DID YOU KNOW?

Only two different teams, France and Wales, won Grand Slams in the 1970s. In the 'eighties and 'nineties, three teams, England, France, and Scotland achieved Grand Slams in each of these two decades. Yet in the first decade of the 21st century, Grand Slams have been shared out amongst no fewer than four countries: England, France, Ireland, and Wales. Never before have more than three countries won Grand Slams in the same decade.

1980

ENGLAND 24 IRELAND 9; at Twickenham; 19th of January 1980

15	Hare [2 PENs, 3 CONs]	15	O'Brien
14	Carleton	14	Kennedy
13	Preston	13	McKibbin
12	Bond	12	McNaughton
11	Slemen [TRY]	11	McLennan
10	Horton. J	10	Campbell [3 PENs]
9	Smith [TRY]	9	Patterson
8	Scott [TRY]	8	Duggan
7	Neary	7	Slattery (c)
6	Uttley	6	O'Driscoll
5	Horton. N	5	Glennon
4	Beaumont (c)	4	Keane
3	Blakeway	3	McLoughlin
2	Wheeler	2	Fitzgerald
1	Cotton	1	Orr

Comments: Phil Blakeway and the replacement Clive Woodward enjoyed the best possible start to their England careers in this convincing victory.

WALES 18 FRANCE 9; at Cardiff; 19th of January 1980

15	Blyth	15	Aguirre
14	Rees [TRY]	14	Bustaffa
13	Richards [TRY]	13	Bertranne
12	Fenwick	12	Codorniou
11	Keen	11	Costes
10	Davies [CON]	10	Caussade [DG, CON]
9	Holmes [TRY]	9	Gallion
8	Butler	8	Maleig
7	Squire (c)	7	Joinel
6	Ringer	6	Rives (c)
5	Wheel	5	Marchal [TRY]
4	Martin	4	Haget
3	Price [TRY]	3	Paparemborde
2	Phillips	2	Paco
1	Williams	1	Salas

Comments: The hosts crossed the try-line three times in the second-half to ensure that it was a happy debut for Eddie Butler and Les Keen.

FRANCE 13 ENGLAND 17; at Parc des Princes; 2nd of February 1980

	France		England
15	Gabernet	15	Hare [PEN]
14	Bustaffa	14	Carleton [TRY]
13	Bertranne	13	Woodward
12	Codorniou	12	Preston [TRY]
11	Averous [TRY]	11	Slemen
10	Caussade [PEN, CON]	10	Horton [2 DGs]
9	Gallion	9	Smith
8	Carpentier	8	Scott
7	Joinel	7	Neary
6	Rives (c) [TRY]	6	Uttley
5	Maleig	5	Colclough
4	Duhard	4	Beaumont (c)
3	Paparemborde	3	Blakeway
2	Dintrans	2	Wheeler
1	Salas	1	Cotton

Comments: John Carleton and Nick Preston were the try-scoring heroes as England overcame their Parisian blues for the first time since the 1960s.

IRELAND 22 SCOTLAND 15; at Lansdowne Road; 2nd of February 1980

	Ireland		Scotland
15	O'Donnell	15	Irvine [PEN, 2 CONs]
14	Kennedy [TRY]	14	Munro
13	McKibbin	13	Renwick
12	McNaughton	12	Johnston [2 TRIES]
11	Moloney	11	Hay
10	Campbell [3 PENs, DG, CON]	10	Rutherford
9	Patterson	9	Laidlaw
8	Spring	8	Beattie
7	Slattery (c)	7	Brewster
6	O'Driscoll	6	Biggar (c)
5	Glennon	5	Gray
4	Keane [TRY]	4	Cuthbertson
3	Fitzpatrick	3	Milne
2	Fitzgerald	2	Deans
1	Orr	1	Burnett

Comments: This was Scotland's 11th successive Five Nations match without a win, in spite of 2 tries from David Johnston, and due to Campbell's 14 points.

ENGLAND 9 WALES 8; at Twickenham; 16th of February 1980

15	Hare [3 PENS]		15	Blyth
14	Carleton		14	Rees [TRY]
13	Woodward		13	Richards
12	Dodge		12	Fenwick
11	Slemen		11	Keen
10	Horton		10	Davies
9	Smith		9	Holmes
8	Scott		8	Butler
7	Neary		7	Squire (c) [TRY]
6	Uttley		6	Ringer [SENT OFF]
5	Colclough		5	Wheel
4	Beaumont (c)		4	Martin
3	Blakeway		3	Price
2	Wheeler		2	Phillips
1	Cotton		1	Williams

Comments: Paul Ringer's sending-off left the visitors reduced to 14 men and they paid the penalty as Dusty Hare kicked England to a pivotal triumph.

SCOTLAND 22 FRANCE 14; at Murrayfield; 16th of February 1980

15	Irvine [2 TRIES, 2 PENs, CON]		15	Gabernet [TRY, PEN]
14	Munro		14	Bustaffa
13	Renwick (CON)		13	Bertranne
12	Johnston		12	Codorniou
11	Hay		11	Averous
10	Rutherford [TRY]		10	Caussade [DG]
9	Laidlaw		9	Gallion [TRY]
8	Beattie		8	Clemente
7	Brewster		7	Joinel
6	Biggar (c)		6	Rives (c)
5	Gray		5	Marchal
4	Tomes		4	Haget
3	Milne		3	Paparemborde
2	Deans		2	Dintrans
1	Burnett		1	Vaquerin

Comments: Andy Irvine helped himself to sixteen points as the Scots came back from a 7-4 interval deficit to finally taste a Five Nations success.

FRANCE 19 IRELAND 18; at Parc des Princes; 1st of March 1980

15	Aguirre [2 PENS, CON]	15	O'Donnell
14	Gourdon [2 TRIES]	14	Kennedy
13	Bertranne	13	Irwin
12	Codorniou	12	McNaughton
11	Costes	11	McLennan [TRY]
10	Pedeutour [DG]	10	Campbell [3 PENs, DG, CON]
9	Gallion	9	Patterson
8	Clemente	8	Spring
7	Joinel	7	Slattery (c)
6	Rives (c)	6	O'Driscoll
5	Marchal	5	Keane
4	Haget	4	Foley
3	Dospital	3	Fitzpatrick
2	Dintrans	2	Fitzgerald
1	Vaquerin	1	Orr

Comments: Jean-Francois Gourdon scored 2 second-half tries as France avoided a whitewash. This was tough on Ollie Campbell who kicked 14 points.

WALES 17 SCOTLAND 6; at Cardiff; 1st of March 1980

15	Blyth [CON]	15	Irvine [CON]
14	Rees	14	Robertson
13	Richards [TRY]	13	Renwick [TRY]
12	Fenwick [PEN]	12	Johnston
11	Keen [TRY]	11	Hay
10	Davies	10	Gossman
9	Holmes [TRY]	9	Laidlaw
8	Butler	8	Beattie
7	Squire (c)	7	Dickson
6	Lane	6	Biggar (c)
5	Wheel	5	Gray
4	Martin	4	Tomes
3	Price	3	Rowan
2	Phillips	2	Lawrie
1	Williams	1	Burnett

Comments: Two second-half tries from the home team ensured that the Welsh could celebrate St. David's Day with two points, after this comfortable win.

IRELAND 21 WALES 7; at Lansdowne Road; 15th of March 1980

15	O'Donnell		15	Blyth [TRY]
14	Kennedy		14	Rees
13	McNaughton		13	Richards
12	Irwin [TRY]		12	Fenwick [PEN]
11	Moloney		11	Keen
10	Campbell [PEN, 3 CONs]		10	Morgan
9	Patterson		9	Holmes
8	Spring		8	Butler
7	Slattery (c)		7	Squire (c)
6	O'Driscoll [TRY]		6	Lane
5	Foley		5	Wheel
4	Keane		4	Martin
3	Fitzpatrick		3	Price
2	Fitzgerald [TRY]		2	Phillips
1	Orr		1	Williams

Comments: Future Ireland and Lions captain Ciaran Fitzgerald scored his only try for Ireland when he charged down a kick in this emphatic triumph.

SCOTLAND 18 ENGLAND 30; at Murrayfield; 15th of March 1980

15	Irvine (c) [2 PENs, 2 CONs]		15	Hare [2 PENs, 2 CONs]
14	Robertson		14	Carleton [3 TRIES]
13	Renwick		13	Woodward
12	Johnston		12	Dodge
11	Hay		11	Slemen [TRY]
10	Rutherford [TRY]		10	Horton
9	Laidlaw		9	Smith [TRY]
8	Beattie		8	Scott
7	Biggar		7	Neary
6	Leslie		6	Uttley
5	Gray		5	Colclough
4	Tomes [TRY]		4	Beaumont (c)
3	Rowan		3	Blakeway
2	Lawrie		2	Wheeler
1	Burnett		1	Cotton

Comments: John Carleton recorded a hat-trick of tries as England grabbed the Grand Slam in spectacular fashion, helped by three first-half tries.

1980 FINAL TABLE

		Points For	Points Against	Total Points
1ST	ENGLAND	80	48	8
2ND	IRELAND	70	65	4
2ND	WALES	50	45	4
4TH	FRANCE	55	75	2
4TH	SCOTLAND	61	83	2

Comments: England scored more points in their four victorious outings than they had in 10 previous Five Nations fixtures.

DID YOU KNOW?

The 1980 British And Irish Lions excursion to South Africa didn't just culminate in a three-one tests defeat for the tourists. The ill-fated campaign also brought to an abrupt end the playing careers of the promising Irish pair, Rodney O'Donnell and Colin Patterson. The former who was notoriously superstitious succumbed to a near-fatal collision with the formidable Danie Gerber. Furthermore, the Lions suffered the loss of England's Fran Cotton who actually departed the rugby field with a suspected heart attack!

1981

FRANCE 16 SCOTLAND 9; at Parc des Princes; 17th of January 1981

15	Gabernet [PEN]		15	Irvine (c) [PEN]
14	Blanco [TRY]		14	Munro
13	Bertranne [TRY]		13	Renwick [CON]
12	Codorniou		12	Robertson
11	Pardo		11	Hay
10	Vivies [PEN]		10	Rutherford [TRY]
9	Berbizier		9	Laidlaw
8	Carpentier		8	Beattie
7	Joinel		7	Dickson
6	Rives (c)		6	Calder
5	Imbernon		5	Gray
4	Revailler		4	Tomes
3	Paparemborde		3	Rowan
2	Dintrans		2	Deans
1	Dospital		1	Aitkin

Comments: Blanco and Bertranne each crossed the try-line to set up the victory. Alain Caussade came off the bench and kicked a conversion for the hosts.

WALES 21 ENGLAND 19; at Cardiff; 17th of January 1981

15	Williams. J		15	Hare [TRY, 5 PENs]
14	Ackerman		14	Carleton
13	Richards		13	Woodward
12	Fenwick (c) [4 PENs, CON]		12	Dodge
11	Nicholas		11	Slemen
10	Davies [DG]		10	Horton
9	Williams. B		9	Smith
8	Williams. G		8	Scott
7	Squire		7	Cooke
6	Lewis		6	Rafter
5	Wheel		5	Colclough
4	Davis [TRY]		4	Beaumont (c)
3	Price		3	Blakeway
2	Phillips		2	Wheeler
1	Stephens		1	Cotton

Comments: The final score was tough on Dusty Hare who recorded all of England's points. Fenwick's goal-kicking was crucial to Wales's narrow success.

IRELAND 13 FRANCE 19; at Lansdowne Road; 7th of February 1981

15	MacNeill [TRY]	15	Gabernet [PEN]
14	Quinn	14	Caussade
13	Irwin	13	Bertranne
12	McNaughton	12	Mesny
11	McLennan	11	Pardo [TRY]
10	Campbell [3 PENs]	10	Laporte [2 PENs, 2 DGs]
9	Robbie	9	Berbizier
8	Duggan	8	Carpentier
7	Slattery (c)	7	Joinel
6	O'Driscoll	6	Rives (c)
5	Foley	5	Imbernon
4	Keane	4	Revailler
3	Fitzpatrick	3	Paparemborde
2	Whelan	2	Dintrans
1	Orr	1	Dospital

Comments: Guy Laporte notched 2 memorable drop goals on his debut. Hugo MacNeill scored a second-half try on his debut but France still held on.

SCOTLAND 15 WALES 6; at Murrayfield; 7th of February 1981

15	Irvine (c) [TRY]	15	Williams. J
14	Munro	14	Ackerman
13	Renwick [PEN, 2 CONs]	13	Richards
12	Robertson	12	Fenwick (c) [2 PENs]
11	Hay	11	Nicholas
10	Rutherford	10	Davies
9	Laidlaw	9	Williams. B
8	Beattie	8	Williams. G
7	Leslie	7	Squire
6	Calder	6	Lewis
5	Tomes [TRY]	5	Wheel
4	Cuthbertson	4	Davis
3	Rowan	3	Price
2	Deans	2	Phillips
1	Aitkin	1	Stephens

Comments: Gwyn Evans came on as a substitute to earn his first cap, but Wales had no answer to a team that crossed the try-line in each half.

ENGLAND 23 SCOTLAND 17; at Twickenham; 21st of February 1981

15	Hare [3 PENs, CON]	15	Irvine (c) [PEN, CON]
14	Carleton	14	Munro [2 TRIES]
13	Woodward [TRY]	13	Renwick
12	Dodge	12	Robertson
11	Slemen [TRY]	11	Hay
10	Davies [TRY]	10	Rutherford
9	Smith	9	Laidlaw
8	Scott	8	Beattie
7	Cooke	7	Leslie
6	Jeavons	6	Calder [TRY]
5	Colclough	5	Tomes
4	Beaumont (c)	4	Cuthbertson
3	Blakeway	3	Rowan
2	Wheeler	2	Deans
1	Smart	1	Aitkin

Comments: Steve Munro scored his only two tries for Scotland in this match, but Huw Davies also crossed the try-line on his debut in this try feast.

WALES 9 IRELAND 8; at Cardiff; 21st of February 1981

15	Evans [2 PENs]	15	MacNeill [TRY]
14	Richards	14	Quinn
13	Gravell	13	Irwin
12	Morgan	12	Campbell
11	Nicholas	11	McLennan
10	Pearce [DG]	10	Ward
9	Williams	9	Robbie
8	Squire (c)	8	Duggan
7	Burgess	7	Slattery (c) [TRY]
6	Lewis	6	O'Driscoll
5	Wheel	5	Spring
4	Martin	4	Keane
3	Price	3	Fitzpatrick
2	Phillips	2	Whelan
1	Stephens	1	Orr

Comments: Gary Pearce slotted home a decisive drop goal as Ireland failed to land a single kick, in spite of having both Campbell and Ward in their team.

FRANCE 19 WALES 15; at Parc des Princes; 7th of March 1981

15	Gabernet [TRY, 2 PENs]	15	Evans [3 PENs, CON]
14	Blanco	14	Rees
13	Bertranne	13	Gravell
12	Codorniou	12	Richards [TRY]
11	Pardo	11	Nicholas
10	Laporte [3 PENs]	10	Pearce
9	Berbizier	9	Williams
8	Joinel	8	Squire (c)
7	Lacans	7	Burgess
6	Rives (c)	6	Lewis
5	Imbernon	5	Wheel
4	Revailler	4	Martin
3	Paparemborde	3	Price
2	Dintrans	2	Phillips
1	Dospital	1	Stephens

Comments: Serge Gabernet's second-half try was the difference between the two teams as Les Bleus completed the third leg of a potential 'Grand Chelem'.

IRELAND 6 ENGLAND 10; at Lansdowne Road; 7th of March 1981

15	MacNeill [DG]	15	Rose [TRY, CON]
14	Quinn	14	Carleton
13	Irwin	13	Woodward
12	Campbell [DG]	12	Dodge [TRY]
11	McLennan	11	Slemen
10	Ward	10	Davies
9	Robbie	9	Smith
8	Duggan	8	Scott
7	Slattery (c)	7	Cooke
6	O'Driscoll	6	Jeavons
5	Foley	5	Colclough
4	Keane	4	Beaumont (c)
3	Fitzpatrick	3	Blakeway
2	Whelan	2	Wheeler
1	Orr	1	Smart

Comments: Tries from Paul Dodge and the debutant Marcus Rose helped England come from behind as Ireland failed again to land a single penalty.

ENGLAND 12 FRANCE 16; at Twickenham; 21st of March 1981

15	Rose [4 PENs]		15	Gabernet
14	Carleton		14	Blanco
13	Woodward		13	Bertranne
12	Dodge		12	Codorniou
11	Slemen		11	Pardo [TRY]
10	Davies		10	Laporte [2 DGs, CON]
9	Smith		9	Berbizier
8	Scott		8	Joinel
7	Cooke		7	Lacans [TRY]
6	Jeavons		6	Rives (c)
5	Colclough		5	Imbernon
4	Beaumont (c)		4	Revailler
3	Blakeway		3	Paparemborde
2	Wheeler		2	Dintrans
1	Smart		1	Dospital

Comments: Rose's four second-half penalties came too late as France raced into a 16-0 interval lead en route to their second Grand Slam in five seasons.

SCOTLAND 10 IRELAND 9; at Murrayfield; 21st of March 1981

15	Irvine (c) [PEN]		15	MacNeill
14	Munro		14	Hooks
13	Renwick		13	Irwin [TRY]
12	Robertson		12	Campbell [PEN, CON]
11	Hay [TRY]		11	McLennan
10	Rutherford [DG]		10	Ward
9	Laidlaw		9	Robbie
8	Beattie		8	Duggan
7	Leslie		7	Slattery (c)
6	Calder		6	O'Driscoll
5	Tomes		5	Foley
4	Cuthbertson		4	Keane
3	Rowan		3	Fitzpatrick
2	Deans		2	Cantrell
1	Aitkin		1	Orr

Comments: Bruce Hay recorded his only Five Nations try as Scotland seized a 10-0 interval lead. Ireland ended a whitewashed season with 4 narrow defeats.

1981 FINAL TABLE

		Points For	Points Against	Total Points
1ST	FRANCE	70	49	8
2ND	ENGLAND	64	60	4
2ND	WALES	51	61	4
2ND	SCOTLAND	51	54	4
5TH	IRELAND	36	48	0

Comments:Remarkably, the Irish conceded less points than all the other teams. This was France's third-ever Grand Slam.

DID YOU KNOW?

The 1981 championship was the second of three tournaments in which a Grand Slam for France was accompanied by a whitewash for Ireland. This peculiar phenomenon also occurred in 1977 and 1998.

1982

SCOTLAND 9 ENGLAND 9; at Murrayfield; 16th of January 1982

15 Irvine (c) [2 PENs]	15 Rose [PEN]
14 Robertson	14 Carleton
13 Renwick	13 Woodward
12 Johnston	12 Dodge [2 PENs]
11 Baird	11 Slemen
10 Rutherford [DG]	10 Davies
9 Laidlaw	9 Smith
8 Paxton	8 Hesford
7 Leslie	7 Winterbottom
6 Calder	6 Jeavons
5 Tomes	5 Colclough
4 Cuthbertson	4 Beaumont (c)
3 Milne	3 Pearce
2 Deans	2 Wheeler
1 Aitkin	1 Smart

Comments: England failed to build upon their 9-6 interval lead in a match that was a far cry from the Calcutta Cup spectacles of 1980 and 1981.

IRELAND 20 WALES 12; at Lansdowne Road; 23rd of January 1982

15 MacNeill	15 Evans [PEN, CON]
14 Ringland [TRY]	14 Ackerman
13 Irwin	13 Richards
12 Dean	12 Daniels
11 Finn [2 TRIES]	11 Rees
10 Campbell [2 PENs, CON]	10 Davies. G (c)
9 McGrath	9 Holmes [TRY]
8 Duggan	8 Squire
7 Slattery	7 Williams
6 O'Driscoll	6 Davies. M
5 Lenihan	5 Moriarty
4 Keane	4 Wheel
3 McLoughlin	3 Price
2 Fitzgerald (c)	2 Phillips
1 Orr	1 Stephens

Comments: Finn bagged a pair of tries as a Campbell-inspired Ireland came from behind to secure victory. Pearce came off the bench to kick a drop goal for Wales.

ENGLAND 15 IRELAND 16; at Twickenham; 6th of February 1982

15	Rose [3 PENs, CON]	15	MacNeill [TRY]
14	Carleton	14	Ringland
13	Woodward	13	Kiernan
12	Bond	12	Dean
11	Slemen [TRY]	11	Finn
10	Davies	10	Campbell [2 PENs, CON]
9	Smith (c)	9	McGrath
8	Scott	8	Duggan
7	Winterbottom	7	Slattery
6	Jeavons	6	O'Driscoll
5	Colclough	5	Lenihan
4	Syddall	4	Keane
3	Blakeway	3	McLoughlin [TRY]
2	Wheeler	2	Fitzgerald (c)
1	Smart	1	Orr

Comments: A late Slemen try flattered England. The match boasted a bizarre try from Gerry 'Ginger' McLoughlin who bulldozed his way over the English line.

WALES 22 FRANCE 12; at Cardiff; 6th of February 1982

15	Evans [6 PENs]	15	Sallefranque [PEN, CON]
14	Ackerman	14	Blanco [TRY]
13	Richards	13	Perrier
12	Gravell	12	Belascain
11	Rees	11	Pardo
10	Davies (c)	10	Lescarboura
9	Holmes [TRY]	9	Martinez [PEN]
8	Squire	8	Rodriguez
7	Lewis	7	Lacans
6	Burgess	6	Rives (c)
5	Moriarty	5	Revailler
4	Sutton	4	Lorieux
3	Price	3	Paparemborde
2	Phillips	2	Dintrans
1	Stephens	1	Cremaschi

Comments: A Blanco try helped France to a 9-6 half-time lead, but a try from Holmes and accurate goal-kicking from Evans ensured a comfortable Welsh win.

FRANCE 15 ENGLAND 27; at Parc des Princes; 20th of February 1982

15	Sallefranque [2 PENs, CON]		15	Hare [5 PENs, 2 CONs]
14	Blanco		14	Carleton [TRY]
13	Perrier		13	Woodward [TRY]
12	Belascain		12	Dodge
11	Pardo [TRY]		11	Slemen
10	Lescarboura [DG]		10	Cusworth
9	Martinez		9	Smith (c)
8	Joinel		8	Scott
7	Buchet		7	Winterbottom
6	Rives (c)		6	Jeavons
5	Rodriguez		5	Colclough
4	Carpentier		4	Bainbridge
3	Dubroca		3	Blakeway
2	Dintrans		2	Wheeler
1	Wolf		1	Smart

Comments: Dusty Hare kicked 19 points as England won in Paris for a second successive time. Steve Bainbridge made his debut in this away-day triumph.

IRELAND 21 SCOTLAND 12; at Lansdowne Road; 20th of February 1982

15	MacNeill		15	Irvine (c) [CON]
14	Finn		14	Robertson
13	Kiernan		13	Renwick [2 PENs]
12	Dean		12	Johnston
11	Crossan		11	Baird
10	Campbell [6 PENs, DG]		10	Rutherford [TRY]
9	McGrath		9	Laidlaw
8	Duggan		8	Paxton. I
7	Slattery		7	Paxton. E
6	O'Driscoll		6	Calder
5	Lenihan		5	Tomes
4	Keane		4	Cuthbertson
3	McLoughlin		3	Milne
2	Fitzgerald (c)		2	Deans
1	Orr		1	Aitkin

Comments: Keith Crossan made his debut as Ireland seized the Triple Crown. Hero of the day was Ollie Campbell who kicked all 21 of the home team's points.

ENGLAND 17 WALES 7; at Twickenham; 6th of March 1982

15	Hare [3 PENs]		15	Evans
14	Carleton [TRY]		14	Ackerman
13	Woodward		13	Gravell
12	Dodge		12	Donovan
11	Slemen [TRY]		11	Rees
10	Cusworth		10	Davies (c) [DG]
9	Smith (c)		9	Holmes
8	Scott		8	Squire
7	Winterbottom		7	Lewis [TRY]
6	Jeavons		6	Burgess
5	Colclough		5	Moriarty
4	Bainbridge		4	Sutton
3	Blakeway		3	Price
2	Wheeler		2	Phillips
1	Smart		1	Stephens

Comments: A solitary Hare penalty was the only score of the second half as England overcame a toothless Wales, for whom the glory years were fading fast.

SCOTLAND 16 FRANCE 7; at Murrayfield; 6th of March 1982

15	Irvine (c) [3 PENs]		15	Sallefranque [PEN]
14	Robertson		14	Blanco
13	Renwick [DG]		13	Perrier
12	Johnston		12	Belascain
11	Baird		11	Pardo
10	Rutherford [TRY]		10	Lescarboura
9	Laidlaw		9	Martinez
8	Paxton		8	Carpentier
7	White		7	Joinel
6	Calder		6	Rives (c) [TRY]
5	Tomes		5	Rodriguez
4	Cuthbertson		4	Revailler
3	Milne		3	Dubroca
2	Deans		2	Dintrans
1	Aitkin		1	Cremaschi

Comments: A try from Jean-Pierre Rives gave the visitors a 7-3 interval lead, but Rutherford's second try of the tournament helped the hosts secure 2 points.

FRANCE 22 IRELAND 9; at Parc des Princes; 20th of March 1982

15	Gabernet [2 PENs, CON]	15	MacNeill
14	Fabre	14	Ringland
13	Mesny [TRY]	13	Kiernan
12	Belascain	12	Dean
11	Blanco [TRY, 2 PENs]	11	Finn
10	Lescarboura	10	Campbell [3 PENs]
9	Berbizier	9	McGrath
8	Joinel	8	O'Driscoll
7	Rodriguez	7	Kearney
6	Rives (c)	6	Slattery
5	Imbernon	5	Lenihan
4	Revailler	4	Keane
3	Paparemborde	3	McLoughlin
2	Dintrans	2	Fitzgerald (c)
1	Dospital	1	Orr

Comments: Ireland's quest for a second-ever Grand Slam ran out of steam in the second half as Blanco and Mesny both touched down for tries.

WALES 18 SCOTLAND 34; at Cardiff; 20th of March 1982

15	Evans [4 PENs, CON]	15	Irvine (c) [4 CONs]
14	Ackerman	14	Pollock [TRY]
13	Gravell	13	Renwick [TRY, DG]
12	Donovan	12	Johnston [TRY]
11	Rees	11	Baird
10	Davies (c)	10	Rutherford [DG]
9	Williams	9	Laidlaw
8	Butler [TRY]	8	Paxton
7	Lewis	7	White [TRY]
6	Burgess	6	Calder [TRY]
5	Moriarty	5	Tomes
4	Norster	4	Cuthbertson
3	Price	3	Milne
2	Phillips	2	Deans
1	Stephens	1	Aitkin

Comments: Scotland ran riot with five tries, including one from debutant Jim Pollock, to win in Cardiff for the first time since the 1960s.

1982 FINAL TABLE

		Points For	Points Against	Total Points
1ST	IRELAND	66	61	6
2ND	ENGLAND	68	47	5
2ND	SCOTLAND	71	55	5
4TH	FRANCE	56	74	2
4TH	WALES	59	83	2

Comments: Scotland scored the most points and England conceded the least points, but this would be a glory year for Ireland.

DID YOU KNOW?

There have been many occasions since 1970 when a rugby team fell at the final hurdle in their quest for a Grand Slam:

1978: France lost away to Wales who took the Grand Slam instead
1982: Ireland lost away to France
1984: France lost away to Scotland who took the Grand Slam instead
1988: Wales lost at home to France
1990: England lost away to Scotland who took the Grand Slam instead
1991: France lost away to England who took the Grand Slam instead
1994: Wales lost away to England
1995: Scotland lost away to England who took the Grand Slam instead
1996: Scotland lost at home to England
1999: England lost away to Wales
2000: England lost away to Scotland
2001: England lost away to Ireland
2003: Ireland lost at home to England who took the Grand Slam instead
2008: France lost away to Wales who took the Grand Slam instead

1983

ENGLAND 15 FRANCE 19; at Twickenham; 15th of January 1983

15	Hare [4 PENs]		15	Blanco [2 CONs]
14	Carleton		14	Sella [TRY]
13	Davies		13	Belascain
12	Dodge		12	Codorniou
11	Swift		11	Esteve [TRY]
10	Cusworth [DG]		10	Camberabero [PEN]
9	Smith (c)		9	Martinez
8	Scott		8	Joinel
7	Winterbottom		7	Rodriguez
6	Jeavons		6	Rives (c)
5	Bainbridge		5	Condom
4	Colclough		4	Orso
3	Pearce		3	Paparemborde [TRY]
2	Wheeler		2	Dintrans
1	Smart		1	Dospital

Comments: Les Francais overcame a 9-3 interval deficit with the help of three tries as this fixture produced an away win for the fourth successive year.

SCOTLAND 13 IRELAND 15; at Murrayfield; 15th of January 1983

15	Dods [2 PENs]		15	MacNeill
14	Robertson		14	Ringland
13	Renwick [DG]		13	Irwin
12	Johnston		12	Kiernan [TRY]
11	Baird		11	Finn
10	Wilson		10	Campbell [3 PENs, CON]
9	Laidlaw (c) [TRY]		9	McGrath
8	Paxton		8	Duggan
7	Leslie		7	O'Driscoll
6	Calder		6	Slattery
5	Tomes		5	Keane
4	Cuthbertson		4	Lenihan
3	Milne		3	McLoughlin
2	Deans		2	Fitzgerald (c)
1	McGuinness		1	Orr

Comments: Peter Dodds slotted home two second-half penalties, but Ireland held on to their half-time lead after Kiernan had scored his first international try.

FRANCE 19 SCOTLAND 15; at Parc des Princes; 5th of February 1983

15	Blanco [3 PENs, CON]		15	Dods [PEN, CON]
14	Sella		14	Robertson [TRY]
13	Codorniou		13	Renwick
12	Belascain		12	Johnston
11	Esteve [2 TRIES]		11	Baird
10	Delage		10	Gossman [2 DGs]
9	Berbizier		9	Laidlaw (c)
8	Joinel		8	Beattie
7	Rodriguez		7	Leslie
6	Rives (c)		6	Calder
5	Orso		5	Tomes
4	Condom		4	Cuthbertson
3	Paparemborde		3	Milne
2	Dupont		2	Deans
1	Dospital		1	Aitkin

Comments: Patrick Esteve's try was the only score of the second half and it separated two teams that had been locked together 15-15 at the interval.

WALES 13 ENGLAND 13; at Cardiff; 5th of February 1983

15	Wyatt [2 PENs]		15	Hare [2 PENs]
14	Rees. E		14	Carleton [TRY]
13	Richards		13	Davies
12	Ring		12	Dodge
11	Rees. C		11	Swift
10	Dacey [DG]		10	Cusworth [DG]
9	Holmes		9	Smith (c)
8	Butler (c)		8	Scott
7	Pickering		7	Winterbottom
6	Squire [TRY]		6	Jeavons
5	Moriarty		5	Bainbridge
4	Norster		4	Boyle
3	Price		3	Pearce
2	James		2	Mills
1	Williams		1	Smart

Comments: Both teams shared the 2 tries, 4 penalties, 2 drop goals, 26 points and 2 tournament points. 6 players won their first caps, including five Welshmen.

IRELAND 22 FRANCE 16; at Lansdowne Road; 19th of February 1983

15	MacNeill	15	Blanco [TRY, 2 PENs, CON]
14	Ringland	14	Sella
13	Irwin	13	Belascain
12	Kiernan	12	Codorniou
11	Finn [2 TRIES]	11	Esteve [TRY]
10	Campbell [4 PENs, CON]	10	Delage
9	McGrath	9	Berbizier
8	Duggan	8	Joinel
7	O'Driscoll	7	Erbani
6	Slattery	6	Rives (c)
5	Keane	5	Imbernon
4	Lenihan	4	Condom
3	McLoughlin	3	Paparemborde
2	Fitzgerald (c)	2	Herrero
1	Orr	1	Dospital

Comments: Moss Finn grabbed a try in each half as the home team's Dads' Army set of forwards, led by Ciaran Fitzgerald, marched towards another victory.

SCOTLAND 15 WALES 19; at Murrayfield; 19th of February 1983

15	Dods [3 PENS, CON]	15	Wyatt [3 PENS, CON]
14	Robertson	14	Rees. E [TRY]
13	Renwick [TRY]	13	Richards
12	Johnston	12	Ackerman
11	Baird	11	Rees. C
10	Gossman	10	Dacey
9	Laidlaw (c)	9	Holmes
8	Beattie	8	Butler (c)
7	Leslie	7	Pickering
6	Calder	6	Squire
5	Tomes	5	Perkins
4	Cuthbertson	4	Norster
3	Milne	3	Eidman
2	Deans	2	James
1	Aitkin	1	Jones [TRY]

Comments: Staff Jones crossed the try-line on his debut as Wales recorded their first away win in the Five Nations since 1979, after seven failed attempts.

ENGLAND 12 SCOTLAND 22; at Twickenham; 5th of March 1983

15	Hare [3 PENs]	15	Dods [3 PENs, CON]
14	Carleton	14	Pollock
13	Davies	13	Renwick
12	Dodge	12	Robertson [DG]
11	Swift	11	Baird
10	Horton [DG]	10	Rutherford
9	Smith (c)	9	Laidlaw [TRY]
8	Scott	8	Beattie
7	Winterbottom	7	Leslie
6	Jeavons	6	Calder
5	Bainbridge	5	Paxton
4	Boyle	4	Smith [TRY]
3	Pearce	3	Milne
2	Wheeler	2	Deans
1	Smart	1	Aitkin (c)

Comments: Roy Laidlaw and the giant debutant Tom Smith were the try-scoring heroes as the Scots won back the Calcutta Cup for the first time since 1976.

WALES 23 IRELAND 9; at Cardiff; 5th of March 1983

15	Wyatt [TRY, 3 PENs, CON]	15	MacNeill [PEN]
14	Rees. E [TRY]	14	Ringland
13	Ackerman	13	Irwin
12	Richards	12	Kiernan
11	Rees. C	11	Finn
10	Dacey	10	Campbell [2 PENs]
9	Holmes [TRY]	9	McGrath
8	Butler (c)	8	Duggan
7	Pickering	7	O'Driscoll
6	Squire	6	Slattery
5	Norster	5	Keane
4	Perkins	4	Lenihan
3	Price	3	McLoughlin
2	James	2	Fitzgerald (c)
1	Jones	1	Orr

Comments: Mark Wyatt helped himself to 15 points as Wales, 12-6 ahead at half-time, registered their most emphatic win since the 1970s.

FRANCE 16 WALES 9; at Parc des Princes; 19th of March 1983

15	Blanco [3 PENs]	15	Wyatt [CON]
14	Sella	14	Rees. E
13	Codorniou	13	Ackerman
12	Belascain	12	Evans [PEN]
11	Esteve [TRY]	11	Rees. C
10	Camberabero [DG]	10	Dacey
9	Martinez	9	Holmes
8	Joinel	8	Butler (c)
7	Erbani	7	Pickering
6	Rives (c)	6	Squire [TRY]
5	Imbernon	5	Norster
4	Condom	4	Perkins
3	Paparemborde	3	Price
2	Dintrans	2	James
1	Dospital	1	Jones

Comments: Esteve's second-half try helped his team to a share of the championship. The winger had crossed the try-line in all of France's matches of 1983.

IRELAND 25 ENGLAND 15; at Lansdowne Road; 19th of March 1983

15	MacNeill	15	Hare [5 PENs]
14	Ringland	14	Carleton
13	Irwin	13	Woodward
12	Kiernan	12	Dodge
11	Finn	11	Trick
10	Campbell [TRY, 5 PENS, CON]	10	Horton
9	McGrath	9	Youngs
8	Duggan	8	Scott (c)
7	O'Driscoll	7	Winterbottom
6	Slattery [TRY]	6	Jeavons
5	Keane	5	Bainbridge
4	Lenihan	4	Boyle
3	McLoughlin	3	Pearce
2	Fitzgerald (c)	2	Wheeler
1	Orr	1	Smart

Comments: Dusty Hare's 15 points was eclipsed by Ollie Campbell's haul of 21 as the men in green earned themselves a share of the Five Nations honours.

1983 FINAL TABLE

		Points For	Points Against	Total Points
1ST	FRANCE	70	61	6
1ST	IRELAND	71	67	6
3RD	WALES	64	53	5
4TH	SCOTLAND	65	65	2
5TH	ENGLAND	55	79	1

Comments: England failed to win a match, but their drawn appearance at the Arms Park ultimately denied Wales a Triple Crown.

DID YOU KNOW?

Scotland's convincing triumph over England at Twickenham in 1983 was the first of five successive Five Nations victories, culminating in the Grand Slam of 1984. However, the Scots have failed to register a single victory in south-west London since their 22-12 win. Twickenham has been an unhappy and fruitless venue for Scotland now in thirteen subsequent visits.

1984

FRANCE 25 IRELAND 12; at Parc des Princes; 21st of January 1984

15	Blanco		15	MacNeill
14	Lagisquet		14	Ringland
13	Sella [TRY]		13	Irwin
12	Codorniou		12	Moroney
11	Esteve		11	Crossan
10	Lescarboura [4 PENs, DG, CON]		10	Campbell [4 PENs]
9	Gallion [TRY]		9	McGrath
8	Joinel		8	Duggan
7	Rodriguez		7	O'Driscoll
6	Rives (c)		6	Slattery
5	Condom		5	Lenihan
4	Lorieux		4	Keane
3	Garuet-Lempirou [SENT OFF]		3	McLoughlin
2	Dintrans		2	Fitzgerald (c)
1	Cremaschi		1	Orr

Comments: Rory Moroney made his debut, but the ageing Irish pack had no answer to the hosts who ran out comfortable winners in the end.

WALES 9 SCOTLAND 15; at Cardiff; 21st of January 1984

15	Davies [PEN, CON]		15	Dods [PEN, 2 CONs]
14	Titley [TRY]		14	Munro
13	Ackerman		13	Johnston
12	Bowen		12	Kennedy
11	Hadley		11	Baird
10	Dacey		10	Rutherford
9	Douglas		9	Laidlaw
8	Butler (c)		8	Paxton [TRY]
7	Pickering		7	Leslie
6	Moriarty		6	Calder
5	Norster		5	Tomes
4	Perkins		4	Cuthbertson
3	Morgan		3	Milne
2	James		2	Deans
1	Jones		1	Aitkin (c) [TRY]

Comments: The Scots' captain, Jim Aitkin, scored his only international try as the tartan warriors won at the Arms Park for the second successive time.

IRELAND 9 WALES 18; at Lansdowne Road; 4th of February 1984

15	MacNeill	15	Davies [2 PENs, CON]
14	Ringland	14	Titley
13	Irwin	13	Ackerman [TRY]
12	Moroney	12	Bowen [2 PENs]
11	Crossan	11	Hadley
10	Campbell [3 PENs]	10	Dacey
9	McGrath	9	Douglas
8	Duggan	8	Butler
7	O'Driscoll	7	Pickering
6	Duncan	6	Moriarty
5	Lenihan	5	Norster
4	Keane	4	Perkins
3	McCoy	3	Eidman
2	Fitzgerald (c)	2	Watkins (c)
1	Orr	1	Stephens

Comments: Mike Watkins was peculiarly awarded the Wales captaincy on his debut. His team were assisted by Rob Ackerman's only international try.

SCOTLAND 18 ENGLAND 6; at Murrayfield; 4th of February 1984

15	Dods [2 PENs, 2 CONs]	15	Hare [2 PENs]
14	Robertson	14	Carleton
13	Kennedy [TRY]	13	Davies
12	Johnston [TRY]	12	Woodward
11	Baird	11	Slemen
10	Rutherford	10	Cusworth
9	Laidlaw	9	Youngs
8	Paxton	8	Scott
7	Leslie	7	Winterbottom
6	Calder	6	Simpson
5	Tomes	5	Bainbridge
4	Cuthbertson	4	Colclough
3	Milne	3	Pearce
2	Deans	2	Wheeler (c)
1	Aitkin (c)	1	White

Comments: Alexander Kennedy recorded his only try for Scotland as the home team made light work of this Calcutta Cup encounter.

ENGLAND 12 IRELAND 9; at Twickenham; 18th of February 1984

15	Hare [3 PENs]	15	MacNeill
14	Carleton	14	Ringland
13	Barley	13	Kiernan
12	Woodward	12	Finn
11	Underwood	11	Crossan
10	Cusworth [DG]	10	Ward [3 PENs]
9	Youngs	9	Doyle
8	Scott	8	Duggan (c)
7	Cooke	7	O'Driscoll
6	Hall	6	Duncan
5	Bainbridge	5	Lenihan
4	Colclough	4	Keane
3	Blakeway	3	Fitzgerald
2	Wheeler (c)	2	Harbison
1	White	1	Orr

Comments: This wooden spoon play-off was decided by a Les Cusworth drop goal as both Dusty Hare and Tony Ward traded three penalties each.

WALES 16 FRANCE 21; at Cardiff; 18th of February 1984

15	Davies [TRY, 2 PENs, CON]	15	Blanco
14	Titley	14	Lagisquet
13	Ackerman	13	Sella [TRY]
12	Bowen	12	Codorniou
11	Hadley	11	Esteve
10	Dacey	10	Lescarboura [4 PENs, DG, CON]
9	Douglas	9	Gallion
8	Butler [TRY]	8	Joinel
7	Pickering	7	Erbani
6	Moriarty	6	Rives (c)
5	Norster	5	Condom
4	Perkins	4	Lorieux
3	Eidman	3	Dubroca
2	Watkins (c)	2	Dintrans
1	Stephens	1	Cremaschi

Comments: Although the Welsh crossed the try-line twice in the second half, they were damaged by a haul of 17 points for Jean-Patrick Lescarboura.

FRANCE 32 ENGLAND 18; at Parc des Princes; 3rd of March 1984

15	Blanco		15	Hare [TRY, 2 PENs, 2 CONs]
14	Begu [TRY]		14	Carleton
13	Sella [TRY]		13	Woodward
12	Codorniou [TRY]		12	Barley
11	Esteve [TRY]		11	Underwood [TRY]
10	Lescarboura [PEN, DG, 3 CONs]		10	Cusworth
9	Gallion [TRY]		9	Youngs
8	Joinel		8	Scott
7	Erbani		7	Winterbottom
6	Rives (c)		6	Hall
5	Condom		5	Bainbridge
4	Lorieux		4	Colclough
3	Dubroca		3	Blakeway
2	Dintrans		2	Wheeler (c)
1	Dospital		1	White

Comments: Dusty Hare accumulated fourteen points but his team were still fourteen points short as France finally secured a home win against England.

IRELAND 9 SCOTLAND 32*; at Lansdowne Road; 3rd of March 1984

15	Murphy [PEN, CON]		15	Dods [TRY, 2 PENs, 3 CONs]
14	Ringland		14	Pollock
13	Kiernan [TRY]		13	Robertson [TRY]
12	Finn		12	Johnston
11	Crossan		11	Baird
10	Ward		10	Rutherford
9	Doyle		9	Laidlaw [2 TRIES]
8	Duggan (c)		8	Paxton
7	McGrath		7	Leslie
6	O'Driscoll		6	Calder
5	Lenihan		5	Tomes
4	Keane		4	Campbell
3	Fitzgerald		3	Milne
2	Harbison		2	Deans
1	Orr		1	Aitkin (c)

Comments: Roy Laidlaw helped himself to a pair of tries while Peter Dods plundered sixteen points as Scotland emphatically seized the Triple Crown.

*Scotland's points included a penalty try.

ENGLAND 15 WALES 24; at Twickenham; 17th of March 1984

15	Hare [5 PENs]		15	Davies [4 PENs, CON]
14	Carleton		14	Titley
13	Barley		13	Ackerman
12	Woodward		12	Bowen
11	Underwood		11	Hadley [TRY]
10	Cusworth		10	Dacey [2 DGs]
9	Youngs		9	Holmes
8	Scott		8	Butler
7	Winterbottom		7	Pickering
6	Dun		6	Moriarty
5	Bainbridge		5	Norster
4	Colclough		4	Perkins
3	Blakeway		3	Eidman
2	Wheeler (c)		2	Watkins (c)
1	Rendall		1	Stephens

Comments: Adrian Hadley scored the match's only try as Wales came from behind to end their campaign with two home defeats and two away wins.

SCOTLAND 21 FRANCE 12; at Parc des Princes; 17th of March 1984

15	Dods [5 PENs, CON]		15	Blanco
14	Pollock		14	Begu
13	Robertson		13	Sella
12	Johnston		12	Codorniou
11	Baird		11	Esteve
10	Rutherford		10	Lescarboura [PEN, DG, CON]
9	Laidlaw		9	Gallion [TRY]
8	Paxton		8	Orso
7	Leslie		7	Joinel
6	Calder [TRY]		6	Rives (c)
5	Tomes		5	Condom
4	Campbell		4	Haget
3	Milne		3	Dubroca
2	Deans		2	Dintrans
1	Aitkin (c)		1	Dospital

Comments: Jim Calder crossed the try-line in the second half and Peter Dods kicked seventeen points to earn Scotland the coveted Grand Slam.

1984 FINAL TABLE

		Points For	Points Against	Total Points
1ST	SCOTLAND	86	36	8
2ND	FRANCE	90	67	6
3RD	WALES	67	60	4
4TH	ENGLAND	51	83	2
5TH	IRELAND	39	87	0

Comments: This was Scotland's first clean sweep since 1925, whilst Ireland were whitewashed for the third time in 8 years.

DID YOU KNOW?

1984 began a period of total dominance by France against Ireland until 2000. The Oirish failed to beat either France or Scotland once in the 'nineties. The French took a perfect twenty points off the men in green in the 1990s. Scotland could only make do with a mere nineteen points!

1985

ENGLAND 9 FRANCE 9; at Twickenham; 2nd of February 1985

15	Martin		15	Blanco
14	Smith		14	Esteve
13	Simms		13	Sella
12	Dodge (c)		12	Codorniou
11	Underwood		11	Lavigne
10	Andrew [2 PENs, DG]		10	Lescarboura [3 DGs]
9	Harding		9	Gallion
8	Hesford		8	Erbani
7	Cooke		7	Rodriguez
6	Hall		6	Gratton
5	Dooley		5	Condom
4	Orwin		4	Haget
3	Pearce		3	Garuet-Lempirou
2	Brain		2	Dintrans (c)
1	Blakeway		1	Dospital

Comments: Jean-Patrick Lescarboura landed a hat-trick of drop goals but both teams had to settle for a share of the points in this try-less contest.

SCOTLAND 15 IRELAND 18; at Murrayfield; 2nd of February 1985

15	Dods [4 PENs]		15	MacNeill
14	Baird		14	Ringland [2 TRIES]
13	Murray		13	Mullin
12	Robertson [DG]		12	Kiernan [PEN, DG, 2 CONs]
11	Tukalo		11	Crossan
10	Rutherford		10	Dean
9	Laidlaw (c)		9	Bradley
8	Beattie		8	Spillane
7	Jeffrey		7	Carr
6	Calder		6	Matthews
5	Smith		5	Anderson
4	Campbell		4	Lenihan
3	Rowan		3	McCoy
2	Deans		2	Fitzgerald (c)
1	McGuinness		1	Orr

Comments: Trevor Ringland's brace of second-half tries overturned the 6-3 interval deficit. The visitors were fielding a new look back row.

FRANCE 11 SCOTLAND 3; at Parc des Princes; 16th of February 1985

	France			Scotland
15	Blanco [2 TRIES]		15	Dods [PEN]
14	Pardo		14	Steven
13	Sella		13	Murray
12	Codorniou		12	Robertson
11	Esteve		11	Pollock
10	Lescarboura [PEN]		10	Rutherford
9	Gallion		9	Laidlaw
8	Joinel		8	Paxton
7	Rodriguez		7	Leslie (c)
6	Gratton		6	Calder
5	Condom		5	Smith
4	Haget		4	Campbell
3	Garuet-Lempirou		3	Milne
2	Dintrans (c)		2	Deans
1	Dospital		1	McGuinness

Comments: All the points were scored in the first half as Serge Blanco demonstrated his attacking abilities with two decisive tries.

IRELAND 15 FRANCE 15; at Lansdowne Road; 2nd of March 1985

	Ireland			France
15	MacNeill		15	Blanco
14	Ringland		14	Pardo
13	Moroney		13	Sella
12	Kiernan [5 PENs]		12	Codorniou [TRY]
11	Crossan		11	Esteve [TRY]
10	Dean		10	Lescarboura [PEN, 2 CONs]
9	Bradley		9	Gallion
8	Spillane		8	Joinel
7	Carr		7	Rodriguez
6	Matthews		6	Gratton
5	Anderson		5	Haget
4	Lenihan		4	Condom
3	McCoy		3	Garuet-Lempirou
2	Fitzgerald (c)		2	Dintrans (c)
1	Orr		1	Dospital

Comments: Brian McCall won his first cap as a replacement in a match where France had to settle for another draw, having scored the only two tries.

SCOTLAND 21 WALES 25; at Murrayfield; 2nd of March 1985

15	Dods [PEN, 2 CONs]	15	Wyatt [4 PENs, CON]
14	Steven	14	Titley
13	Murray	13	Ackerman
12	Robertson	12	Ring
11	Baird	11	Lewis
10	Rutherford [2 DGs]	10	Davies [DG]
9	Hunter	9	Holmes (c)
8	Paxton [2 TRIES]	8	Moriarty
7	Leslie (c)	7	Pickering [2 TRIES]
6	Calder	6	Morris
5	Tomes	5	Norster
4	Campbell	4	Perkins
3	Milne	3	Eidman
2	Deans	2	James
1	McGuinness	1	Whitefoot

Comments: Mark Wyatt kicked fourteen points in this high-scoring match in which the four tries were shared. Martyn Morris won his first cap for Wales.

ENGLAND 10 SCOTLAND 7; at Twickenham; 16th of March 1985

15	Martin	15	Dods [PEN]
14	Smith [TRY]	14	Steven
13	Simms	13	Wyllie
12	Dodge (c)	12	Robertson [TRY]
11	Underwood	11	Baird
10	Andrew [2 PENs]	10	Rutherford
9	Harding	9	Hunter
8	Hesford	8	Paxton
7	Cooke	7	Leslie (c)
6	Hall	6	Jeffrey
5	Dooley	5	Tomes
4	Orwin	4	Campbell
3	Pearce	3	Milne
2	Brain	2	Deans
1	Blakeway	1	McGuinness

Comments: Simon Smith crossed the try-line in the second half as Scotland were condemned to a whitewash, having trailed 6-4 at the interval.

WALES 9 IRELAND 21; at Cardiff; 16th of March 1985

15	Wyatt [CON]	15	MacNeill
14	Titley	14	Ringland [TRY]
13	Ackerman	13	Mullin
12	Ring	12	Kiernan [3 PENs, 2 CONs]
11	Lewis [TRY]	11	Crossan [TRY]
10	Davies [DG]	10	Dean
9	Holmes (c)	9	Bradley
8	Moriarty	8	Spillane
7	Pickering	7	Carr
6	Morris	6	Matthews
5	Norster	5	Anderson
4	Perkins	4	Lenihan
3	Eidman	3	McCoy
2	James	2	Fitzgerald (c)
1	Whitefoot	1	Orr

Comments: The Ulster wingers, Trevor Ringland and Keith Crossan, scored a try in each half as Ireland won at the Arms Park for the first time since the 1960s.

FRANCE 14 WALES 3; at Parc des Princes; 30th of March 1985

15	Blanco	15	Thorburn [PEN]
14	Bonneval	14	Lewis
13	Sella	13	Ackerman
12	Codorniou	12	Ring
11	Esteve [TRY]	11	Hadley
10	Lescarboura [2 PENs]	10	Davies
9	Gallion [TRY]	9	Holmes(c)
8	Joinel	8	Moriarty
7	Rodriguez	7	Pickering
6	Gratton	6	Morris
5	Condom	5	Norster
4	Orso	4	Perkins
3	Garuet-Lempirou	3	Evans
2	Dintrans (c)	2	James
1	Dospital	1	Whitefoot

Comments: Paul Thorburn landed a penalty on his debut but Les Bleus took both points, courtesy of a try in each half.

IRELAND 13 ENGLAND 10; at Lansdowne Road; 30th of March 1985

15	MacNeill	15	Martin
14	Ringland	14	Smith
13	Mullin [TRY]	13	Simms
12	Kiernan [2 PENs, DG]	12	Dodge (c)
11	Crossan	11	Underwood [TRY]
10	Dean	10	Andrew [2 PENs]
9	Bradley	9	Melville
8	Spillane	8	Hesford
7	Carr	7	Cooke
6	Matthews	6	Hall
5	Anderson	5	Dooley
4	Lenihan	4	Orwin
3	McCoy	3	Pearce
2	Fitzgerald (c)	2	Brain
1	Orr	1	Blakeway

Comments: Michael Kiernan landed a late drop goal as Ireland grabbed another Triple Crown. Ciaran Fitzgerald was the victorious captain again.

WALES 24 ENGLAND 15; at Cardiff; 20th of April 1985

15	Thorburn [3 PENs, 2 CONs]	15	Martin
14	Lewis	14	Smith [TRY]
13	Ackerman	13	Simms
12	Hopkins	12	Dodge (c)
11	Hadley	11	Underwood
10	Davies. J [TRY, DG]	10	Andrew [2 PENs, DG, CON]
9	Holmes (c)	9	Melville
8	Davies. P	8	Hesford
7	Pickering	7	Cooke
6	Roberts [TRY]	6	Hall
5	Norster	5	Dooley
4	Perkins	4	Orwin
3	Evans	3	Pearce
2	James	2	Brain
1	Whitefoot	1	Sheppard

Comments: Jonathan Davies helped himself to a try and a drop goal on his debut. This was a repeat of the score between the two neighbours the year before.

1985 FINAL TABLE

		Points For	Points Against	Total Points
1ST	IRELAND	67	49	7
2ND	FRANCE	49	30	6
3RD	WALES	61	71	4
4TH	ENGLAND	44	53	3
5TH	SCOTLAND	46	64	0

Comments: Scotland slid from Grand Slam in 1984 to whitewash in 1985. Ireland went from whitewash in 1984 to Triple Crown.

DID YOU KNOW?

In 1985 Ireland registered their first win at the Arms Park since a 3-0 there in 1967. After 1983, the Irish have astonishingly won eleven times, drawn once, and lost only once on their away matches against Wales. In fact, 1983 proved to be Ireland's last defeat at the Arms Park. Even at the Millennium Stadium, during an era of two Welsh Grand Slams, Ireland have still recorded four wins out of five.

1986

ENGLAND 21 WALES 18; at Twickenham; 18th of January 1986

15	Davies		15	Thorburn [3 PENs, CON]
14	Smith		14	Lewis
13	Halliday		13	Devereux
12	Salmon		12	Bowen [TRY]
11	Underwood		11	Hadley
10	Andrew [6 PENs, DG]		10	Davies. J [DG]
9	Melville (c)		9	Jones
8	Robbins		8	Davies. P
7	Winterbottom		7	Pickering (c)
6	Hall		6	Brown
5	Colclough		5	Waters
4	Dooley		4	Perkins
3	Pearce		3	Eidman
2	Brain		2	James
1	Rendall		1	Whitefoot

Comments: Rob Andrew was largely responsible for this narrow win as his seven successful kicks were England's sole source of points.

SCOTLAND 18 FRANCE 17; at Murrayfield; 18th of January 1986

15	Hastings. G [6 PENs]		15	Blanco
14	Duncan		14	Lafond
13	Johnston		13	Sella [TRY]
12	Hastings. S		12	Chadebech
11	Baird		11	Esteve
10	Rutherford		10	Laporte [2 PENs, DG]
9	Laidlaw		9	Berbizier [TRY]
8	Beattie		8	Joinel
7	Calder		7	Erbani
6	Jeffrey		6	Gratton
5	Campbell-Lamerton		5	Condom
4	Campbell		4	Haget
3	Milne		3	Garuet-Lempirou
2	Deans (c)		2	Dubroca (c)
1	Sole		1	Marocco

Comments: The Hastings brothers, Gavin and Scot, made a happy debut for Scotland, with the former landing six penalties, just like Rob Andrew at Twickenham.

FRANCE 29 IRELAND 9; at Parc des Princes; 1st of February 1986

	France			Ireland
15	Blanco [PEN]		15	MacNeill
14	Lafond [DG]		14	Ringland
13	Sella [TRY]		13	Mullin
12	Chadebech		12	Kiernan [3 PENs]
11	Esteve		11	Finn
10	Laporte [3 PENs, CON]		10	Dean
9	Berbizier [TRY]		9	Bradley
8	Joinel		8	Spillane
7	Erbani		7	Morrow
6	Champ		6	Kearney
5	Condom		5	Anderson
4	Haget		4	Lenihan
3	Garuet-Lempirou		3	McCoy
2	Dubroca (c)		2	Fitzgerald (c)
1	Marocco [TRY]		1	Orr

Comments: David Morrow won his first cap but this was another unhappy Irish excursion to Paris. Pierre Berbizier scored a try for the second successive match.

WALES 22 SCOTLAND 15; at Cardiff; 1st of February 1986

	Wales			Scotland
15	Thorburn [5 PENs]		15	Hastings. G [PEN]
14	Lewis		14	Duncan [TRY]
13	Devereux		13	Johnston
12	Bowen		12	Hastings. S [TRY]
11	Hadley [TRY]		11	Baird
10	Davies. J [DG]		10	Rutherford
9	Jones		9	Laidlaw
8	Davies. P		8	Beattie
7	Pickering (c)		7	Calder
6	Brown		6	Jeffrey [TRY]
5	Waters		5	Paxton
4	Perkins		4	Campbell
3	Eidman		3	Milne
2	James		2	Deans (c)
1	Whitefoot		1	Sole

Comments: The visitors won the try count three to one, but left the Arms Park empty-handed thanks to Paul Thorburn's five accurate penalty attempts.

IRELAND 12 WALES 19; at Lansdowne Road; 15th of February 1986

15	MacNeill		15	Thorburn [3 PENs, CON]
14	Ringland [TRY]		14	Lewis [TRY]
13	Mullin		13	Devereux
12	Kiernan [2 PENs, CON]		12	Bowen
11	Finn		11	Hadley
10	Dean		10	Davies. J
9	Bradley		9	Jones
8	Spillane		8	Davies. P [TRY]
7	Carr		7	Pickering (c)
6	Kearney		6	Moriarty
5	Holland		5	Waters
4	Lenihan		4	Perkins
3	Fitzgerald. D		3	Eidman
2	Fitzgerald. C (c)		2	James
1	Kennedy		1	Whitefoot

Comments: In a tale of two halves, Wales scored fifteen points after the interval without reply. This was the ideal start for their new recruit Paul Moriarty.

SCOTLAND 33 ENGLAND 6; at Murrayfield; 15th of February 1986

15	Hastings. G [5 PENs, 3 CONs]		15	Davies
14	Duncan [TRY]		14	Smith
13	Johnston		13	Halliday
12	Hastings. S [TRY]		12	Salmon
11	Baird		11	Harrison
10	Rutherford [TRY]		10	Andrew [2 PENs]
9	Laidlaw		9	Melville (c)
8	Beattie		8	Robbins
7	Calder		7	Winterbottom
6	Jeffrey		6	Hall
5	Paxton		5	Colclough
4	Campbell		4	Dooley
3	Milne		3	Pearce
2	Deans (c)		2	Brain
1	Brewster		1	Rendall

Comments: It was Bannockburn revisited as one mobile pack gave the other immobile pack the run-around. The Hastings brothers registered a mere 25 points.

ENGLAND 25* IRELAND 20; at Twickenham; 1st of March 1986

	England		Ireland
15	Davies [TRY]	15	MacNeill
14	Harrison	14	Ringland [TRY]
13	Simms	13	Mullin [TRY]
12	Clough	12	Kiernan [2 PENs, CON]
11	Underwood	11	Crossan
10	Andrew [PEN, 3 CONs]	10	Keyes
9	Melville (c)	9	Bradley
8	Richards [2 TRIES]	8	Spillane
7	Rees	7	Carr
6	Winterbottom	6	Morrow
5	Colclough	5	Lenihan
4	Dooley	4	McCall [TRY]
3	Pearce	3	Fitzgerald. D
2	Brain	2	Fitzgerald. C (c)
1	Chilcott	1	Kennedy

Comments: Dean Richards scored two tries on his debut as England destroyed the Irish pack which failed to cope with scrums near their own try-line.

*England's points included a penalty try.

WALES 15 FRANCE 23; at Cardiff; 1st of March 1986

	Wales		France
15	Thorburn [5 PENs]	15	Blanco [TRY]
14	Titley	14	Lafond [2 TRIES]
13	Devereux	13	Sella [TRY]
12	Bowen	12	Charvet
11	Hadley	11	Bonneval
10	Davies. J	10	Laporte [DG, 2 CONs]
9	Jones	9	Berbizier
8	Davies. P	8	Joinel
7	Pickering (c)	7	Erbani
6	Moriarty	6	Champ
5	Waters	5	Condom
4	Perkins	4	Haget
3	Eidman	3	Garuet-Lempirou
2	James	2	Dubroca (c)
1	Whitefoot	1	Marocco

Comments: The pacy Denis Charvet won his first cap as France ran in four tries. Wales again relied upon the boot of Paul Thorburn for all of their points.

FRANCE 29* ENGLAND 10; at Parc des Princes; 15th of March 1986

15	Blanco [TRY]	15	Davies
14	Lafond	14	Harrison
13	Sella [TRY]	13	Samms
12	Charvet	12	Clough
11	Bonneval	11	Underwood
10	Laporte [TRY, 3 PENs, 2 CONs]	10	Andrew
9	Berbizier	9	Melville (c)
8	Joinel	8	Richards
7	Erbani	7	Rees
6	Champ	6	Winterbottom
5	Condom	5	Colclough
4	Haget	4	Dooley [TRY]
3	Garuet-Lempirou	3	Pearce
2	Dubroca (c)	2	Brain
1	Marocco	1	Chilcott

Comments: Philippe Sella completed his clean sweep of a try in each match. Stuart Barnes came on as a replacement and kicked two penalties for England.

*France's points included a penalty try.

IRELAND 9 SCOTLAND 10; at Lansdowne Road; 15th of March 1986

15	MacNeill	15	Hastings. G [2 PENs]
14	Ringland [TRY]	14	Robertson
13	Mullin	13	Johnston
12	Kiernan [PEN, CON]	12	Hastings. S
11	Crossan	11	Baird
10	Ward	10	Rutherford
9	Bradley	9	Laidlaw [TRY]
8	Anderson	8	Beattie
7	Carr	7	Calder
6	Morrow	6	Jeffrey
5	Lenihan	5	Paxton
4	McCall	4	Campbell
3	Fitzgerald. D	3	Milne
2	Fitzgerald. C (c)	2	Deans (c)
1	Orr	1	Brewster

Comments: Scotland trailed 9-0 at the interval, but Roy Laidlaw scored another try against Ireland and then Kiernan missed a straight-forward late penalty.

1986 FINAL TABLE

		Points For	Points Against	Total Points
1ST	FRANCE	98	52	6
1ST	SCOTLAND	76	54	6
3RD	WALES	74	71	4
3RD	ENGLAND	62	100	4
5TH	IRELAND	50	83	0

Comments: In spite of two home wins, England conceded an embarrassing ton of points. Ireland were whitewashed again.

DID YOU KNOW?

Scotland's drubbing of England in 1986 was something of a freak result. Although England have subsequently enjoyed the upper hand in many of their fixtures, there have been many close encounters of the Calcutta Cup kind since 1970:

ENGLAND 15 SCOTLAND 16; at Twickenham; 20th of March 1971
SCOTLAND 16 ENGLAND 14; at Murrayfield; 2nd of February 1974
ENGLAND 7 SCOTLAND 6; at Twickenham; 15th of March 1975
ENGLAND 7 SCOTLAND 7; at Twickenham; 3rd of February 1979
ENGLAND 23 SCOTLAND 17; at Twickenham; 21st of February 1981
SCOTLAND 9 ENGLAND 9; at Murrayfield; 16th of January 1982
ENGLAND 10 SCOTLAND 7; at Twickenham; 16th of March 1985
SCOTLAND 6 ENGLAND 9; at Murrayfield; 5th of March 1988
ENGLAND 12 SCOTLAND 12; at Twickenham; 4th of February 1989
SCOTLAND 13 ENGLAND 7; at Murrayfield; 17th of March 1990
SCOTLAND 14 ENGLAND 15; at Murrayfield; 5th of February 1994
ENGLAND 24 SCOTLAND 21; at Twickenham; 20th of February 1999
SCOTLAND 19 ENGLAND 13; at Murrayfield; 2nd of April 2000
SCOTLAND 18 ENGLAND 12; at Murrayfield; 25th of February 2006
SCOTLAND 15 ENGLAND 9; at Murrayfield; 8th of March 2008

1987

FRANCE 16 WALES 9; at Parc des Princes; 7th of February 1987

	France		Wales
15	Blanco	15	Thorburn [3 PENs]
14	Berot [2 PENs, CON]	14	Webbe
13	Sella	13	Devereux
12	Charvet	12	Hopkins
11	Bonneval [TRY]	11	Evans. I
10	Mesnel [TRY]	10	Davies. J
9	Berbizier	9	Jones
8	Rodriguez	8	Davies. P
7	Erbani	7	Pickering (c)
6	Champ	6	Moriarty
5	Condom	5	Norster
4	Lorieux	4	Sutton
3	Garuet-Lempirou	3	Evans. S
2	Dubroca (c)	2	Phillips
1	Ondarts	1	Whitefoot

Comments: Les Bleus crossed the try-line twice in the second-half, having trailed 9-3 at the interval. This was the debut for Ieuan Evans and Kevin Phillips.

IRELAND 17 ENGLAND 0; at Lansdowne Road; 7th of February 1987

	Ireland		England
15	MacNeill	15	Rose
14	Ringland	14	Harrison
13	Mullin	13	Salmon
12	Kiernan [TRY, PEN, CON]	12	Simms
11	Crossan [TRY]	11	Underwood
10	Dean	10	Andrew
9	Bradley	9	Hill (c)
8	Anderson	8	Simpson
7	Carr	7	Winterbottom
6	Matthews [TRY]	6	Hall
5	Glennon	5	Cusani
4	Lenihan (c)	4	Redman
3	Fitzgerald	3	Pearce
2	Harbison	2	Dawe
1	Orr	1	Rendall

Comments: Dave Cusani and Graham Dawe had a miserable debut as England failed to 'trouble the scorer' in unpleasant weather conditions.

ENGLAND 15 FRANCE 19; at Twickenham; 21st of February 1987

15	Rose [4 PENs]	15	Blanco [DG]
14	Harrison	14	Berot [PEN, CON]
13	Salmon	13	Sella [TRY]
12	Simms	12	Charvet
11	Underwood	11	Bonneval [TRY]
10	Andrew [DG]	10	Mesnel [DG]
9	Hill (c)	9	Berbizier
8	Hall	8	Rodriguez
7	Rees	7	Erbani
6	Winterbottom	6	Champ
5	Bainbridge	5	Condom
4	Dooley	4	Lorieux
3	Pearce	3	Garuet-Lempirou
2	Dawe	2	Dubroca (c)
1	Rendall	1	Ondarts

Comments: The visitors scored a try in each half to secure another narrow win that left them halfway towards un autre Grand Chelem.

SCOTLAND 16 IRELAND 12; at Murrayfield; 21st of February 1987

15	Hastings. G [CON]	15	MacNeill
14	Duncan	14	Ringland
13	Wylie	13	Mullin
12	Hastings. S	12	Kiernan [PEN, DG, CON]
11	Tukalo [TRY]	11	Crossan
10	Rutherford [2 DGs]	10	Dean
9	Laidlaw [TRY]	9	Bradley
8	Beattie	8	Anderson
7	Calder	7	Carr
6	Jeffrey	6	Matthews
5	Paxton	5	Glennon
4	Tomes	4	Lenihan (c) [TRY]
3	Milne	3	Fitzgerald
2	Deans (c)	2	Harbison
1	Sole	1	Orr

Comments: Donal Lenihan recorded his only international try, but the Irish conceded yet another try to their nemesis, the diminutive Roy Laidlaw.

FRANCE 28 SCOTLAND 22; at Parc des Princes; 7th of March 1987

15	Blanco		15	Hastings. G [TRY, 4 PENs, CON]
14	Berot [TRY, 3 PENs]		14	Duncan
13	Sella		13	Wyllie
12	Charvet		12	Hastings. S
11	Bonneval [3 TRIES]		11	Tukalo
10	Mesnel [DG]		10	Rutherford
9	Berbizier		9	Laidlaw
8	Rodriguez		8	Beattie [TRY]
7	Erbani		7	Calder
6	Champ		6	Jeffrey
5	Condom		5	Paxton
4	Haget		4	Tomes
3	Garuet-Lempirou		3	Milne
2	Dubroca (c)		2	Deans (c)
1	Ondarts		1	Sole

Comments: Philippe Berot registered thirteen points for the hosts, but he was upstaged by his fellow-winger Eric Bonneval who grabbed a hat-trick of tries.

WALES 19 ENGLAND 12; at Cardiff; 7th of March 1987

15	Thorburn [5 PENs]		15	Rose [4 PENs]
14	Webbe		14	Harrison
13	Devereux		13	Simms
12	Hopkins		12	Salmon
11	Evans. I		11	Underwood
10	Davies. J		10	Andrew
9	Jones		9	Hill (c)
8	Davies. P		8	Hall
7	Pickering (c)		7	Rees
6	Moriarty		6	Winterbottom
5	Norster		5	Bainbridge
4	Sutton		4	Dooley
3	Evans. S [TRY]		3	Pearce
2	James		2	Dawe
1	Whitefoot		1	Chilcott

Comments: While both full-backs slotted nine penalties between them, Ieuan Evans scored the decisive try in the second half to ensure a home win.

IRELAND 13 FRANCE 19; at Lansdowne Road; 21st of March 1987

15	MacNeill	15	Blanco
14	Ringland [TRY]	14	Berot [3 PENs, CON]
13	Mullin	13	Sella
12	Kiernan [PEN, CON]	12	Charvet
11	Crossan	11	Bonneval
10	Dean	10	Mesnel
9	Bradley [TRY]	9	Berbizier
8	Spillane	8	Rodriguez
7	Anderson	7	Erbani
6	Matthews	6	Champ [2 TRIES]
5	Glennon	5	Condom
4	Lenihan (c)	4	Haget
3	Fitzgerald	3	Garuet-Lempirou
2	Harbison	2	Dubroca (c)
1	Orr	1	Ondarts

Comments: Eric Champ's pair of second-half tries turned this match around after Ireland had led 10-0. This was France's third Grand Slam in ten years.

SCOTLAND 21 WALES 15; at Murrayfield; 21st of March 1987

15	Hastings. G [2 PENs, 2 CONs]	15	Wyatt [2 PENs, CON]
14	Duncan	14	Webbe
13	Robertson	13	Devereux
12	Hastings. S	12	Hopkins
11	Tukalo	11	Evans
10	Rutherford [DG]	10	Davies [DG]
9	Laidlaw	9	Jones. R
8	Beattie [TRY]	8	Jones. M [TRY]
7	Calder	7	Pickering (c)
6	Jeffrey [TRY]	6	Moriarty
5	Paxton	5	Norster
4	White	4	Sutton
3	Milne	3	Francis
2	Deans (c)	2	James
1	Sole	1	Whitefoot

Comments: Mark Jones helped himself to a debut try, but Scotland held on for victory, thanks to tries from the back row forwards John Beattie and John Jeffrey.

ENGLAND 21 SCOTLAND 12; at Twickenham; 4th of April 1987

15	Rose [TRY, 3 PENs, 2 CONs]	15	Hastings [2 PENs, CON]
14	Harrison (c) [TRY]	14	Duncan
13	Halliday	13	Robertson [TRY]
12	Salmon	12	Baird
11	Underwood	11	Tukalo
10	Williams	10	Rutherford
9	Harding	9	Laidlaw
8	Richards	8	Beattie
7	Rees	7	Calder
6	Hall	6	Jeffrey
5	Bainbridge	5	Paxton
4	Redman	4	White
3	Pearce	3	Milne
2	Moore	2	Deans (c)
1	Rendall	1	Sole

Comments: Brian Moore and Peter Williams won their first caps in this comfortable home win. Mike Harrison and Marcus Rose provided England's tries.

WALES 11 IRELAND 15; at Cardiff; 4th of April 1987

15	Wyatt [PEN]	15	MacNeill
14	Evans [TRY]	14	Ringland
13	Devereux	13	Mullin [TRY]
12	Ring	12	Kiernan [PEN, 2 CONs]
11	Hadley	11	Crossan
10	Davies. J	10	Dean [TRY]
9	Jones	9	Bradley
8	Davies. P	8	Spillane
7	Collins	7	Carr
6	Moriarty	6	Matthews
5	Norster [TRY]	5	Anderson
4	Sutton	4	Lenihan (c)
3	Blackmore	3	Fitzgerald
2	James (c)	2	Harbison
1	Whitefoot	1	Orr

Comments: Uncharacteristically, Ireland started slowly but they fought back after conceding two tries. Wales only led 8-6 at the interval.

1987 FINAL TABLE

		Points For	Points Against	Total Points
1ST	FRANCE	82	59	8
2ND	IRELAND	57	46	4
2ND	SCOTLAND	71	76	4
4TH	WALES	54	64	2
4TH	ENGLAND	48	67	2

Comments: As in 1981, France won all four matches by a narrow margin. All the teams now braced themselves for the World Cup.

THE WORLD CUPS, 1987 TO 2007

1987 semi-final: Australia 24 France 30; in Sydney; 13th of June
1987 semi-final: New Zealand 49 Wales 6; in Brisbane; 14th of June
1987 FINAL: NEW ZEALAND 29 France 9; in Auckland; 20th of June
1991 semi-final: Scotland 6 England 9; in Edinburgh; 26th of October
1991 semi-final: Australia 16 New Zealand 6; in Dublin; 27th of October
1991 FINAL: AUSTRALIA 12 England 6; in London; 2nd of November
1995 semi-final: South Africa 19 France 15; in Durban; 17th of June
1995 semi-final: New Zealand 45 England 29; in Cape Town; 18th of June
1995 FINAL: SOUTH AFRICA 15 New Zealand 12; in Johannesburg; 24th of June
1999 semi-final: Australia 27 South Africa 21; in London; 30th of October
1999 semi-final: France 43 New Zealand 31; in London; 31st of October
1999 FINAL: AUSTRALIA 35 France 12; in Cardiff; 6th of November
2003 semi-final: Australia 22 New Zealand 10; in Sydney; 15th of November
2003 semi-final: England 24 France 7; in Sydney; 16th of November
2003 FINAL: ENGLAND 20 Australia 17; in Sydney; 22nd of November
2007 semi-final: France 9 England 14; in St-Denis; 13th of October
2007 semi-final: South Africa 37 Argentina 13; in St-Denis; 14th of October
2007 FINAL: SOUTH AFRICA 15 England 6; in St-Denis; 20th of October

1988

FRANCE 10 ENGLAND 9; at Parc des Princes; 16th of January 1988

15	Blanco		15	Webb [2 PENs]
14	Berot [2 PENs]		14	Harrison (c)
13	Sella		13	Carling
12	Andrieu		12	Simms
11	Bonneval		11	Underwood
10	Mesnel		10	Cusworth [DG]
9	Berbizier		9	Melville
8	Rodriguez [TRY]		8	Richards
7	Erbani		7	Winterbottom
6	Champ		6	Skinner
5	Serriere		5	Dooley
4	Condom		4	Orwin
3	Garuet-Lempirou		3	Probyn
2	Dubroca (c)		2	Moore
1	Ondarts		1	Rendall

Comments: Will Carling, Jeff Probyn, and Mickey Skinner won their first caps as England succumbed to an unlucky defeat to the reigning champions.

IRELAND 22 SCOTLAND 18; at Lansdowne Road; 16th of January 1988

15	Danaher		15	Hastings. G [2 PENs, 2 CONs]
14	Ringland		14	Duncan
13	Mullin [TRY]		13	Tait
12	Kiernan [PEN, DG, 2 CONs]		12	Hastings. S [TRY]
11	Crossan		11	Baird
10	Dean		10	Cramb
9	Bradley [TRY]		9	Laidlaw [TRY]
8	Gibson		8	Paxton
7	Sexton		7	Calder
6	Matthews		6	Jeffrey
5	Anderson		5	Cronin
4	Lenihan (c)		4	White
3	Fitzgerald. D		3	Rowan
2	Kingston		2	Callander (c)
1	Fitzgerald. J		1	Sole

Comments: Hugo MacNeill was dropped in favour of the debutant Phil Danaher, but he came on as a replacement and scored one of the three Irish tries.

ENGLAND 3 WALES 11; at Twickenham; 6th of February 1988

15	Webb [PEN]		15	Clement
14	Harrison (c)		14	Evans
13	Carling		13	Ring
12	Simms		12	Bowen (c)
11	Underwood		11	Hadley [2 TRIES]
10	Cusworth		10	Davies [DG]
9	Melville		9	Jones. R
8	Richards		8	Moriarty
7	Winterbottom		7	Collins
6	Skinner		6	Phillips. R
5	Dooley		5	Norster
4	Orwin		4	May
3	Probyn		3	Young
2	Moore		2	Phillips. K
1	Rendall		1	Jones. S

Comments: Adrian Hadley was the Welsh hero, courtesy of his brace of tries. This match had been peculiarly scoreless at the interval.

SCOTLAND 23 FRANCE 12; at Murrayfield; 6th of February 1988

15	Hastings. G [TRY, 4 PENs]		15	Blanco
14	Duncan		14	Berot [PEN, CON]
13	Tait		13	Sella
12	Hastings. S		12	Andrieu
11	Tukalo [TRY]		11	Lagisquet [TRY]
10	Cramb [DG]		10	Lescarboura [DG]
9	Laidlaw		9	Berbizier
8	White		8	Rodriguez
7	Calder		7	Erbani
6	Turnbull		6	Champ
5	Cronin		5	Condom
4	Campbell		4	Lorieux
3	Rowan		3	Garuet-Lempirou
2	Callander (c)		2	Dubroca (c)
1	Sole		1	Armary

Comments: The home team's two tries came in the first half as France failed to win in Edinburgh for the fifth successive time.

FRANCE 25 IRELAND 6; at Parc des Princes; 20th of February 1988

15	Blanco [TRY]		15	Danaher
14	Berot [CON]		14	Ringland
13	Sella [TRY]		13	Mullin
12	Andrieu		12	Kiernan [2 PENs]
11	Lagisquet [TRY]		11	Crossan
10	Camberabero [TRY, DG]		10	Dean
9	Berbizier		9	Bradley
8	Rodriguez		8	Gibson
7	Carminati [TRY]		7	Whittle
6	Cecillon		6	Matthews
5	Orso		5	Anderson
4	Lorieux		4	Lenihan (c)
3	Ondarts		3	Fitzgerald. D
2	Dubroca (c)		2	Kingston
1	Armary		1	Fitzgerald. J

Comments: The French crossed the try-line four times in the second half. The nineteen points winning margin flattered the hapless visitors.

WALES 25 SCOTLAND 20; at Cardiff; 20th of February 1988

15	Thorburn [PEN, 2 CONs]		15	Hastings. G [4 PENs]
14	Evans [TRY]		14	Duncan [TRY]
13	Ring		13	Tait
12	Bowen (c)		12	Hastings. S
11	Hadley		11	Tukalo
10	Davies [TRY, 2 DGs]		10	Ker
9	Jones. R		9	Laidlaw
8	Moriarty		8	White
7	Collins		7	Calder [TRY]
6	Phillips		6	Jeffrey
5	Norster		5	Cronin
4	May		4	Campbell
3	Young		3	Rowan
2	Watkins [TRY]		2	Callander (c)
1	Jones. S		1	Sole

Comments: The hosts responded impressively after trailing 17-10 at the interval and now could set their sights on a possible Triple Crown.

IRELAND 9 WALES 12; at Lansdowne Road; 5th of March 1988

15	Danaher	15	Thorburn [PEN, CON]
14	Ringland	14	Evans
13	Mullin	13	Ring
12	Kiernan [PEN, CON]	12	Bowen (c)
11	Crossan	11	Hadley
10	Dean	10	Davies [DG]
9	Bradley	9	Jones
8	Gibson	8	Moriarty [TRY]
7	McBride	7	Collins
6	Matthews	6	Phillips
5	Anderson	5	Norster
4	Lenihan (c)	4	May
3	Fitzgerald	3	Young
2	Kingston [TRY]	2	Watkins
1	Clancy	1	Buchanan

Comments: Paul Moriarty scored the crucial second-half try as Wales came from behind to land their first Triple Crown of a barren decade.

SCOTLAND 6 ENGLAND 9; at Murrayfield; 5th of March 1988

15	Hastings [2 PENs]	15	Webb [2 PENs]
14	Duncan	14	Underwood
13	Tait	13	Carling
12	Robertson	12	Halliday
11	Tukalo	11	Oti
10	Ker	10	Andrew [DG]
9	Laidlaw	9	Melville (c)
8	Paxton	8	Richards
7	Calder	7	Winterbottom
6	Turnbull	6	Skinner
5	Cronin	5	Dooley
4	White	4	Orwin
3	Rowan	3	Probyn
2	Callander (c)	2	Moore
1	Sole	1	Rendall

Comments: Chris Oti made his debut as England won in Edinburgh for the first time since 1980. Rob Andrew slotted home a vital drop goal.

ENGLAND 35 IRELAND 3; at Twickenham; 19th of March 1988

15	Webb [PEN, CON]	15	MacNeill
14	Underwood [2 TRIES]	14	Ringland
13	Carling	13	Mullin
12	Halliday	12	Kiernan [PEN]
11	Oti [3 TRIES]	11	Crossan
10	Andrew [3 CONs]	10	Dean
9	Melville (c)	9	Bradley
8	Richards	8	Anderson
7	Rees [TRY]	7	McBride
6	Skinner	6	Matthews
5	Dooley	5	Moylett
4	Orwin	4	Lenihan (c)
3	Probyn	3	Fitzgerald
2	Moore	2	Kingston
1	Rendall	1	Clancy

Comments: In this remarkable match, Ireland actually led 3-0 at the interval. Then England ran riot with the wingers, Oti and Underwood, sharing five tries.

WALES 9 FRANCE 10; at Cardiff; 19th of March 1988

15	Thorburn [PEN, CON]	15	Blanco
14	Evans [TRY]	14	Lafond [2 PENs]
13	Ring	13	Sella
12	Bowen (c)	12	Andrieu
11	Hadley	11	Lagisquet
10	Davies	10	Lescarboura [TRY]
9	Jones. R	9	Berbizier
8	Moriarty	8	Rodriguez
7	Collins	7	Carminati
6	Phillips	6	Cecillon
5	Norster	5	Condom
4	May	4	Lorieux
3	Young	3	Ondarts
2	Watkins	2	Dubroca (c)
1	Jones. S	1	Armary

Comments: In spite of a Ieuan Evans second-half try, the French foiled the Grand Slam attempt, thanks to a try from Jean-Patrick Lescarboura.

1988 FINAL TABLE

		Points For	Points Against	Total Points
1ST	WALES	57	42	6
1ST	FRANCE	57	47	6
3RD	ENGLAND	56	30	4
4TH	SCOTLAND	67	68	2
4TH	IRELAND	40	90	2

Comments: Wales enjoyed a brief revival, but the seeds of future English domination of Europe were sown in this tournament.

DID YOU KNOW?

1988 saw Wales's last successful trip to Twickenham until 2008. In the intervening twenty years, neither Scotland nor Wales were able to win at Fortress Twickenham. Peculiarly, Ireland managed three wins there during that lifespan even though they never shared nor won a championship during that period.

1989

IRELAND 21 FRANCE 26; at Lansdowne Road; 21st of January 1989

15	Danaher		15	Blanco [TRY]
14	Sexton		14	Lafond [TRY, 2 PENs, 2 CONs]
13	Mullin [TRY]		13	Sella
12	Irwin		12	Andrieu
11	Kiernan [5 PENs, CON]		11	Lagisquet [2 TRIES]
10	Dean		10	Mesnel
9	Aherne		9	Berbizier (c)
8	Mannion		8	Rodriguez
7	O'Hara		7	Carminati
6	Matthews (c)		6	Cecillon
5	Anderson		5	Condom
4	Lenihan		4	Bourguignon
3	McCoy		3	Portolan
2	Smith		2	Marocco
1	Clancy		1	Ondarts

Comments: The Irish led 18-7 at half-time with the help of another try from Brendan Mullin, but the visitors fought back with four tries after the interval.

SCOTLAND 23 WALES 7; at Murrayfield; 21st of January 1989

15	Dods [2 PENs, CON]		15	Thorburn (c)
14	Duncan		14	Hall [TRY]
13	Hastings		13	Davies. N
12	Lineen		12	Devereux
11	Tukalo		11	Davies. C
10	Chalmers [TRY, DG]		10	Bowen [PEN]
9	Armstrong [TRY]		9	Griffiths. J
8	White [TRY]		8	Jones
7	Jeffrey		7	Bryant
6	Calder (c)		6	Phillips
5	Cronin		5	Davies. P
4	Gray		4	Moseley
3	Milne. I		3	Young
2	Milne. K		2	Watkins
1	Sole		1	Griffiths. M

Comments: Craig Chalmers dropped a goal and scored a try on his debut. Wales were a mere 19-0 behind at half-time in this non-contest.

ENGLAND 12 SCOTLAND 12; at Twickenham; 4th of February 1989

15	Webb [2 PENs]	15	Dods [2 PENs, CON]
14	Underwood	14	Robertson
13	Carling (c)	13	Hastings
12	Halliday	12	Lineen
11	Oti	11	Tukalo
10	Andrew [2 PENs]	10	Chalmers
9	Morris	9	Armstrong
8	Richards	8	White
7	Robinson	7	Jeffrey [TRY]
6	Teague	6	Calder (c)
5	Ackford	5	Cronin
4	Dooley	4	Gray
3	Probyn	3	Burnell
2	Moore	2	Milne
1	Rendall	1	Sole

Comments: John Jeffrey scored the match's only try in the first half, but England came from behind to claim a draw on the debut of Scotland's Paul Burnell.

WALES 13 IRELAND 19; at Cardiff; 4th of February 1989

15	Thorburn (c) [3 PENs]	15	Dunlea
14	Evans	14	Kiernan [3 PENs, CON]
13	Devereux	13	Mullin
12	Davies. N	12	Irwin
11	Hall	11	Crossan
10	Bowen	10	Dean [TRY]
9	Jones. R	9	Aherne
8	Jones. M [TRY]	8	Mannion [TRY]
7	Bryant	7	O'Hara
6	Phillips	6	Matthews (c)
5	Moseley	5	Anderson
4	Davies. P	4	Lenihan
3	Delaney	3	McCoy
2	Watkins	2	Smith
1	Griffiths	1	Clancy

Comments: The away team trailed 6-0 at half-time, but they secured a third consecutive Cardiff triumph with the help of an interception try from Noel Mannion.

FRANCE 31 WALES 12; at Parc des Princes; 18th of February 1989

15 Blanco [2 TRIES]	15 Thorburn (c) [4 PENS]
14 Lafond [2 PENs, 3 CONs]	14 Evans. I
13 Sella	13 Evans. D
12 Andrieu	12 Hall
11 Lagisquet	11 Davies. C
10 Mesnel [DG]	10 Turner
9 Berbizier (c) [TRY]	9 Jones. R
8 Carminati	8 Jones. M
7 Erbani	7 Bryant
6 Champ	6 Jones. G
5 Condom	5 Norster
4 Lorieux	4 Davies. P
3 Ondarts	3 Delaney
2 Dintrans [TRY]	2 Watkins
1 Armary	1 Griffiths

Comments: Paul Thorburn landed four penalties, but France won comfortably, scoring four tries, including a pair of tries from the great Serge Blanco.

IRELAND 3 ENGLAND 16; at Lansdowne Road; 18th of February 1989

15 Dunlea	15 Webb
14 Kiernan [PEN]	14 Underwood
13 Mullin	13 Carling (c)
12 Irwin	12 Halliday
11 Haycock	11 Oti
10 Dean	10 Andrew [2 PENs, CON]
9 Aherne	9 Morris
8 Mannion	8 Richards [TRY]
7 O'Hara	7 Robinson
6 Matthews (c)	6 Teague
5 Anderson	5 Ackford
4 Lenihan	4 Dooley
3 McCoy	3 Probyn
2 Smith	2 Moore [TRY]
1 Clancy	1 Rendall

Comments: Paul Haycock won his only Irish cap as England's forward power proved decisive. The two tries came from the pack, for Brian Moore and Dean Richards.

ENGLAND 11 FRANCE 0; at Twickenham; 4th of March 1989

15	Webb	15	Blanco
14	Underwood	14	Lafond
13	Carling (c) [TRY]	13	Sella
12	Halliday	12	Andrieu
11	Oti	11	Lagisquet
10	Andrew [PEN]	10	Mesnel
9	Morris	9	Berbizier (c)
8	Richards	8	Rodriguez
7	Robinson [TRY]	7	Erbani
6	Teague	6	Cecillon
5	Ackford	5	Condom
4	Dooley	4	Bourguignon
3	Chilcott	3	Portolan
2	Moore	2	Dintrans
1	Rendall	1	Ondarts

Comments: England secured their first home win against France since 1979 with a try in each half. The try heroes were the captain Will Carling and Andy Robinson.

SCOTLAND 37 IRELAND 21; at Murrayfield; 4th of March 1989

15	Dods [3 PENs, 4 CONs]	15	Dunlea [TRY]
14	Robertson	14	Kiernan [PEN, 3 CONs]
13	Hastings	13	Mullin [2 TRIES]
12	Lineen	12	Irwin
11	Tukalo [3 TRIES]	11	Crossan
10	Chalmers	10	Dean
9	Armstrong	9	Aherne
8	White	8	Mannion
7	Calder (c)	7	McBride
6	Jeffrey [TRY]	6	Matthews (c)
5	Cronin [TRY]	5	Francis
4	Gray	4	Lenihan
3	Burnell	3	McCoy
2	Milne	2	Smith
1	Sole	1	Clancy

Comments: Scotland actually trailed 21-19 at the interval. Hero of the day was Iwan Tukalo with his hat-trick of tries in this try-scoring bonanza.

FRANCE 19 SCOTLAND 3; at Parc des Princes; 18th of March 1989

15	Blanco [TRY]	15	Dods [PEN]
14	Berot [PEN, 2 CONs]	14	Robertson
13	Sella	13	Hastings
12	Andrieu	12	Lineen
11	Lagisquet [TRY]	11	Tukalo
10	Mesnel	10	Chalmers
9	Berbizier (c) [TRY]	9	Armstrong
8	Rodriguez	8	White
7	Carminati	7	Calder (c)
6	Champ	6	Jeffrey
5	Condom	5	Cronin
4	Erbani	4	Gray
3	Garuet-Lempirou	3	Burnell
2	Dintrans	2	Milne
1	Armary	1	Sole

Comments: Les Bleus only led 6-3 at half-time, but they won convincingly as this fixture produced the eleventh successive home win between the two teams.

WALES 12 ENGLAND 9; at Cardiff; 18th of March 1989

15	Thorburn (c) [2 PENs, CON]	15	Webb
14	Evans. I	14	Underwood
13	Evans. D	13	Carling (c)
12	Hall [TRY]	12	Halliday
11	Emyr	11	Oti
10	Turner	10	Andrew [2 PENs, DG]
9	Jones. R	9	Morris
8	Jones. M	8	Richards
7	Bryant	7	Robinson
6	Jones. G	6	Teague
5	Norster	5	Ackford
4	Davies	4	Dooley
3	Delaney	3	Chilcott
2	Watkins	2	Moore
1	Griffiths	1	Rendall

Comments: Arthur Emyr made his debut and Mike Hall scored the match's only try as Wales overturned the 9-6 interval deficit to avoid the dreaded whitewash.

1989 FINAL TABLE

		Points For	Points Against	Total Points
1ST	FRANCE	76	47	6
2ND	ENGLAND	48	27	5
2ND	SCOTLAND	75	59	5
4TH	IRELAND	64	92	2
4TH	WALES	44	82	2

Comments: Ireland and Wales had now assumed the role of tournament also-rans, a label which would linger for several years.

DID YOU KNOW?

1989 began an eleven-year era of dominance by Scotland over Ireland until 2000. Remarkably, Scotland only failed once to beat Ireland in the 1990s which also included a World Cup win in 1991 and Ireland only failed to beat Scotland once in the first decade of the 21st century in the Six Nations.

1990

ENGLAND 23 IRELAND 0; at Twickenham; 20th of January 1990

15	Hodgkinson [PEN, 2 CONs]	15	Murphy
14	Underwood [TRY]	14	Kiernan
13	Carling (c)	13	Mullin
12	Guscott [TRY]	12	Irwin
11	Bailey	11	Crossan
10	Andrew	10	Russell
9	Hill	9	Aherne
8	Egerton [TRY]	8	Mannion
7	Winterbottom	7	O'Hara
6	Skinner	6	Matthews
5	Ackford	5	Anderson (c)
4	Dooley	4	Lenihan
3	Probyn [TRY]	3	Halpin
2	Moore	2	Smith
1	Rendall	1	Fitzgerald

Comments: The home team achieved 3 tries after the interval in this rout. This was the first time Ireland had failed to score since they lost to England in 1977.

WALES 19 FRANCE 29; at Cardiff; 20th of January 1990

15	Thorburn [4 PENs]	15	Lafond [TRY]
14	Titley [TRY]	14	Andrieu
13	Ring	13	Sella [TRY]
12	Hall	12	Charvet
11	Emyr	11	Lagisquet [TRY]
10	Evans [DG]	10	Camberabero [TRY, PEN, 3 CONs]
9	Jones. R (c)	9	Berbizier (c)
8	Jones. M	8	Roumat
7	Jones. G	7	Champ
6	Davies	6	Rodriguez [TRY]
5	Allen	5	Erbani
4	Moseley [SENT OFF]	4	Devergie
3	Young	3	Garuet-Lempirou
2	Phillips	2	Armary
1	Griffiths	1	Ondarts

Comments: Wales led 13-9 at half-time with the help of a Mark Titley try. However, their chances of a victory were ruined by the dismissal of Kevin Moseley.

FRANCE 7 ENGLAND 26; at Parc des Princes; 3rd of February 1990

	France		England
15	Blanco	15	Hodgkinson [4 PENs, CON]
14	Andrieu	14	Underwood [TRY]
13	Sella	13	Carling (c) [TRY]
12	Charvet [PEN]	12	Guscott [TRY]
11	Lagisquet [TRY]	11	Bailey
10	Mesnel	10	Andrew
9	Berbizier (c)	9	Hill
8	Rodriguez	8	Teague
7	Champ	7	Winterbottom
6	Roumat	6	Skinner
5	Erbani	5	Ackford
4	Devergie	4	Dooley
3	Garuet-Lempirou	3	Probyn
2	Armary	2	Moore
1	Ondarts	1	Rendall

Comments: Three of the visitors' back division recorded tries as a rampant England pursued their first Grand Slam after ten barren years.

IRELAND 10 SCOTLAND 13; at Lansdowne Road; 3rd of February 1990

	Ireland		Scotland
15	Murphy	15	Hastings. G
14	Kiernan [2 PENs]	14	Stanger
13	Mullin	13	Hastings. S
12	Irwin	12	Lineen
11	Crossan	11	Tukalo
10	Smith	10	Chalmers [PEN, CON]
9	Aherne	9	Armstrong
8	Mannion	8	White [2 TRIES]
7	O'Hara	7	Calder
6	Matthews	6	Jeffrey
5	Lenihan	5	Cronin
4	Anderson (c)	4	Gray
3	Fitzgerald. D	3	Burnell
2	McDonald	2	Milne
1	Fitzgerald. J [TRY]	1	Sole (c)

Comments: After trailing 7-0 at half-time, the away team bounced back with a brace of tries from Derek White. John Fitzgerald scored his only try for Ireland.

ENGLAND 34 WALES 6; at Twickenham; 17th of February 1990

15	Hodgkinson [4 PENs, 3 CONs]	15	Thorburn [CON]
14	Halliday	14	Titley
13	Carling (c) [TRY]	13	Ring
12	Guscott	12	Hall
11	Underwood [2 TRIES]	11	Emyr
10	Andrew	10	Evans
9	Hill [TRY]	9	Jones. R (c)
8	Teague	8	Jones. M
7	Winterbottom	7	Collins
6	Skinner	6	Davies [TRY]
5	Ackford	5	Allen
4	Dooley	4	Llewellyn
3	Probyn	3	Delaney
2	Moore	2	Phillips
1	Rendall	1	Griffiths

Comments: Phil Davies's second-half try was merely a consolation as Wales were put to the sword. Rory Underwood was a double try-scoring hero for the hosts.

SCOTLAND 21 FRANCE 0; at Murrayfield; 17th of February 1990

15	Hastings. G [PEN]	15	Blanco
14	Stanger	14	Hontas
13	Hastings. S	13	Sella
12	Lineen	12	Mesnel
11	Tukalo [TRY]	11	Lagisquet
10	Chalmers [2 PENs, 2 CONs]	10	Camberabero
9	Armstrong	9	Sanz
8	White	8	Rodriguez (c)
7	Calder [TRY]	7	Lhermet
6	Jeffrey	6	Carminati [SENT OFF]
5	Cronin	5	Roumat
4	Gray	4	Devergie
3	Burnell	3	Ondarts
2	Milne	2	Armary
1	Sole (c)	1	Pujolle

Comments: Finlay Calder and Iwan Tukalo both crossed the try-line after the interval as Scotland humiliated the fourteen-man French.

FRANCE 31 IRELAND 12; at Parc des Princes; 3rd of March 1990

15	Blanco		15	Murphy
14	Hontas		14	Hooks
13	Sella		13	Kiernan [4 PENs]
12	Mesnel [2 TRIES]		12	Danaher
11	Lagisquet [TRY]		11	Crossan
10	Camberabero [5 PENs, 2 CONs]		10	Smith
9	Sanz		9	Aherne
8	Rodriguez (c)		8	Mannion
7	Lhermet		7	O'Hara
6	Roumat		6	McBride
5	Devergie		5	Lenihan (c)
4	Condom		4	Francis
3	Ondarts		3	Fitzgerald. D
2	Armary		2	Kingston
1	Pujolle		1	Fitzgerald. J

Comments: France doled out another routine Parisian thrashing of Ireland with a pair of tries from Franck Mesnel and 19 points from the boot of Camberabero.

WALES 9 SCOTLAND 13; at Cardiff; 3rd of March 1990

15	Thorburn [PEN, CON]		15	Hastings. G
14	Hall		14	Stanger
13	Ring		13	Hastings. S
12	Bateman		12	Lineen
11	Emyr [TRY]		11	Tukalo
10	Evans		10	Chalmers [3 PENs]
9	Jones. R (c)		9	Armstrong
8	Jones. M		8	White
7	Collins		7	Calder
6	Perego		6	Jeffrey
5	Davies		5	Cronin [TRY]
4	Llewellyn		4	Gray
3	Pugh		3	Burnell
2	Phillips		2	Milne
1	Williams		1	Sole (c)

Comments: A Damian Cronin try in the first half helped Scotland take a 10-3 lead at the halfway stage. They held on to their lead to make it three wins out of three.

SCOTLAND 13 ENGLAND 7; at Murrayfield; 17th of March 1990

15	Hastings. G		15	Hodgkinson [PEN]
14	Stanger [TRY]		14	Halliday
13	Hastings. S		13	Carling (c)
12	Lineen		12	Guscott [TRY]
11	Tukalo		11	Underwood
10	Chalmers [3 PENs]		10	Andrew
9	Armstrong		9	Hill
8	White		8	Teague
7	Calder		7	Winterbottom
6	Jeffrey		6	Skinner
5	Cronin		5	Ackford
4	Gray		4	Dooley
3	Burnell		3	Probyn
2	Milne		2	Moore
1	Sole (c)		1	Rendall

Comments: Tony Stanger's second half try earned Scotland their third-ever Grand Slam. England piled on the pressure thereafter, but their hopes were dashed.

IRELAND 14 WALES 8; at Lansdowne Road; 24th of March 1990

15	Murphy		15	Thorburn
14	Hooks		14	Ford [TRY]
13	Kiernan [CON]		13	Ring
12	Mullin		12	Bateman
11	Crossan		11	Emyr
10	Smith [TRY]		10	Evans
9	Bradley		9	Jones. R (c)
8	Mannion		8	Jones. M
7	O'Hara		7	Collins
6	McBride [TRY]		6	Morris
5	Lenihan (c)		5	Allen
4	Francis		4	Llewellyn [TRY]
3	Fitzgerald. D		3	Williams-Jones
2	Kingston [TRY]		2	Phillips
1	Fitzgerald. J		1	Williams

Comments: Steve Ford crossed the try-line on his debut but Ireland led throughout this basement clash. Whitewashed Wales failed to kick a single point.

1990 FINAL TABLE

	Points For	Points Against	Total Points
1ST SCOTLAND	60	26	8
2ND ENGLAND	90	26	6
3RD FRANCE	67	78	4
4TH IRELAND	36	75	2
5TH WALES	42	90	0

Comments: This tournament represented humiliation for Wales, heartbreak for England, and glory for unfancied Scotland.

DID YOU KNOW?

England have three times in the modern era gone to Murrayfield on the last match of their campaign in search of the Grand Slam. Peculiarly, the occasions have been at the ten year intervals of 1980, 1990, and 2000. Only in the first match of this sequence was the English rugby invasion of Edinburgh a successful one.

1991

FRANCE 15 SCOTLAND 9; at Parc des Princes; 19th of January 1991

15	Blanco (c) [DG]	15	Hastings. G
14	Lafond	14	Stanger
13	Mesnel	13	Lineen
12	Charvet	12	Hastings. S
11	Lagisquet	11	Moore
10	Camberabero [2 PENs, 2 DGs]	10	Chalmers [2 PENs, DG]
9	Berbizier	9	Armstrong
8	Cecillon	8	White
7	Cabannes	7	Turnbull
6	Blond	6	Jeffrey
5	Roumat	5	Cronin
4	Tachdjian	4	Gray
3	Ondarts	3	Burnell
2	Marocco	2	Milne
1	Lascube	1	Sole (c)

Comments: Craig Chalmers kicked all of Scotland's points but he was upstaged by the other fly half Didier Camberabero, who slotted 2 drop goals and 2 penalties.

WALES 6 ENGLAND 25; at Cardiff; 19th of January 1991

15	Thorburn (c) [PEN]	15	Hodgkinson [7 PENs]
14	Evans	14	Heslop
13	Ring	13	Carling (c)
12	Gibbs	12	Guscott
11	Ford	11	Underwood
10	Jenkins [PEN]	10	Andrew
9	Jones	9	Hill
8	Arnold	8	Richards
7	George	7	Winterbottom
6	Carter	6	Teague [TRY]
5	Llewellyn. GO	5	Ackford
4	Llewellyn. GD	4	Dooley
3	Knight	3	Probyn
2	Phillips	2	Moore
1	Williams	1	Leonard

Comments: England thrashed the Welsh again, with Mike Teague registering a second-half try. Most of the damage came courtesy of Simon Hodgkinson's penalties.

IRELAND 13 FRANCE 21; at Lansdowne Road; 2nd of February 1991

15	Murphy		15	Blanco (c)
14	Geoghegan		14	Lafond
13	Mullin		13	Mesnel
12	Kiernan [3 PENs]		12	Charvet
11	Hooks		11	Lagisquet [TRY]
10	Smith. B		10	Camberabero [3 PENs, 2 CONs]
9	Saunders (c)		9	Berbizier
8	Robinson		8	Cecillon
7	Hamilton		7	Cabannes [TRY]
6	Matthews		6	Blond
5	Rigney		5	Roumat
4	Galwey		4	Tachdjian
3	Fitzgerald. D		3	Ondarts
2	Smith. S [TRY]		2	Marocco
1	Fitzgerald. J		1	Lascube

Comments: Six Irishmen won their first caps and although Steve Smith's try helped the hosts to lead at half time, they folded after the interval yet again.

SCOTLAND 32 WALES 12; at Murrayfield; 2nd of February 1991

15	Hastings. G [2 PENs, CON]		15	Thorburn (c) [2 PENs, CON]
14	Stanger		14	Evans
13	Lineen		13	Ring
12	Hastings. S		12	Gibbs
11	Moore		11	Ford [TRY]
10	Chalmers [TRY, PEN, DG, CON]		10	Jenkins
9	Armstrong [TRY]		9	Jones
8	White [2 TRIES]		8	Arnold
7	Jeffrey		7	George
6	Turnbull		6	Carter
5	Cronin		5	Llewellyn. GO
4	Gray		4	Llewellyn. GD
3	Burnell		3	Knight
2	Allan		2	Phillips
1	Sole (c)		1	Williams

Comments: Derek White obtained another double helping of tries as woeful Wales slipped to their tenth defeat in their last eleven Five Nations contests.

ENGLAND 21 SCOTLAND 12; at Twickenham; 16th of February 1991

15	Hodgkinson [5 PENs, CON]	15	Hastings. G
14	Heslop [TRY]	14	Stanger
13	Carling (c)	13	Lineen
12	Guscott	12	Hastings. S
11	Underwood	11	Moore
10	Andrew	10	Chalmers [4 PENs]
9	Hill	9	Armstrong
8	Richards	8	White
7	Winterbottom	7	Jeffrey
6	Teague	6	Turnbull
5	Ackford	5	Cronin
4	Dooley	4	Gray
3	Probyn	3	Burnell
2	Moore	2	Milne
1	Leonard	1	Sole (c)

Comments: Craig Chalmers slotted home 4 penalties, but England were not to be denied their revenge for their 1990 heartbreak. Nigel Heslop scored the only try.

WALES 21 IRELAND 21; at Cardiff; 16th of February 1991

15	Thorburn (c) [2 PENs, 2 CONs]	15	Staples [TRY]
14	Evans	14	Geoghegan [TRY]
13	Ring	13	Mullin [TRY]
12	Gibbs	12	Curtis
11	Ford	11	Clarke [TRY]
10	Jenkins [TRY, DG]	10	Smith. B [DG, CON]
9	Bridges	9	Saunders (c)
8	Davies. P	8	Robinson
7	Lewis	7	Hamilton
6	Morris	6	Matthews
5	Arnold [TRY]	5	Rigney
4	Llewellyn	4	Galwey
3	Davies. J	3	Fitzgerald. D
2	Phillips	2	Smith. S
1	Griffiths	1	Fitzgerald. J

Comments: Jack Clarke and Jim Staples achieved tries on their debut, but both the celtic tournament also-rans had to share a point in this six-tries bonanza.

FRANCE 36 WALES 3; at Parc des Princes; 2nd of March 1991

15	Blanco (c) [TRY, CON]	15	Thorburn (c) [PEN]
14	Lafond [TRY]	14	Evans
13	Mesnel [TRY]	13	Ring
12	Sella [TRY]	12	Gibbs
11	Saint-Andre [TRY]	11	Emyr
10	Camberabero [2 PENs, 2 CONs]	10	Jenkins
9	Berbizier	9	Bridges
8	Deslandes	8	Davies. P
7	Cabannes	7	Lewis
6	Blond	6	Morris
5	Roumat [TRY]	5	Arnold
4	Gourragne	4	Llewellyn
3	Ondarts	3	Davies. J
2	Marocco	2	Phillips
1	Lascube	1	Griffiths

Comments: Poor Wales reached new depths as France recorded their 9th successive win against them. Wales had now failed to win their last 8 Five Nations matches.

IRELAND 7 ENGLAND 16; at Lansdowne Road; 2nd of March 1991

15	Staples	15	Hodgkinson [2 PENs, CON]
14	Geoghegan [TRY]	14	Heslop
13	Mullin	13	Carling (c)
12	Curtis	12	Guscott
11	Crossan	11	Underwood [TRY]
10	Smith. B [PEN]	10	Andrew
9	Saunders (c)	9	Hill
8	Robinson	8	Richards
7	Hamilton	7	Winterbottom
6	Matthews	6	Teague [TRY]
5	Rigney	5	Ackford
4	Francis	4	Dooley
3	Fitzgerald. D	3	Probyn
2	Smith. S	2	Moore
1	Fitzgerald. J	1	Leonard

Comments: This match was deadlocked 3-3 at the halfway point, but tries from Mike Teague and Rory Underwood yielded England their first Triple Crown since 1980.

ENGLAND 21 FRANCE 19; at Twickenham; 16th of March 1991

15	Hodgkinson [4 PENs, CON]	15	Blanco (c)
14	Heslop	14	Lafond
13	Carling (c)	13	Mesnel [TRY]
12	Guscott	12	Sella
11	Underwood [TRY]	11	Saint-Andre [TRY]
10	Andrew [DG]	10	Camberabero [TRY, PEN, 2 CONs]
9	Hill	9	Berbizier
8	Richards	8	Benazzi
7	Winterbottom	7	Cabannes
6	Teague	6	Blond
5	Ackford	5	Roumat
4	Dooley	4	Tachdjian
3	Probyn	3	Ondarts
2	Moore	2	Marocco
1	Leonard	1	Lascube

Comments: Rory Underwood's first-half try and Hodgkinson's accurate kicks ensured the coveted Grand Slam. A late flourish from France almost paid dividends.

SCOTLAND 28 IRELAND 25; at Murrayfield; 16th of March 1991

15	Hastings. G [TRY, PEN]	15	Staples
14	Stanger [TRY]	14	Geoghegan [TRY]
13	Lineen	13	Mullin [TRY]
12	Hastings. S [TRY]	12	Curtis
11	Tukalo	11	Crossan [TRY]
10	Chalmers [3 PENs, 2 CONs]	10	Smith. B [DG, 3 CONs]
9	Armstrong	9	Saunders (c)
8	White	8	Robinson [TRY]
7	Jeffrey	7	Hamilton
6	Turnbull	6	Matthews
5	Cronin	5	Rigney
4	Gray	4	Francis
3	Burnell	3	Fitzgerald. D
2	Allan	2	Smith. S
1	Sole (c)	1	Fitzgerald. J

Comments: The visitors crossed the try-line 4 times for the second successive away match and again failed to win. Three penalties from Chalmers proved decisive.

1991 FINAL TABLE

		Points For	Points Against	Total Points
1ST	ENGLAND	83	44	8
2ND	FRANCE	91	46	6
3RD	SCOTLAND	81	73	4
4TH	IRELAND	66	86	1
4TH	WALES	42	114	1

Comments: Ten years earlier France had collected the Grand Slam at Twickenham. This season saw a reversal of that occasion.

DID YOU KNOW?

Although a Grand Slam might be expected to be the start of a golden era for the worthy winners, it sometimes galvanises the other teams to do likewise the following year. There have been several instances since 1970 where a Grand Slam for one country has been followed immediately by another Slam for a different team: The Grand Slam turnovers are as follows:

1976 Wales and 1977 France
1977 France and 1978 Wales
1980 England and 1981 France
1990 Scotland and 1991 England
2002 France and 2003 England
2003 England and 2004 France
2004 France and 2005 Wales
2008 Wales and 2009 Ireland.

1992

IRELAND 15 WALES 16; at Lansdowne Road; 18th of January 1992

15	Staples		15	Clement
14	Wallace [TRY]		14	Evans (c)
13	Mullin		13	Gibbs
12	Curtis		12	Jenkins. N [3 PENs]
11	Crossan		11	Hall
10	Keyes [3 PENs, CON]		10	Stephens [DG]
9	Saunders		9	Jones
8	Robinson		8	Davies [TRY]
7	Fitzgibbon		7	Webster
6	Matthews (c)		6	Lewis
5	Francis		5	Copsey
4	Lenihan		4	Llewellyn
3	Fitzgerald		3	Delaney
2	Smith		2	Jenkins. G
1	Popplewell		1	Griffiths

Comments: Stuart Davies scored a second-half try on his debut as Wales overturned the 9-6 half-time deficit to make the best possible start to the Five Nations.

SCOTLAND 7 ENGLAND 25; at Murrayfield; 18th of January 1992

15	Hastings. G [PEN]		15	Webb [4 PENs, CON]
14	Stanger		14	Halliday
13	Hastings. S		13	Carling (c)
12	Lineen		12	Guscott [DG]
11	Tukalo		11	Underwood [TRY]
10	Chalmers		10	Andrew
9	Nicol		9	Morris [TRY]
8	White [TRY]		8	Rodber
7	Smith		7	Winterbottom
6	McIvor		6	Skinner
5	Morrison		5	Dooley
4	Weir		4	Bayfield
3	Burnell		3	Probyn
2	Milne		2	Moore
1	Sole (c)		1	Leonard

Comments: England only led 10-7 at the interval but thereafter they dominated. This was the debut for Tim Rodber and sweet revenge for the 1990 Grand Slam loss.

ENGLAND 38 IRELAND 9; at Twickenham; 1st of February 1992

15	Webb [2 TRIES, 2 PENs, 4 CONs]		15	Staples
14	Halliday [TRY]		14	Wallace
13	Carling (c)		13	Mullin
12	Guscott [TRY]		12	Curtis
11	Underwood [TRY]		11	Geoghegan
10	Andrew		10	Keyes [TRY, PEN, CON]
9	Morris [TRY]		9	Aherne
8	Rodber		8	Robinson
7	Winterbottom		7	Fitzgibbon
6	Skinner		6	Matthews (c)
5	Dooley		5	Francis
4	Bayfield		4	Galwey
3	Probyn		3	Halpin
2	Moore		2	Smith
1	Leonard		1	Popplewell

Comments: Jonathan Webb registered twenty-two points in this no contest. The rampant home team were already a mere 24-9 ahead at the halfway stage.

WALES 9 FRANCE 12; at Cardiff; 1st of February 1992

15	Clement		15	Lafond [CON]
14	Evans (c)		14	Saint-Andre [TRY]
13	Gibbs		13	Sella (c)
12	Jenkins. N [3 PENs]		12	Mesnel
11	Hall		11	Viars [PEN]
10	Stephens		10	Penaud [DG]
9	Jones		9	Galthie
8	Davies		8	Cecillon
7	Webster		7	Cabannes
6	Lewis		6	Tordo
5	Copsey		5	Mougeot
4	Llewellyn		4	Cadieu
3	Delaney		3	Gimbert
2	Jenkins. G		2	Moscato
1	Griffiths		1	Lascube

Comments: France scored all their points in the first 40 minutes and Wales replied with theirs in the second half. Saint-Andre's try largely decided the result.

FRANCE 13 ENGLAND 31*; at Parc des Princes; 15th of February 1992

15	Lafond	15	Webb [TRY, 3 PENs, 3 CONs]
14	Saint-Andre	14	Halliday
13	Mesnel	13	Carling (c)
12	Sella (c)	12	Guscott
11	Viars [TRY, PEN, CON]	11	Underwood [TRY]
10	Penaud [TRY]	10	Andrew
9	Galthie	9	Morris [TRY]
8	van Heerden	8	Richards
7	Cabannes	7	Winterbottom
6	Tordo	6	Skinner
5	Mougeot	5	Dooley
4	Cecillon	4	Bayfield
3	Gimbert	3	Probyn
2	Moscato [SENT OFF]	2	Moore
1	Lascube [SENT OFF]	1	Leonard

Comments: Webb only managed 19 points this time. 13 proved unlucky for some as thirteen-man France could only muster thirteen points against the visitors.

*England's points included a penalty try.

IRELAND 10 SCOTLAND 18; at Lansdowne Road; 15th of February 1992

15	Murphy	15	Hastings. G [2 PENs, 2 CONs]
14	Wallace [TRY]	14	Stanger [TRY]
13	Mullin	13	Hastings. S
12	Danaher	12	Lineen
11	Geoghegan	11	Tukalo
10	Keyes [2 PENs]	10	Chalmers
9	Aherne	9	Nicol [TRY]
8	Robinson	8	White
7	Fitzgibbon	7	Smith
6	Matthews (c)	6	McIvor
5	Francis	5	Weir
4	Galwey	4	Edwards
3	Halpin	3	Burnell
2	Smith	2	Milne
1	Popplewell	1	Sole (c)

Comments: The Scots recorded a try in each half against their hapless hosts. Rob Wainwright came on as a replacement to win his first Scottish cap.

ENGLAND 24 WALES 0; at Twickenham; 7th of March 1992

15	Webb [2 PENs, 3 CONs]	15	Clement
14	Halliday	14	Evans (c)
13	Carling (c) [TRY]	13	Jenkins. N
12	Guscott	12	Gibbs
11	Underwood	11	Hall
10	Andrew	10	Stephens
9	Morris	9	Jones
8	Richards	8	Davies
7	Winterbottom	7	Webster
6	Skinner [TRY]	6	Morris
5	Bayfield	5	Copsey
4	Dooley [TRY]	4	Llewellyn
3	Probyn	3	Delaney
2	Moore	2	Jenkins. G
1	Leonard	1	Griffiths

Comments: The ruthless home team had already crossed the try-line twice in the first half as Wales failed to score in a match for the first time since 1970.

SCOTLAND 10 FRANCE 6; at Murrayfield; 7th of March 1992

15	Hastings. G [2 PENs]	15	Sadourny
14	Stanger	14	Lafond [2 PENs]
13	Hastings. S	13	Mesnel
12	Lineen	12	Sella (c)
11	Tukalo	11	Saint-Andre
10	Chalmers	10	Penaud
9	Nicol	9	Galthie
8	White	8	van Heerden
7	Wainwright	7	Cabannes
6	McIvor	6	Tordo
5	Weir	5	Roumat
4	Edwards [TRY]	4	Cecillon
3	Burnell	3	Gallart
2	Milne	2	Genet
1	Sole (c)	1	Armary

Comments: Neil Edwards scored his only international try to give Scotland a narrow 4-3 lead at half-time. Yet again toothless France flopped at Murrayfield.

FRANCE 44 IRELAND 12; at Parc des Princes; 21st of March 1992

15	Sadourny [TRY]	15	Murphy
14	Saint-Andre	14	Wallace
13	Mesnel	13	Curtis
12	Sella (c)	12	Danaher (c)
11	Viars [2 TRIES, 5 CONs, 2 PENs]	11	Geoghegan
10	Penaud [2 TRIES]	10	McAleese [4 PENs]
9	Galthie	9	Aherne
8	Cabannes [TRY]	8	Robinson
7	van Heerden [TRY]	7	Fitzgibbon
6	Tordo	6	Hogan
5	Roumat	5	Galwey
4	Cadieu	4	Rigney
3	Gallart	3	Halpin
2	Genet	2	Smith
1	Armary	1	Popplewell

Comments: The Irish finished a miserable whitewash campaign by conceding 7 tries to a French team, clearly hurting from their losses to England and Scotland.

WALES 15 SCOTLAND 12; at Cardiff; 21st of March 1992

15	Clement	15	Hastings. G [PEN]
14	Evans (c)	14	Stanger
13	Bidgood	13	Hastings. S
12	Gibbs	12	Lineen
11	Hall	11	Tukalo
10	Jenkins. N [3 PENs, CON]	10	Chalmers [2 PENs, DG]
9	Jones	9	Nicol
8	Davies	8	White
7	Webster [TRY]	7	Smith
6	Lewis	6	McIvor
5	Copsey	5	Weir
4	Llewellyn	4	Edwards
3	Williams-Jones	3	Burnell
2	Jenkins. G	2	Milne
1	Griffiths	1	Sole (c)

Comments: Richard Webster's only try for Wales helped them to their first home win in the Five Nations since March 1989.

1992 FINAL TABLE

		Points For	Points Against	Total Points
1ST	ENGLAND	118	29	8
2ND	FRANCE	75	62	4
2ND	SCOTLAND	47	56	4
2ND	WALES	40	63	4
5TH	IRELAND	46	116	0

Comments: England won the first back-to-back Grand Slams since 1924, averaging an impressive 29. 5 points per triumph.

DID YOU KNOW?

Between the end of the 1992 championship and the start of the 1993 tournament, the value of a try was increased to five points in a renewed effort to ensure that matches were decided by running rugby rather than merely a penalty kick-fest. In fact, until the 1973 Five Nations, a try was merely worth a scandalous three points and deemed to be of identical value to a penalty or drop goal!

1993

ENGLAND 16 FRANCE 15; at Twickenham; 16th of January 1993

15	Webb [3 PENs, CON]	15	Lafond
14	Hunter [TRY]	14	Saint-Andre [2 TRIES]
13	Carling (c)	13	Sella
12	Guscott	12	Lacroix
11	Underwood	11	Hontas
10	Andrew	10	Camberabero [PEN, CON]
9	Morris	9	Hueber
8	Clarke	8	Cecillon
7	Winterbottom	7	Cabannes
6	Teague	6	Benetton
5	Bayfield	5	Roumat
4	Johnson	4	Benazzi
3	Probyn	3	Seigne
2	Moore	2	Tordo (c)
1	Leonard	1	Armary

Comments: Martin Johnson made his debut as both teams merely added a penalty each to the half-time score of 13-12, with all tries having come in the first half.

SCOTLAND 15 IRELAND 3; at Murrayfield; 16th of January 1993

15	Hastings. G (c) [PEN, CON]	15	Wilkinson
14	Stanger [TRY]	14	Geoghegan
13	Hastings. S	13	Cunningham
12	Shiel	12	Danaher
11	Stark [TRY]	11	Wallace
10	Chalmers	10	Malone [PEN]
9	Armstrong	9	Bradley (c)
8	Weir	8	Robinson
7	Morrison	7	McBride
6	Turnbull	6	Lawlor
5	Reed	5	Costello
4	Cronin	4	Johns
3	Burnell	3	McCarthy
2	Milne	2	Smith
1	Watt	1	Popplewell

Comments: Each team fielded three new recruits. One of them, Derek Stark, scored one of the two tries as Scotland led comfortably 15-0 at the halfway stage.

FRANCE 11 SCOTLAND 3; at Parc des Princes; 6th of February 1993

15	Lafond	15	Hastings. G (c) [PEN]
14	Saint-Andre	14	Stanger
13	Sella	13	Hastings. S
12	Lacroix [TRY]	12	Shiel
11	Hontas	11	Stark
10	Camberabero [2 PENs]	10	Chalmers
9	Hueber	9	Armstrong
8	Cecillon	8	Weir
7	Cabannes	7	Morrison
6	Benetton	6	Turnbull
5	Roumat	5	Reed
4	Benazzi	4	Cronin
3	Seigne	3	Burnell
2	Tordo (c)	2	Milne
1	Armary	1	Wright

Comments: Both teams swapped a penalty each in the first 40 minutes. It took a Thierry Lacroix try and another Didier Camberabero penalty to settle the outcome.

WALES 10 ENGLAND 9; at Cardiff; 6th of February 1993

15	Rayer	15	Webb [2 PENs]
14	Evans. I (c) [TRY]	14	Hunter
13	Hall	13	Carling (c)
12	Gibbs	12	Guscott [DG]
11	Proctor	11	Underwood
10	Jenkins [PEN, CON]	10	Andrew
9	Jones	9	Morris
8	Davies	8	Clarke
7	Webster	7	Winterbottom
6	Lewis	6	Teague
5	Copsey	5	Bayfield
4	Llewellyn	4	Dooley
3	Williams-Jones	3	Probyn
2	Meek	2	Moore
1	Evans. R	1	Leonard

Comments: Ricky Evans won his first cap, while another Evans, the captain Ieuan, scored the decisive try. All the points came in the first half.

IRELAND 6 FRANCE 21; at Lansdowne Road; 20th of February 1993

15	Clarke		15	Lafond
14	Geoghegan		14	Saint-Andre [TRY]
13	Cunningham		13	Sella [TRY]
12	Danaher		12	Lacroix
11	Wallace		11	Hontas
10	Malone [2 PENs]		10	Camberabero [2 PENs, DG, CON]
9	Bradley (c)		9	Hueber
8	Galwey		8	Cecillon
7	McBride		7	Cabannes
6	O'Hara		6	Benetton
5	Francis		5	Roumat
4	Johns		4	Benazzi
3	Clohessy		3	Seigne
2	Kingston		2	Tordo (c)
1	Popplewell		1	Armary

Comments: Yet again Ireland ran out of steam after being level at the interval. The 2 Philippes, Saint-Andre and Sella, crossed the try-line in the second half.

SCOTLAND 20 WALES 0; at Murrayfield; 20th of February 1993

15	Hastings. G (c) [5 PENs]		15	Rayer
14	Stanger		14	Evans. I (c)
13	Hastings. S		13	Hall
12	Shiel		12	Gibbs
11	Stark		11	Proctor
10	Chalmers		10	Jenkins
9	Armstrong		9	Jones
8	Weir		8	Davies
7	Morrison		7	Webster
6	Turnbull [TRY]		6	Lewis
5	Reed		5	Copsey
4	Cronin		4	Llewellyn
3	Wright		3	Williams-Jones
2	Milne		2	Meek
1	Burnell		1	Evans. R

Comments: After the euphoria of their England win, Wales fell to earth with this humiliation. Derek Turnbull scored a try as Scotland took a 14-0 interval lead.

ENGLAND 26 SCOTLAND 12; at Twickenham; 6th of March 1993

15	Webb [3 PENs, CON]	15	Hastings. G (c) [3 PENs]
14	Underwood. T [TRY]	14	Stanger
13	Carling (c)	13	Hastings. S
12	Guscott [TRY]	12	Shiel
11	Underwood. R [TRY]	11	Stark
10	Barnes	10	Chalmers [DG]
9	Morris	9	Armstrong
8	Clarke	8	Weir
7	Winterbottom	7	Morrison
6	Teague	6	Turnbull
5	Bayfield	5	Reed
4	Dooley	4	Cronin
3	Probyn	3	Wright
2	Moore	2	Milne
1	Leonard	1	Burnell

Comments: Both the Underwood brothers crossed the try-line to wreck Scotland's Triple Crown quest. Gregor Townsend won his first Scottish cap as a replacement.

WALES 14 IRELAND 19; at Cardiff; 6th of March 1993

15	Rayer	15	Clarke [DG]
14	Evans. I (c) [TRY]	14	Geoghegan
13	Hall	13	Cunningham
12	Gibbs	12	Danaher
11	Walker	11	Wallace
10	Jenkins [3 PENs]	10	Elwood [3 PENs, CON]
9	Jones	9	Bradley (c)
8	Davies	8	Robinson [TRY]
7	Webster	7	McBride
6	Lewis	6	O'Hara
5	Copsey	5	Francis
4	Llewellyn	4	Johns
3	Williams-Jones	3	Clohessy
2	Meek	2	Kingston
1	Evans. R	1	Popplewell

Comments: Nigel Walker made his debut for Wales, but it was another new face Eric Elwood who contributed enormously to another Irish win in the principality.

FRANCE 26 WALES 10; at Parc des Princes; 20th of March 1993

15	Lafond [TRY, CON]		15	Clement
14	Saint-Andre		14	Evans. I (c)
13	Lacroix		13	Davies. N
12	Sella		12	Gibbs
11	Hontas		11	Walker [TRY]
10	Mesnel [3 PENs]		10	Jenkins [PEN, CON]
9	Hueber		9	Moon
8	Cecillon		8	Lewis
7	Cabannes		7	Webster
6	Benetton [2 TRIES]		6	Perego
5	Roumat		5	Davies. P
4	Benazzi		4	Llewellyn
3	Seigne		3	Williams-Jones
2	Tordo (c)		2	Lamerton
1	Armary		1	Evans. R

Comments: Philippe Benetton was the double try-scoring hero as France ran out comfortable winners. Wales were already struggling at 16-3 behind at the interval.

IRELAND 17 ENGLAND 3; at Lansdowne Road; 20th of March 1993

15	O'Shea		15	Webb [PEN]
14	Geoghegan		14	Underwood. T
13	Field		13	Carling (c)
12	Danaher		12	Guscott
11	Wallace		11	Underwood. R
10	Elwood [2 PENs, 2 DGs]		10	Barnes
9	Bradley (c)		9	Morris
8	Robinson		8	Clarke
7	McBride		7	Winterbottom
6	O'Hara		6	Teague
5	Galwey [TRY]		5	Bayfield
4	Johns		4	Dooley
3	Clohessy		3	Probyn
2	Kingston		2	Moore
1	Popplewell		1	Leonard

Comments: England suffered their second successive away defeat as the unfancied Irish upset the form book. Mick Galwey was the only try-scorer in this contest.

1993 FINAL TABLE

		Points For	Points Against	Total Points
1ST	FRANCE	73	35	6
2ND	SCOTLAND	50	40	4
2ND	ENGLAND	54	54	4
2ND	IRELAND	45	53	4
5TH	WALES	34	74	2

Comments: France took advantage when a complacent England crash landed.
Only 4 times did a team reach 20 points in a match.

THE BRITISH AND IRISH LIONS, 1990 TO 2009

LOST 20-18 v New Zealand; in Christchurch; 12th of June 1993
WON 20-7 v New Zealand; in Wellington; 26th of June 1993
LOST 30-13 v New Zealand; in Auckland; 3rd of July 1993
WON 25-16 v South Africa; in Cape Town; 21st of June 1997
WON 18-15 v South Africa; in Durban; 28th of June 1997
LOST 35-16 v South Africa; in Johannesburg; 5th of July 1997
WON 29-13 v Australia; in Brisbane; 30th of June 2001
LOST 35-14 v Australia; in Melbourne; 7th of July 2001
LOST 29-23 v Australia; in Sydney; 14th of July 2001
DREW 25-25 v Argentina; in Cardiff; 23rd of May 2005
LOST 21-3 v New Zealand; in Christchurch; 25th of June 2005
LOST 48-18 v New Zealand; in Wellington; 2nd of July 2005
LOST 38-19 v New Zealand; in Auckland; 9th of July 2005
LOST 26-21 v South Africa; in Durban; 20th of June 2009
LOST 28-25 v South Africa; in Pretoria; 27th of June 2009
WON 28-9 v South Africa; in Johannesburg; 4th of July 2009

1994

FRANCE 35 IRELAND 15; at Parc des Princes; 15th of January 1994

15	Sadourny		15	O'Shea
14	Bernat-Salles		14	Geoghegan
13	Sella		13	Cunningham
12	Lacroix [TRY, 3 PENs, 3 CONs]		12	Danaher
11	Saint-Andre [TRY]		11	Wallace
10	Penaud		10	Elwood [5 PENs]
9	Galthie		9	Bradley (c)
8	Cecillon		8	Robinson
7	Benazzi [TRY]		7	O'Connell
6	Benetton [TRY]		6	Galwey
5	Roumat (c)		5	Francis
4	Merle		4	Johns
3	Gallart		3	Clohessy
2	Gonzalez		2	Kingston
1	Armary		1	Popplewell

Comments: The Oirish suffered another ritual humiliation in Paris. Thierry Lacroix feasted himself with twenty points in this four-try victory.

WALES 29 SCOTLAND 6; at Cardiff; 15th of January 1994

15	Clement		15	Hastings (c) [2 PENs]
14	Evans. I (c) [TRY]		14	Stanger
13	Hall		13	Townsend
12	Davies. N		12	Jardine
11	Walker		11	Logan
10	Jenkins. N [4 PENs, CON]		10	Chalmers
9	Moon		9	Nicol
8	Quinnell		8	Wainwright
7	Perego		7	Morrison
6	Lewis		6	Turnbull
5	Llewellyn		5	Munro
4	Davies. P		4	Edwards
3	Davies. J		3	Burnell
2	Jenkins. G		2	Milne
1	Evans. R		1	Wright

Comments: Mike Rayer came on as a substitute and promptly recorded two tries in this convincing win. Wales's captain, Ieuan Evans, scored the other try.

IRELAND 15 WALES 17; at Lansdowne Road; 5th of February 1994

15	O'Shea	15	Clement
14	Wallace	14	Evans. I (c)
13	McCall	13	Hall
12	Danaher	12	Davies. N
11	Geoghegan	11	Proctor
10	Elwood [5 PENs]	10	Jenkins. N [TRY, 4 PENs]
9	Bradley (c)	9	Moon
8	Johns	8	Quinnell
7	McBride	7	Perego
6	Robinson	6	Lewis
5	Francis	5	Davies. P
4	Galwey	4	Llewellyn
3	Clohessy	3	Davies. J
2	Kingston	2	Jenkins. G
1	Popplewell	1	Evans. R

Comments: Neil Jenkins scored the match's only try in the first half but his team still trailed 9-8 at half-time. Elwood was again the only Irish points scorer.

SCOTLAND 14 ENGLAND 15; at Murrayfield; 5th of February 1994

15	Hastings. G (c) [2 PENs]	15	Callard [5 PENs]
14	Stanger	14	Underwood. T
13	Hastings. S	13	Carling (c)
12	Wyllie	12	de Glanville
11	Logan	11	Underwood. R
10	Townsend [DG]	10	Andrew
9	Armstrong	9	Bracken
8	Weir	8	Clarke
7	Wainwright [TRY]	7	Back
6	Walton	6	Hall
5	Reed	5	Bayfield
4	Munro	4	Johnson
3	Burnell	3	Ubogu
2	Milne	2	Moore
1	Sharp	1	Leonard

Comments: Jon Callard slotted 4 second-half penalties as England narrowly held on to the Calcutta Cup. Rob Wainwright had earlier scored the match's only try.

ENGLAND 12 IRELAND 13; at Twickenham; 19th of February 1994

15	Callard [4 PENs]		15	O'Shea
14	Underwood. T		14	Wallace
13	Carling (c)		13	Field
12	de Glanville		12	Danaher
11	Underwood. R		11	Geoghegan [TRY]
10	Andrew		10	Elwood [2 PENs, CON]
9	Bracken		9	Bradley (c)
8	Ojomoh		8	Johns
7	Back		7	McBride
6	Rodber		6	Robinson
5	Bayfield		5	Francis
4	Johnson		4	Galwey
3	Ubogu		3	Clohessy
2	Moore		2	Kingston
1	Leonard		1	Popplewell

Comments: Simon Geoghegan scored an excellent first-half try, but this match is remembered for a winning Eric Elwood penalty which was perhaps unjustly awarded.

WALES 24 FRANCE 15; at Cardiff; 19th of February 1994

15	Rayer		15	Sadourny
14	Hill		14	Ntamack
13	Hall		13	Sella [TRY]
12	Clement		12	Lacroix [PEN, CON]
11	Walker [TRY]		11	Saint-Andre
10	Jenkins. N [4 PENs, CON]		10	Penaud
9	Moon		9	Galthie
8	Quinnell [TRY]		8	Cecillon
7	Perego		7	Benazzi
6	Lewis		6	Benetton
5	Davies. P		5	Roumat (c) [TRY]
4	Llewellyn (c)		4	Merle
3	Davies. J		3	Gallart
2	Jenkins. G		2	Gonzalez
1	Evans		1	Armary

Comments: Both teams shared 4 tries but the trusty boot of Neil Jenkins was decisive in securing Wales her first Five Nations win over France in twelve years.

FRANCE 14 ENGLAND 18; at Parc des Princes; 5th of March 1994

15	Sadourny	15	Pears
14	Saint-Andre	14	Hunter
13	Sella	13	Carling (c)
12	Lacroix [3 PENs]	12	de Glanville
11	Techoueyres	11	Underwood
10	Penaud	10	Andrew [5 PENs, DG]
9	Galthie	9	Morris
8	Benetton	8	Ojomoh
7	Cabannes	7	Clarke
6	Benazzi [TRY]	6	Rodber
5	Roumat (c)	5	Redman
4	Merle	4	Johnson
3	Gallart	3	Ubogu
2	Gonzalez	2	Moore
1	Benezech	1	Leonard

Comments: England failed to find a try for the fourth successive Five Nations outing but they still earned a commendable win, thanks to Rob Andrew's goal kicks.

IRELAND 6 SCOTLAND 6; at Lansdowne Road; 5th of March 1994

15	O'Shea	15	Hastings. G (c) [2 PENs]
14	Wallace	14	Stanger
13	Field	13	Hastings. S
12	Danaher	12	Wyllie
11	Geoghegan	11	Logan
10	Elwood [2 PENs]	10	Townsend
9	Bradley (c)	9	Armstrong
8	Johns	8	Weir
7	McBride	7	Smith
6	Robinson	6	Walton
5	Francis	5	Reed
4	Galwey	4	Munro
3	Clohessy	3	Burnell
2	Kingston	2	Milne
1	Popplewell	1	Sharp

Comments: Eric Elwood and Gavin Hastings converted a brace of penalties each in this bore draw. This was Scotland's only point in a disappointing campaign.

ENGLAND 15 WALES 8; at Twickenham; 19th of March 1994

15	Hunter		15	Rayer
14	Underwood. T		14	Evans. I (c)
13	Carling (c)		13	Hall
12	de Glanville		12	Davies. N
11	Underwood. R [TRY]		11	Walker [TRY]
10	Andrew [PEN, CON]		10	Jenkins. N [PEN]
9	Morris		9	Moon
8	Richards		8	Quinnell
7	Clarke		7	Perego
6	Rodber [TRY]		6	Lewis
5	Redman		5	Davies. P
4	Johnson		4	Llewellyn
3	Ubogu		3	Davies. J
2	Moore		2	Jenkins. G
1	Leonard		1	Evans. R

Comments: Rodber was amongst the try-scorers as England's juggernaut pack foiled Wales's attempt at seizing the Grand Slam but Wales still won the Five Nations.

SCOTLAND 12 FRANCE 20; at Murrayfield; 19th of March 1994

15	Hastings. G (c) [4 PENs]		15	Sadourny [TRY]
14	Stanger		14	Saint-Andre (c) [TRY]
13	Hastings. S		13	Sella
12	Wyllie		12	Delaigue
11	Logan		11	Techoueyres
10	Townsend		10	Lacroix [2 PENs, CON]
9	Redpath		9	Macabiau
8	Weir		8	Benazzi
7	Smith		7	Cabannes
6	Walton		6	Benetton
5	Reed		5	Merle
4	Munro		4	Brouzet
3	Burnell		3	Seigne
2	Milne		2	Gonzalez
1	Sharp		1	Benezech

Comments: This was France's first successful invasion of Murrayfield since 1978. Pierre Montlaur came on as a replacement to convert one of the two tries.

1994 FINAL TABLE

	Points For	Points Against	Total Points
1ST WALES	78	51	6
2ND ENGLAND	60	49	6
3RD FRANCE	84	69	4
4TH IRELAND	49	70	3
5TH SCOTLAND	38	70	1

Comments: Ireland ruined England's Grand Slam hopes; England ruined Wales's Grand Slam hopes; and Scotland finished winless.

DID YOU KNOW?

1994's Calcutta Cup clash saw a pair of brothers on each team. Scotland fielded the Hastings brothers, Gavin and Scott, whilst England featured the wingers Rory and Tony Underwood. Other brothers who have appeared in the Five Nations and Six Nations since 1970 have included Delon and Steffon Armitage of England; Mauro and Mirco Bergamasco of Italy; Rory and Simon Best of Ireland; Gordon and Peter Brown of Scotland; Finlay and Jim Calder of Scotland; Michael and Peter Dods of Scotland; Guy and Simon Easterby of Ireland; Max and Thom Evans of Scotland; Rory and Sean Lamont of Scotland; John and Martin Leslie of Scotland; Marc et Thomas Lievremont of France; Iain and Kenny Milne of Scotland; Paul and Richard Moriarty of Wales; Craig and Scott Quinnell of Wales; Claude et Walter Spanghero of France; David, Paul and Richard Wallace of Ireland.

1995

FRANCE 21 WALES 9; at Parc des Princes; 21st of January 1995

15	Sadourny	15	Clement
14	Ntamack [TRY]	14	Hill
13	Sella	13	Taylor
12	Lacroix [3 PENs, CON]	12	Hall
11	Saint-Andre (c) [TRY]	11	Walker
10	Deylaud	10	Jenkins. N [3 PENs]
9	Accoceberry	9	Jones. R
8	Benetton	8	Davies. P
7	Cabannes	7	Collins
6	Benazzi	6	Davies. S
5	Roumat	5	Jones. D
4	Merle	4	Llewellyn (c)
3	Califano	3	Davies. J
2	Gonzalez	2	Jenkins. G
1	Benezech	1	Evans

Comments: Emile Ntamack and Philippe Saint-Andre scored first-half tries while Thierry Lacroix added two second-half penalties in this comfortable triumph.

IRELAND 8 ENGLAND 20; at Lansdowne Road; 21st of January 1995

15	O'Shea	15	Catt
14	Geoghegan	14	Underwood. T [TRY]
13	Mullin (c)	13	Carling (c) [TRY]
12	Danaher	12	Guscott
11	Woods	11	Underwood. R
10	Burke [PEN]	10	Andrew [PEN, CON]
9	Hogan	9	Bracken
8	Johns	8	Richards
7	Corkery	7	Clarke [TRY]
6	Foley [TRY]	6	Rodber
5	Francis	5	Bayfield
4	Galwey	4	Johnson
3	Clohessy	3	Ubogu
2	Wood	2	Moore
1	Popplewell	1	Leonard

Comments: Anthony Foley recorded a second-half try on his debut, but the English had already crossed the try-line twice in the first forty minutes.

ENGLAND 31 FRANCE 10; at Twickenham; 4th of February 1995

15 Catt	15 Sadourny
14 Underwood. T [2 TRIES]	14 Bernat-Salles
13 Carling (c)	13 Sella
12 Guscott [TRY]	12 Lacroix [PEN, CON]
11 Underwood. R	11 Saint-Andre (c)
10 Andrew [4 PENs, 2 CONs]	10 Deylaud
9 Bracken	9 Accoceberry
8 Richards	8 Benetton
7 Clarke	7 Cabannes
6 Rodber	6 Benazzi
5 Bayfield	5 Roumat
4 Johnson	4 Brouzet
3 Ubogu	3 Califano
2 Moore	2 Gonzalez
1 Leonard	1 Benezech

Comments: Three tries and sixteen points from Rob Andrew contributed to an emphatic demolition. The replacement Sebastien Viars scored France's only try.

SCOTLAND 26 IRELAND 13; at Murrayfield; 4th of February 1995

15 Hastings (c) [4 PENs, 2 CONs]	15 O'Shea
14 Joiner [TRY]	14 Geoghegan
13 Townsend	13 Mullin [TRY]
12 Jardine	12 Danaher
11 Logan	11 Bell [TRY]
10 Chalmers	10 Burke [PEN]
9 Redpath	9 Bradley (c)
8 Peters	8 Cronin
7 Morrison	7 McBride
6 Wainwright	6 Foley
5 Campbell	5 Fulcher
4 Cronin [TRY]	4 Johns
3 Wright	3 Clohessy
2 Milne	2 Wood
1 Hilton	1 Popplewell

Comments: Although both teams shared four tries, Scotland were indebted to Gavin Hastings who kicked sixteen crucial points as Ireland lost again in Edinburgh.

FRANCE 21 SCOTLAND 23; at Parc des Princes; 18th of February 1995

15	Sadourny [TRY]	15	Hastings (c) [TRY, 3 PENs, 2 CONs]
14	Bernat-Salles	14	Joiner
13	Sella	13	Townsend [TRY]
12	Lacroix [PEN]	12	Jardine
11	Saint-Andre (c) [2 TRIES]	11	Logan
10	Deylaud [DG]	10	Chalmers
9	Accoceberry	9	Redpath
8	Benetton	8	Peters
7	Cabannes	7	Morrison
6	Benazzi	6	Wainwright
5	Roumat	5	Campbell
4	Brouzet	4	Cronin
3	Seigne	3	Wright
2	Gonzalez	2	Milne
1	Califano	1	Hilton

Comments: Although Saint-Andre notched a pair of tries, he ended up on the losing team as tries from Gavin Hastings and Gregor Townsend produced an away win.

WALES 9 ENGLAND 23; at Cardiff; 18th of February 1995

15	Clement	15	Catt
14	Evans (c)	14	Underwood. T
13	Taylor. M	13	Carling (c)
12	Davies. N	12	Guscott
11	Walker	11	Underwood. R [2 TRIES]
10	Jenkins. N [3 PENs]	10	Andrew [2 PENs, CON]
9	Jones. R	9	Bracken
8	Lewis	8	Richards
7	Collins	7	Clarke
6	Taylor. H	6	Rodber
5	Jones. D	5	Bayfield
4	Llewellyn	4	Johnson
3	Davies. J [SENT OFF]	3	Ubogu [TRY]
2	Jenkins. G	2	Moore
1	Griffiths	1	Leonard

Comments: The dismissal of John Davies ruined Wales's chances as England went three-quarters of the way to their third Grand Slam of the 1990s.

IRELAND 7 FRANCE 25; at Lansdowne Road; 4th of March 1995

15	Staples		15	Sadourny
14	Geoghegan [TRY]		14	Ntamack [TRY, PEN, CON]
13	Mullin		13	Mesnel
12	Danaher		12	Sella
11	Woods		11	Saint-Andre (c) [TRY]
10	Elwood [CON]		10	Delaigue [TRY]
9	Bradley (c)		9	Accoceberry
8	Foley		8	Cecillon [TRY]
7	McBride		7	Benetton
6	Halvey		6	Benazzi
5	Fulcher		5	Brouzet
4	Tweed		4	Merle
3	Clohessy		3	Califano
2	Kingston		2	Gonzalez
1	Popplewell		1	Armary

Comments: France only led three-nil at the interval but eventually the floodgates opened and Ireland characteristically wilted in the second half.

SCOTLAND 26 WALES 13; at Murrayfield; 4th of March 1995

15	Hastings. G (c) [4 PENs, 2 CONs]		15	Back
14	Joiner		14	Evans (c)
13	Hastings. S		13	Hall
12	Townsend		12	Davies
11	Logan		11	Proctor
10	Chalmers		10	Jenkins. N [2 PENs, CON]
9	Redpath		9	Jones. R [TRY]
8	Peters [TRY]		8	Lewis
7	Morrison		7	Collins
6	Wainwright		6	Taylor
5	Campbell		5	Llewellyn
4	Weir		4	Jones. D
3	Wright		3	John
2	Milne		2	Jenkins. G
1	Hilton [TRY]		1	Griffiths

Comments: All the tries came in the first forty minutes, with Dave Hilton scoring his only Scotland try as the hosts took a 20-7 lead into the second half.

ENGLAND 24 SCOTLAND 12; at Twickenham; 18th of March 1995

15	Catt	15	Hastings. G (c) [2 PENs]
14	Underwood. T	14	Joiner
13	Carling (c)	13	Hastings. S
12	Guscott	12	Townsend
11	Underwood. R	11	Logan
10	Andrew [7 PENs, DG]	10	Chalmers [2 DGs]
9	Bracken	9	Redpath
8	Richards	8	Peters
7	Clarke	7	Morrison
6	Rodber	6	Wainwright
5	Bayfield	5	Campbell
4	Johnson	4	Weir
3	Ubogu	3	Wright
2	Moore	2	Milne
1	Leonard	1	Hilton

Comments: It was 1990 reversed as England won the Grand Slam decider. Rob Andrew was the hero with twelve points kicked in each half.

WALES 12 IRELAND 16; at Cardiff; 18th of March 1995

15	Back	15	Staples
14	Evans (c)	14	Wallace
13	Davies. N	13	Mullin [TRY]
12	Hall	12	Danaher
11	Proctor	11	Geoghegan
10	Jenkins. N [4 PENs]	10	Elwood
9	Jones	9	Hogan
8	Lewis	8	Johns
7	Collins	7	Halvey
6	Gibbs	6	Foley
5	Llewellyn	5	Fulcher
4	Davies. P	4	Tweed
3	John	3	Clohessy
2	Jenkins. G	2	Kingston (c)
1	Griffiths	1	Popplewell

Comments: Paul Burke came on as a replacement and kicked eleven points, including a drop goal and a conversion of Brendan Mullin's first-half try.

1995 FINAL TABLE

		Points For	Points Against	Total Points
1ST	ENGLAND	98	39	8
2ND	SCOTLAND	87	71	6
3RD	FRANCE	77	70	4
4TH	IRELAND	44	83	2
5TH	WALES	43	86	0

Comments: England enjoyed their third Grand Slam of the 1990s while Wales suffered their second whitewash of the decade.

THE HEINEKEN EUROPEAN CUPS, 1995 TO 2009

1995 beaten semi-finalists: Leinster and Swansea
1996 FINAL: TOULOUSE beat Cardiff 21-18; in Cardiff
1996 beaten semi-finalists: Cardiff and Toulouse
1997 FINAL: BRIVE beat Leicester 28-9; in Cardiff
1997 beaten semi-finalists: Pau and Toulouse
1998 FINAL: BATH beat Brive 19-18; in Bordeaux
1998 beaten semi-finalists: Perpignan and Stade Francais
1999 FINAL: ULSTER beat Colomiers 21-6; in Dublin
2000 beaten semi-finalists: Llanelli and Toulouse
2000 FINAL: NORTHAMPTON beat Munster 9-8; in London
2001 beaten semi-finalists: Gloucester and Munster
2001 FINAL: LEICESTER beat Stade Francais 34-30; in Paris
2002 beaten semi-finalists: Castres and Llanelli
2002 FINAL: LEICESTER beat Munster 15-9; in Cardiff
2003 beaten semi-finalists: Leinster and Munster
2003 FINAL: TOULOUSE beat Perpignan 22-17; in Dublin
2004 beaten semi-finalists: Biarritz and Munster
2004 FINAL: LONDON WASPS beat Toulouse 27-20; in London
2005 beaten semi-finalists: Biarritz and Leicester
2005 FINAL: TOULOUSE beat Stade Francais 18-12; in Edinburgh
2006 beaten semi-finalists: Bath and Leinster
2006 FINAL: MUNSTER beat Biarritz 23-19; in Cardiff
2007 beaten semi-finalists: Llanelli and Northampton
2007 FINAL: LONDON WASPS beat Leicester 25-9; in London
2008 beaten semi-finalists: London Irish and Saracens
2008 FINAL: MUNSTER beat Toulouse 16-13; in Cardiff
2009 beaten semi-finalists: Cardiff and Munster
2009 FINAL: LEINSTER beat Leicester 19-16; in Edinburgh

1996

FRANCE 15 ENGLAND 12; at Parc des Princes; 20th of January 1996

15	Sadourny		15	Catt
14	Ntamack		14	Sleightholme
13	Dourthe		13	Carling (c)
12	Castaignede [DG]		12	Guscott
11	Saint-Andre (c)		11	Underwood
10	Lacroix [3 PENs, DG]		10	Grayson [2 PENs, 2 DGs]
9	Carbonneau		9	Dawson
8	Pelous		8	Clarke
7	Cabannes		7	Dallaglio
6	Benazzi		6	Ojomoh
5	Roumat		5	Bayfield
4	Merle		4	Johnson
3	Califano		3	Leonard
2	Gonzalez		2	Regan
1	Perie		1	Rowntree

Comments: Thierry Lacroix and Paul Grayson each kicked 12 points in this try-less encounter as France came from 6-3 behind at half-time to collect both points.

IRELAND 10 SCOTLAND 16; at Lansdowne Road; 20th of January 1996

15	Staples (c)		15	Shepherd
14	Wallace		14	Joiner
13	Bell		13	Hastings
12	McQuilkin		12	Jardine
11	Geoghegan		11	Dods [TRY, PEN]
10	Elwood [PEN, CON]		10	Townsend [DG]
9	Saverimutto		9	Redpath
8	Johns		8	Peters
7	Corkery		7	Smith
6	Davidson		6	Wainwright (c)
5	Francis		5	Weir
4	Fulcher		4	Campbell
3	Clohessy [TRY]		3	Wright
2	Kingston		2	McKenzie [TRY]
1	Popplewell		1	Hilton

Comments: Kevin McKenzie registered his only international try as Scotland stormed into a 16-3 interval lead en route to two more points in Dublin.

ENGLAND 21 WALES 15; at Twickenham; 3rd of February 1996

15	Catt		15	Thomas. J
14	Sleightholme		14	Evans
13	Carling (c)		13	Davies. L
12	Guscott [TRY]		12	Davies. N
11	Underwood [TRY]		11	Proctor
10	Grayson [3 PENs, CON]		10	Thomas. A [PEN, CON]
9	Dawson		9	Howley [TRY]
8	Clarke		8	Taylor [TRY]
7	Dallaglio		7	Jones. G
6	Rodber		6	Lewis. E
5	Bayfield		5	Jones. D
4	Johnson		4	Llewellyn
3	Leonard		3	Davies. P
2	Regan		2	Humphreys (c)
1	Rowntree		1	Lewis. A

Comments: Each team scored a try in each half. Rory Underwood crossed the try-line again while there was a debut try for Rob Howley but it was to no avail.

SCOTLAND 19 FRANCE 14; at Murrayfield; 3rd of February 1996

15	Shepherd		15	Sadourny
14	Joiner		14	Ntamack
13	Hastings		13	Penaud
12	Jardine		12	Castaignede [PEN]
11	Dods [2 TRIES, 3 PENs]		11	Saint-Andre (c)
10	Townsend		10	Lacroix [2 PENs]
9	Redpath		9	Carbonneau
8	Peters		8	Pelous
7	Smith		7	Cabannes
6	Wainwright (c)		6	Benazzi [TRY]
5	Weir		5	Roumat
4	Campbell		4	Merle
3	Wright		3	Califano
2	McKenzie		2	Gonzalez
1	Hilton		1	Perie

Comments: Abdel Benazzi recorded a try in the first half, but his effort was eclipsed by Michael Dods who helped himself to 19 points, with 2 tries of his own.

FRANCE 45 IRELAND 10*; at Parc des Princes; 17th of February 1996

15	Sadourny	15	Staples (c)
14	Ntamack [2 TRIES]	14	Wallace
13	Campan [TRY]	13	Bell
12	Lacroix	12	McQuilkin
11	Saint-Andre (c) [TRY]	11	Woods
10	Castaignede [5 CONs]	10	Humphreys [PEN, CON]
9	Accoceberry [TRY]	9	Hogan
8	Pelous	8	Costello
7	Cabannes	7	Corkery
6	Castel [2 TRIES]	6	Davidson
5	Roumat	5	Fulcher
4	Benazzi	4	Johns
3	Tournaire	3	Clohessy
2	Gonzalez	2	Kingston
1	Califano	1	Popplewell

Comments: Richard Castel scored two tries on his debut as France blitzed Ireland with a seven-try massacre on the debut of David Humphreys.

*Ireland's points included a penalty try.

WALES 14 SCOTLAND 16; at Cardiff; 17th of February 1996

15	Thomas. J	15	Shepherd
14	Evans	14	Joiner
13	Davies. L	13	Hastings
12	Davies. N	12	Jardine
11	Proctor [TRY]	11	Dods [3 PENs, CON]
10	Thomas. A [3 PENs]	10	Townsend [TRY]
9	Howley	9	Redpath
8	Taylor	8	Peters
7	Jones. G	7	Smith
6	Lewis. E	6	Wainwright (c)
5	Jones. D	5	Campbell
4	Llewellyn	4	Weir
3	Davies. J	3	Wright
2	Humphreys (c)	2	McKenzie
1	Lewis. A	1	Hilton

Comments: Gregor Townsend and Wayne Proctor both scored second-half tries. The trouble for Wales was that Proctor's wasn't converted and they lost by 2 points.

IRELAND 30 WALES 17; at Lansdowne Road; 3rd of March 1996

15	Mason [2 PENs, 2 CONs]	15	Thomas. J
14	Geoghegan [TRY]	14	Evans [2 TRIES]
13	Bell	13	Davies. L
12	Field	12	Davies. N
11	Woods [TRY]	11	Proctor
10	Humphreys	10	Thomas. A [PEN, 2 CONs]
9	Hogan (c)	9	Howley
8	Costello	8	Taylor
7	McBride	7	Jones. G
6	Corkery [TRY]	6	Lewis. E
5	Davidson	5	Jones. D
4	Fulcher [TRY]	4	Llewellyn
3	Wallace	3	Davies. J
2	Clarke	2	Humphreys (c)
1	Popplewell	1	Lewis. A

Comments: Ieuan Evans's pair of tries were in a losing cause. Simon Mason kicked ten points on his debut in addition to the four tries that the hosts recorded.

SCOTLAND 9 ENGLAND 18; at Murrayfield; 2nd of March 1996

15	Shepherd	15	Catt
14	Joiner	14	Sleightholme
13	Hastings	13	Carling(c)
12	Jardine	12	Guscott
11	Dods [3 PENs]	11	Underwood
10	Townsend	10	Grayson [6 PENs]
9	Redpath	9	Dawson
8	Peters	8	Richards
7	Smith	7	Dallaglio
6	Wainwright (c)	6	Clarke
5	Campbell	5	Archer
4	Weir	4	Johnson
3	Wright	3	Leonard
2	McKenzie	2	Regan
1	Hilton	1	Rowntree

Comments: Michael Dods and Paul Grayson each kicked two penalties in the second half, but the damage had already been done with England 12-3 ahead at half-time.

ENGLAND 28 IRELAND 15; at Twickenham; 16th of March 1996

15	Catt		15	Mason [4 PENs]
14	Sleightholme [TRY]		14	Geoghegan
13	Carling (c)		13	Bell
12	Guscott		12	Field
11	Underwood		11	Woods
10	Grayson [6 PENs, DG, CON]		10	Humphreys [DG]
9	Dawson		9	Hogan (c)
8	Richards		8	Costello
7	Dallaglio		7	McBride
6	Clarke		6	Corkery
5	Archer		5	Davidson
4	Johnson		4	Fulcher
3	Leonard		3	Wallace
2	Regan		2	Clarke
1	Rowntree		1	Popplewell

Comments: A try from Jon Sleightholme in the second-half was sufficient to ensure the capture of the Triple Crown, after Ireland had led 15-12 at the interval.

WALES 16 FRANCE 15; at Cardiff; 16th of March 1996

15	Thomas. J		15	Sadourny
14	Evans		14	Ntamack [TRY]
13	Davies. L		13	Glas
12	Davies. N		12	Campan
11	Thomas. G		11	Saint-Andre (c)
10	Jenkins [3 PENs, CON]		10	Castaignede [TRY, PEN, CON]
9	Howley [TRY]		9	Accoceberry
8	Taylor		8	Dispagne
7	Jones. G		7	Cabannes
6	Lewis		6	Castel
5	Jones. D		5	Roumat
4	Llewellyn		4	Benazzi
3	Davies. J		3	Tournaire
2	Humphreys (c)		2	Gonzalez
1	Loader		1	Califano

Comments: Although France crossed the try-line in each half, Wales avoided a second successive whitewash thanks to a first-half try from Rob Howley.

1996 FINAL TABLE

		Points For	Points Against	Total Points
1ST	ENGLAND	79	54	6
2ND	SCOTLAND	60	56	6
3RD	FRANCE	89	57	4
4TH	WALES	62	82	2
5TH	IRELAND	65	106	2

Comments: England had now achieved back-to-back Triple Crowns for the second time in the decade.

THE ENGLISH PREMIERSHIP

The professional era of the English rugby union Premiership dates from the 1996-1997 season. The champions since then are:

1997: Wasps RFC
1998: Newcastle Falcons
1999: Leicester Tigers
2000: Leicester Tigers
2001: Leicester Tigers won both the league and the play-off final
2002: Leicester Tigers, though Gloucester won the play-off final
2003: London Wasps, though Gloucester won the league
2004: London Wasps, though Bath won the league
2005: London Wasps, though Leicester Tigers won the league
2006: Sale Sharks won both the play-off final and the league
2007: Leicester Tigers, though Gloucester won the league
2008: London Wasps, though Gloucester won the league
2009: Leicester Tigers won both the play-off final and the league

---

1997

IRELAND 15 FRANCE 32; at Lansdowne Road; 18th of January 1997

15	O'Shea		15	Sadourny
14	Topping		14	Ntamack
13	Bell		13	Glas
12	Field		12	Castaignede [2 PENs, 3 CONs]
11	Crotty		11	Venditti [3 TRIES]
10	Elwood [5 PENs]		10	Penaud
9	Hogan		9	Galthie [TRY]
8	Miller		8	Pelous
7	McBride		7	Benetton
6	Corkery		6	Benazzi (c)
5	Davidson		5	Miorin
4	Johns		4	Merle
3	Wallace		3	Tournaire
2	Wood (c)		2	Dal Maso
1	Popplewell		1	Califano

Comments: David Venditti achieved a hat-trick of tries as France dished out their customary thrashing of the Irish who had to rely on Elwood for their points.

SCOTLAND 19 WALES 34; at Murrayfield; 18th of January 1997

15	Shepherd [3 PENs, CON]		15	Jenkins [TRY, 2 PENs, 4 CONs]
14	Stanger		14	Evans [TRY]
13	Hastings [TRY]		13	Bateman
12	Townsend		12	Gibbs
11	Logan		11	Thomas. G
10	Chalmers [DG]		10	Thomas. A [TRY]
9	Armstrong		9	Howley
8	Wainwright (c)		8	Quinnell [TRY]
7	Wallace		7	Charvis
6	Walton		6	Williams
5	Reed		5	Rowley
4	Weir		4	Llewellyn
3	Stewart		3	Young
2	Ellis		2	Humphreys (c)
1	Hilton		1	Loader

Comments: Neil Jenkins accumulated 19 points to earn Wales their first win away to Scotland since 1985. He was one of four try-scorers for the men in red.

ENGLAND 41* SCOTLAND 13; at Twickenham; 1st of February 1997

15	Stimpson	15	Shepherd [2 PENs, CON]
14	Sleightholme	14	Stark
13	Carling [TRY]	13	Stanger
12	de Glanville (c) [TRY]	12	Eriksson [TRY]
11	Underwood	11	Logan
10	Grayson [5 PENs, 3 CONs]	10	Townsend
9	Gomersall [TRY]	9	Redpath
8	Rodber	8	Wainwright (c)
7	Hill	7	Smith. I
6	Dallaglio	6	Walton
5	Shaw	5	Reed
4	Johnson	4	Weir
3	Leonard	3	Stewart
2	Regan	2	Ellis
1	Rowntree	1	Smith. T

Comments: Paul Grayson provided 21 points as England ran riot against a team that had now conceded 75 points in 2 matches. This was the debut for Richard Hill.

*England's points included a penalty try.

WALES 25 IRELAND 26; at Cardiff; 1st of February 1997

15	Jenkins [2 PENs, 2 CONs]	15	Staples (c)
14	Evans [2 TRIES]	14	Hickie [TRY]
13	Thomas. G	13	Bell [TRY]
12	Gibbs	12	Field
11	James	11	Crotty
10	Thomas. A	10	Elwood [3 PENs, CON]
9	Howley	9	Hogan
8	Quinnell [TRY]	8	Miller [TRY]
7	Charvis	7	McBride
6	Williams	6	Corkery
5	Rowley	5	Davidson
4	Llewellyn	4	Johns
3	Young	3	Wallace
2	Humphreys (c)	2	Nesdale
1	Loader	1	Popplewell

Comments: Ieuan Evans took his total to four tries in two matches against Ireland and still Wales lost again. Denis Hickie scored a try on his first appearance.

FRANCE 27 WALES 22; at Parc des Princes; 15th of February 1997

15	Sadourny	15	Jenkins [PEN, 2 CONs]
14	Leflamand [2 TRIES]	14	Evans
13	Dourthe [CON]	13	Bateman [TRY]
12	Glas	12	Gibbs
11	Venditti [TRY]	11	Thomas. G [TRY]
10	Lamaison	10	Thomas. A
9	Carbonneau	9	Howley [TRY]
8	Pelous	8	Quinnell
7	Castel	7	Charvis
6	Benazzi (c)	6	Jones
5	Miorin	5	Rowley
4	Merle [TRY]	4	Llewellyn
3	Jordana	3	Young
2	Dal Maso	2	Humphreys (c)
1	Califano	1	Loader

Comments: Wales fought back with two second-half tries but France grabbed both points. David Aucagne came on as a substitute and kicked five points.

IRELAND 6 ENGLAND 46; at Lansdowne Road; 15th of February 1997

15	Staples (c)	15	Stimpson
14	Hickie	14	Sleightholme [2 TRIES]
13	Bell	13	Carling
12	Field	12	de Glanville (c)
11	Topping	11	Underwood [2 TRIES]
10	Elwood [2 PENs]	10	Grayson [4 PENs, 2 CONs]
9	Hogan	9	Gomersall [TRY]
8	Miller	8	Rodber
7	McBride	7	Hill [TRY]
6	Corkery	6	Dallaglio
5	Davidson	5	Shaw
4	Johns	4	Johnson
3	Wallace	3	Leonard
2	Nesdale	2	Regan
1	Popplewell	1	Rowntree

Comments: England scored 35 points without reply in the second half in a rout that featured pairs of tries for both Jon Sleightholme and Tony Underwood.

ENGLAND 20 FRANCE 23; at Twickenham; 1st of March 1997

15	Stimpson	15	Sadourny
14	Sleightholme	14	Leflamand [TRY]
13	Carling	13	Lamaison [TRY, 2 PENs, DG, 2 CONs]
12	de Glanville (c)	12	Glas
11	Underwood	11	Venditti
10	Grayson [4 PENs, DG]	10	Penaud
9	Gomersall	9	Carbonneau
8	Rodber	8	Pelous
7	Hill	7	Magne
6	Dallaglio [TRY]	6	Benazzi (c)
5	Shaw	5	Miorin
4	Johnson	4	Merle
3	Leonard	3	Tournaire
2	Regan	2	Dal Maso
1	Rowntree	1	Califano

Comments: Christophe Lamaison was the star of the show as his 18 points were crucial in allowing France to overcome their foes who had led 14-6 at the interval.

SCOTLAND 38 IRELAND 10; at Lansdowne Road; 1st of March 1997

15	Shepherd [PEN, 5 CONs]	15	Staples (c)
14	Stanger [TRY]	14	Hickie [TRY]
13	Tait [TRY]	13	Field
12	Townsend [TRY]	12	McQuilkin
11	Logan	11	Bell
10	Chalmers	10	Humphreys [PEN, CON]
9	Redpath	9	O'Meara
8	Walton [TRY]	8	Cronin
7	Smith. I	7	McBride
6	Wainwright (c)	6	Corkery
5	Reed	5	Davidson
4	Weir [TRY]	4	Johns
3	Stewart	3	Wallace
2	Ellis	2	Nesdale
1	Smith. T	1	Flavin

Comments: This match was deadlocked at 7-7 at the halfway stage before the Scots ran in 4 more tries. This rout yielded Scotland's only points in a poor season.

FRANCE 47 SCOTLAND 20; at Parc des Princes; 15th of March 1997

15	Sadourny [DG]		15	Shepherd [2 PENs, 2 CONs]
14	Leflamand [TRY]		14	Stanger
13	Lamaison [6 PENs, 3 CONs]		13	Tait [2 TRIES]
12	Glas		12	Townsend
11	Venditti		11	Logan
10	Aucagne		10	Chalmers
9	Accoceberry		9	Redpath
8	Pelous		8	Walton
7	Magne [TRY]		7	Smith. I
6	Benazzi (c) [TRY]		6	Wainwright (c)
5	Miorin		5	Reed
4	Merle		4	Weir
3	Tournaire [TRY]		3	Stewart
2	Dal Maso		2	Ellis
1	Califano		1	Smith. T

Comments: The hosts seized Le Grand Chelem in emphatic style, courtesy of four more tries as well as 24 points from the lethal boot of Christophe Lamaison.

WALES 13 ENGLAND 34; at Cardiff; 15th of March 1997

15	Jenkins		15	Stimpson [TRY]
14	Hill		14	Sleightholme
13	Bateman		13	Carling
12	Davies. N		12	de Glanville (c) [TRY]
11	Thomas		11	Underwood [TRY]
10	Davies. J [2 PENs, CON]		10	Catt [2 PENs, 4 CONs]
9	Howley [TRY]		9	Healey
8	Quinnell		8	Rodber
7	Jones		7	Hill [TRY]
6	Williams		6	Clarke
5	Voyle		5	Shaw
4	Llewellyn		4	Johnson
3	Young		3	Leonard
2	Humphreys (c)		2	Regan
1	Loader		1	Rowntree

Comments: The last Five Nations fixture at the Arms Park saw England grab four second-half tries en route to another humiliation of their next-door neighbours.

1997 FINAL TABLE

		Points For	Points Against	Total Points
1ST	FRANCE	129	77	8
2ND	ENGLAND	141	55	6
3RD	WALES	94	106	2
4TH	SCOTLAND	90	132	2
5TH	IRELAND	57	141	2

Comments: France recorded her first Grand Slam in ten years and England won the Triple Crown in a high-scoring tournament.

DID YOU KNOW?

Wales played four 'home matches' in England in 1998 and 1999 at Wembley Stadium, whilst work was completed on Cardiff's Millennium Stadium. Wales's 'home matches' in the alien territory of London resulted in two wins and two defeats. However, the Welsh conceded a total of 124 points in these four encounters, averaging out at 31 points per fixture. Given this fact, they must have been relieved to return to the safe haven of the principality.

1998

FRANCE 24 ENGLAND 17; at Stade de France; 7th of February 1998

15	Sadourny [DG]	15	Catt
14	Bernat-Salles [TRY]	14	Rees
13	Lamaison [2 PENs, CON]	13	Greenwood
12	Glas	12	Guscott
11	Dominici [TRY]	11	Healey
10	Castaignede [DG]	10	Grayson [4 PENs]
9	Carbonneau	9	Bracken
8	Lievremont	8	Hill
7	Magne	7	Back [TRY]
6	Benetton	6	Dallaglio (c)
5	Pelous	5	Archer
4	Brouzet	4	Johnson
3	Tournaire	3	Garforth
2	Ibanez (c)	2	Regan
1	Califano	1	Leonard

Comments: A debut try for Christophe Dominici helped the hosts to win on the inaugural Five Nations contest at their new ground, the Stade de France.

IRELAND 16* SCOTLAND 17; at Lansdowne Road; 7th of February 1998

15	O'Shea	15	Shepherd [2 PENs]
14	Wallace. R	14	Joiner
13	Maggs	13	Tait [TRY]
12	McCall	12	Townsend
11	Hickie	11	Logan
10	Humphreys [2 PENs, DG, CON]	10	Chalmers [2 PENs]
9	O'Meara	9	Armstrong (c)
8	Miller	8	Walton
7	Dawson	7	Holmes
6	Corkery	6	Wainwright
5	O'Kelly	5	Weir
4	Johns	4	Cronin
3	Wallace. P	3	Stewart
2	Wood (c)	2	Bulloch
1	Corrigan	1	Graham

Comments: The visitors led by one point at the halfway stage (11-10) and won by one point. They had a knack of coming away from Dublin with narrow victories.

*Ireland's points included a penalty try.

ENGLAND 60 WALES 26; at Twickenham; 21st of February 1998

15	Perry	15	Jenkins [3 CONs]
14	Rees [2 TRIES]	14	Thomas. G [TRY]
13	Greenwood [TRY]	13	Bateman [2 TRIES]
12	Guscott	12	Gibbs [TRY]
11	Healey [TRY]	11	Walker
10	Grayson [2 PENs, 7 CONs]	10	Thomas. A
9	Bracken [TRY]	9	Howley (c)
8	Hill	8	Quinnell
7	Back [TRY]	7	Williams. M
6	Dallaglio (c) [TRY]	6	Charvis
5	Archer	5	Voyle
4	Johnson	4	Llewellyn
3	Vickery	3	Young
2	Cockerill	2	Williams. B
1	Leonard	1	Lewis

Comments: England became the first team to score 60 points in a Five Nations match, winning the try count 8-4. Matt Dawson came off the bench and scored a try.

SCOTLAND 16 FRANCE 51; at Murrayfield; 21st of February 1998

15	Lee	15	Sadourny
14	Stanger [TRY]	14	Bernat-Salles [2 TRIES]
13	Tait	13	Lamaison [PEN, 2 CONs]
12	Townsend	12	Glas
11	Logan	11	Dominici
10	Chalmers [3 PENs, CON]	10	Castaignede [TRY, PEN, 3 CONs]
9	Armstrong (c)	9	Carbonneau [TRY]
8	Walton	8	Lievremont. T
7	Holmes	7	Magne
6	Wainwright	6	Lievremont. M [TRY]
5	Weir	5	Pelous
4	Cronin	4	Brouzet [TRY]
3	Stewart	3	Tournaire
2	Bulloch	2	Ibanez (c)
1	Hilton	1	Califano [TRY]

Comments: Not to be outdone, France became the first team to score 50 points in a Five Nations away fixture. They could only manage seven tries in this triumph.

FRANCE 18 IRELAND 16; at Stade de France; 7th of March 1998

15	Sadourny		15	O'Shea
14	Bernat-Salles [TRY]		14	Wallace. R
13	Lamaison [2 PENs, CON]		13	Henderson
12	Glas		12	Maggs
11	Dominici		11	Hickie [TRY]
10	Castaignede		10	Elwood [3 PENs, CON]
9	Carbonneau		9	McGuinness
8	Lievremont. T		8	Costello
7	Magne		7	Ward
6	Lievremont. M		6	Corkery
5	Pelous		5	O'Kelly
4	Brouzet		4	Johns
3	Tournaire		3	Wallace. P
2	Ibanez (c) [TRY]		2	Wood (c)
1	Califano		1	Corrigan

Comments: A Denis Hickie first-half try nearly yielded the unthinkable – an Irish win in France, but the hosts fought back from their 13-6 half-time arrears.

WALES 19 SCOTLAND 13; at Wembley; 7th of March 1998

15	Morgan		15	Lee
14	Proctor [TRY]		14	Stanger
13	Bateman		13	Townsend [TRY]
12	Gibbs		12	Tait
11	Thomas		11	Longstaff
10	Jenkins. N [PEN]		10	Chalmers [PEN]
9	Howley (c)		9	Armstrong (c)
8	Charvis		8	Peters
7	Jones		7	Roxburgh
6	Appleyard		6	Wainwright
5	Moore		5	Weir
4	Voyle		4	Cronin [TRY]
3	Young		3	Stewart
2	Jenkins. G		2	Bulloch
1	Lewis		1	Hilton

Comments: Arwel Thomas came on as a replacement and kicked 11 points which provided Wales with a home win on the foreign soil of their new home, Wembley!

IRELAND 21 WALES 30; at Lansdowne Road; 21st of March 1998

15	Clarke		15	Morgan [TRY]
14	Wallace. R		14	Proctor
13	Maggs		13	Bateman [TRY]
12	Henderson		12	Davies
11	Hickie		11	Thomas
10	Elwood [3 PENs, CON]		10	Jenkins. N [TRY, 3 PENs, 3 CONs]
9	McGuinness		9	Howley (c)
8	Costello [TRY]		8	Charvis
7	Ward [TRY]		7	Jones
6	Corkery		6	Appleyard
5	O'Kelly		5	Moore
4	Johns		4	Voyle
3	Wallace. P		3	Young
2	Wood (c)		2	Jenkins. G
1	Corrigan		1	Lewis

Comments: 2 tries after the interval helped Wales to an away win after Ireland had crossed the try-line twice in the first half. Neil Jenkins scored 20 points.

SCOTLAND 20 ENGLAND 34*; at Murrayfield; 22nd of March 1998

15	Lee [2 CONs]		15	Perry
14	Stanger [TRY]		14	Adebayo
13	Townsend		13	Greenwood
12	Tait		12	Guscott
11	Longstaff [TRY]		11	Healey [TRY]
10	Chalmers [2 PENs]		10	Grayson [TRY, PEN, DG, 4 CONs]
9	Armstrong (c)		9	Dawson [TRY]
8	Peters		8	Ryan
7	Roxburgh		7	Back
6	Wainwright		6	Dallaglio (c)
5	Weir		5	Archer
4	Cronin		4	Johnson
3	Burnell		3	Garforth
2	Bulloch		2	Cockerill
1	Hilton		1	Leonard

Comments: The first Five Nations Sunday fixture was delicately poised at 6-6 at the halfway stage. Then England broke loose with four tries to grab both points.

*England's points included a penalty try.

ENGLAND 35 IRELAND 17; at Twickenham; 4th of April 1998

15	Perry [TRY]		15	Clarke
14	Catt [TRY]		14	Wallace. R
13	Greenwood		13	Maggs
12	Guscott		12	McCall
11	Healey		11	Hickie [2 TRIES]
10	Grayson [3 PENs, 3 CONs]		10	Elwood [PEN, 2 CONs]
9	Dawson		9	McGuinness
8	Diprose		8	Costello
7	Back		7	Ward
6	Dallaglio (c)		6	Corkery
5	Archer		5	O'Kelly
4	Johnson		4	Johns
3	Garforth		3	Wallace. P
2	Cockerill [TRY]		2	Wood (c)
1	Leonard		1	Corrigan

Comments: Phil de Glanville came on as a replacement to score a try as England cruised to victory. Jonny Wilkinson also came off the bench to make his debut.

WALES 0 FRANCE 51; at Wembley; 5th of April 1998

15	Morgan		15	Sadourny [2 TRIES]
14	Proctor		14	Bernat-Salles
13	Davies. L		13	Lamaison [2 PENs, 5 CONs]
12	Boobyer		12	Glas [TRY]
11	Thomas		11	Garbajosa [2 TRIES]
10	Jenkins. N		10	Castaignede
9	Howley (c)		9	Carbonneau
8	Davies. S		8	Lievremont. T [TRY]
7	Charvis		7	Magne
6	Appleyard		6	Lievremont. M
5	Moore		5	Pelous
4	Voyle		4	Brouzet
3	Young		3	Tournaire
2	Jenkins. G		2	Ibanez (c)
1	Lewis		1	Califano

Comments: Garbajosa and Sadourny shared four tries while Galthie came off the bench to score a try in a display of running rugby that has rarely been bettered.

1998 FINAL TABLE

		Points For	Points Against	Total Points
1ST	FRANCE	144	49	8
2ND	ENGLAND	146	87	6
3RD	WALES	75	145	4
4TH	SCOTLAND	66	120	2
5TH	IRELAND	70	100	0

Comments:It was deja-vu as France and England repeated 1997's Grand Slam and Triple Crown successes.

DID YOU KNOW?

Although France have beaten off Italy's five challenges at the Stade de France, they have been less comfortable at this new venue against the other nations. Ireland managed to win there in 2000, while Scotland did likewise in 1999. The hosts have managed twenty-two wins out of 29, but they have suffered two home defeats to England in 2000 and 2008, and three losses against the Welsh in 1999, 2001 and 2005.

1999

IRELAND 9 FRANCE 10; at Lansdowne Road; 6th of February 1999

15	O'Shea		15	Ntamack
14	Bishop		14	Bernat-Salles
13	Maggs		13	Dourthe [TRY]
12	Bell		12	Comba
11	Dempsey		11	Lombard
10	Humphreys [3 PENs]		10	Castaignede [PEN, CON]
9	McGuinness		9	Carbonneau
8	Costello		8	Lievremont
7	O'Cuinneagain		7	Magne
6	Miller		6	Benetton
5	Davidson		5	Pelous
4	Johns (c)		4	Brouzet
3	Wallace		3	Tournaire
2	Wood		2	Ibanez (c)
1	Clohessy		1	Califano

Comments: France trailed 6-0 at the halfway stage and had to rely on a try from Emile Ntamack to see them over the finishing line by the narrowest of margins.

SCOTLAND 33 WALES 20; at Murrayfield; 6th of February 1999

15	Metcalfe		15	Howarth
14	Murray. C		14	Robinson
13	Townsend [TRY]		13	Bateman
12	Leslie. J [TRY]		12	Gibbs [TRY]
11	Logan [2 PENs, 2 CONs]		11	James [TRY]
10	Hodge [PEN]		10	Jenkins [2 PENs, 2 CONs]
9	Armstrong (c)		9	Howley (c)
8	Peters		8	Quinnell
7	Leslie. M		7	Williams
6	Walton		6	Charvis
5	Weir		5	Wyatt
4	Murray. S [TRY]		4	Gough
3	Burnell		3	Anthony
2	Bulloch		2	Humphreys
1	Smith		1	Morris

Comments: Three second-half tries provided Scotland with maximum points. Alan Tait came on as a substitute and also crossed the try-line for the host team.

ENGLAND 24 SCOTLAND 21; at Twickenham; 20th of February 1999

15 Beal [TRY]	15 Metcalfe
14 Rees	14 Murray. C
13 Wilkinson [PEN, 3 Cons]	13 Tait [2 TRIES]
12 Guscott	12 Leslie. J
11 Luger [TRY]	11 Logan [3 CONs]
10 Catt	10 Townsend [TRY]
9 Dawson	9 Armstrong (c)
8 Hill	8 Peters
7 Back	7 Leslie. M
6 Dallaglio (c)	6 Walton
5 Rodber [TRY]	5 Grimes
4 Johnson	4 Murray. S
3 Garforth	3 Burnell
2 Cockerill	2 Bulloch
1 Leonard	1 Smith

Comments: A brace of tries for Alan Tait ensured that Scotland matched England's try count, but the teams were only separated by a Jonny Wilkinson penalty.

WALES 23 IRELAND 29; at Wembley; 20th of February 1999

15 Howarth [TRY]	15 O'Shea
14 Robinson	14 Bishop
13 Taylor	13 Maggs [TRY]
12 Gibbs	12 Bell
11 James	11 Woods
10 Jenkins [3 PENs, 2 CONs]	10 Humphreys [3 PENs, 2 DGs, 2 CONs]
9 Howley (c)	9 McGuinness
8 Quinnell. S	8 Miller
7 Williams. M	7 Ward
6 Charvis	6 O'Cuinneagain
5 Wyatt	5 Davidson
4 Quinnell. C [TRY]	4 Johns (c)
3 Young	3 Wallace
2 Williams. B	2 Wood [TRY]
1 Morris	1 Clohessy

Comments: Two dropped goals from David Humphreys were the major difference between the two teams as Ireland won another away match against Wales.

FRANCE 33 WALES 34; at Stade de France; 6th of March 1999

	France		Wales
15	Ntamack [3 TRIES]	15	Howarth
14	Bernat-Salles	14	Robinson
13	Dourthe	13	Taylor
12	Comba	12	Gibbs
11	Lombard	11	James [TRY]
10	Castaignede [TRY, 3 PENs, 2 CONs]	10	Jenkins. N [5 PENs, 2 CONs]
9	Carbonneau	9	Howley (c)
8	Lievremont	8	Quinnell. S
7	Raynaud	7	Sinkinson
6	Benetton	6	Charvis [TRY]
5	Pelous	5	Wyatt
4	Brouzet	4	Quinnell. C [TRY]
3	Tournaire	3	Evans
2	Ibanez (c)	2	Jenkins. G
1	Califano	1	Rogers

Comments: Not even a hat-trick of tries for Ntamack could stop Wales recording a massive upset. 3 tries gave Wales their first away win in France since 1975.

IRELAND 15 ENGLAND 27; at Lansdowne Road; 6th of March 1999

	Ireland		England
15	O'Shea	15	Perry [TRY]
14	Bishop	14	Rees
13	Maggs	13	Wilkinson [4 PENs, CON]
12	Henderson	12	Guscott
11	Dempsey [PEN]	11	Luger
10	Humphreys [4 PENs]	10	Grayson [DG]
9	McGuinness	9	Bracken
8	Costello	8	Dallaglio (c)
7	Ward	7	Back
6	O'Cuinneagain	6	Hill
5	Davidson	5	Rodber [TRY]
4	Johns (c)	4	Johnson
3	Wallace	3	Garforth
2	Wood	2	Cockerill
1	Clohessy	1	Leonard

Comments: Matt Perry and Tim Rodber were the try-scoring heroes as England moved towards a possible fifth consecutive Triple Crown.

ENGLAND 21 FRANCE 10; at Twickenham; 20th of March 1999

15	Perry		15	Ntamack
14	Rees		14	Garbajosa
13	Wilkinson [7 PENs]		13	Giordani
12	Guscott		12	Comba [TRY]
11	Luger		11	Dominici
10	Catt		10	Castaignede [PEN, CON]
9	Bracken		9	Carbonneau
8	Dallaglio (c)		8	Juillet
7	Back		7	Castel
6	Hill		6	Lievremont
5	Rodber		5	Pelous
4	Johnson		4	Brouzet
3	Garforth		3	Tournaire
2	Cockerill		2	Ibanez (c)
1	Leonard		1	Marconnet

Comments: Jonny Wilkinson kicked three penalties in the first half and another four in the second as England jumped the third hurdle of a potential Grand Slam.

SCOTLAND 30 IRELAND 13*; at Murrayfield; 20th of March 1999

15	Metcalfe		15	O'Shea
14	Murray. C [2 TRIES]		14	Bishop
13	Tait		13	Maggs
12	Leslie. J		12	Bell
11	Logan [2 PENs, 2 CONs]		11	Dempsey
10	Townsend [TRY]		10	Humphreys [2 PENs, CON]
9	Armstrong (c)		9	McGuinness
8	Peters		8	Miller
7	Leslie. M		7	Ward
6	Walton		6	O'Cuinneagain
5	Grimes [TRY]		5	Davidson
4	Murray. S		4	Johns (c)
3	Burnell		3	Wallace
2	Bulloch		2	Wood
1	Smith		1	Clohessy

Comments: Half of Scotland's four tries came from Cameron Murray. The Scots had now taken 19 points out of 20 against their celtic opponents in the 1990s.

*Ireland's points included a penalty try.

FRANCE 22 SCOTLAND 36; at Stade de France; 10th of April 1999

15	Ntamack [TRY]	15	Metcalfe
14	Garbajosa	14	Murray. C
13	Giordani	13	Tait [2 TRIES]
12	Comba	12	Leslie. J
11	Dominici [TRY]	11	Logan [PEN, 4 CONs]
10	Castaignede	10	Townsend [TRY]
9	Carbonneau	9	Armstrong (c)
8	Juillet [TRY]	8	Leslie. M [2 TRIES]
7	Labit	7	Reid
6	Castel	6	Pountney
5	Cleda	5	Grimes
4	Brouzet	4	Murray. S
3	Tournaire	3	Burnell
2	Ibanez (c)	2	Bulloch
1	Califano	1	Hilton

Comments: Aucagne came off the bench and kicked 7 points as Scotland scored all 5 tries in an amazing first half that ended with them leading 33 points to 22.

WALES 32 ENGLAND 31; at Wembley; 11th of April 1999

15	Howarth [TRY]	15	Perry
14	Thomas	14	Luger [TRY]
13	Taylor	13	Wilkinson [4 PENs, 2 CONs]
12	Gibbs [TRY]	12	Mather
11	James	11	Hanley [TRY]
10	Jenkins. N [6 PENs, 2 CONs]	10	Catt
9	Howley (c)	9	Dawson
8	Quinnell. S	8	Dallaglio (c)
7	Sinkinson	7	Back
6	Charvis	6	Hill [TRY]
5	Wyatt	5	Rodber
4	Quinnell. C	4	Johnson
3	Evans	3	Garforth
2	Jenkins. G	2	Cockerill
1	Rogers	1	Leonard

Comments: Wales denied England a clean sweep, with Gibbs scoring the crucial try and Jenkins kicking 22 points. This London outing was an England away match!

1999 FINAL TABLE

		Points For	Points Against	Total Points
1ST	SCOTLAND	120	79	6
2ND	ENGLAND	103	78	6
3RD	WALES	109	126	4
4TH	FRANCE	75	100	2
5TH	IRELAND	66	90	2

Comments: Scotland totalled more tournament points than England for the first time since 1989.

DID YOU KNOW?

1999 was the last year of the Five Nations tournament as new recruits Italy joined the other five in 2000. Italy's first decade in the Six Nations has yet to yield a win against England, France, or Ireland, and they have managed merely four wins against Scotland and two wins and a draw against Wales. Only one win in Edinburgh and a draw in Cardiff has been their three points on their travels thus far.

2000

ENGLAND 50 IRELAND 18; at Twickenham; 5th of February 2000

15	Perry	15	O'Shea
14	Healey [2 TRIES]	14	Bishop
13	Tindall [TRY]	13	O'Driscoll
12	Catt	12	Mullins
11	Cohen [2 TRIES]	11	Maggs [TRY]
10	Wilkinson [4 PENs, 4 CONs]	10	Humphreys [2 PENs, CON]
9	Dawson (c)	9	Tierney
8	Dallaglio	8	Foley
7	Back [TRY]	7	Dawson
6	Hill	6	O'Cuinneagain
5	Shaw	5	O'Kelly
4	Archer	4	Casey
3	Vickery	3	Wallace
2	Greening	2	Wood (c)
1	Leonard	1	Clohessy

Comments: New caps Ben Cohen and Mike Tindall shared 3 tries between them as England inflicted a rout. Galwey came off the bench to score a try for the Irish.

ITALY 34 SCOTLAND 20; at Rome; 5th of February 2000

15	Pini	15	Metcalfe
14	Dallan. D	14	Longstaff
13	Dallan. M	13	Mayer
12	Martin	12	Leslie. J (c)
11	Stoica	11	Logan [CON]
10	Dominguez [6 PENs, 3 DGs, CON]	10	Townsend [PEN, DG, CON]
9	Troncon (c)	9	Redpath
8	Visser	8	Simpson
7	Bergamasco	7	Pountney
6	Giovanelli	6	Leslie. M [TRY]
5	Gritti	5	Grimes
4	Checchinato	4	Murray
3	Paoletti	3	Stewart
2	Moscardi	2	Bulloch [TRY]
1	Cuttitta	1	Smith

Comments: Diego Dominguez racked up a mere 29 points as Italy made a fine start to the new Six Nations. De Carli came off the bench and scored their only try.

WALES 3 FRANCE 36; at the Millennium Stadium; 5th of February 2000

15	Howarth	15	Castaignede [TRY]
14	Thomas	14	Ntamack [TRY]
13	Taylor	13	Lombard
12	Jones-Hughes	12	Dourthe
11	James	11	Dominici
10	Jenkins. N [PEN]	10	Lamaison [4 PENs, DG, 3 CONs]
9	Howley	9	Galthie
8	Quinnell	8	Pelous (c)
7	Sinkinson	7	Magne [TRY]
6	Charvis	6	Benazzi
5	Wyatt	5	Brouzet
4	Gough	4	Matiu
3	Young (c)	3	Tournaire
2	Jenkins. G	2	Dal Maso
1	Rogers	1	Califano

Comments: This match was in the balance at 9-3 to Les Bleus at the interval, but they then scored 3 tries to settle the outcome. Lamaison contributed 21 points.

FRANCE 9 ENGLAND 15; at Stade de France; 19th of February 2000

15	Dourthe [3 PENs]	15	Perry
14	Ntamack	14	Healey
13	Venditti	13	Tindall
12	Lombard	12	Catt
11	Dominici	11	Cohen
10	Castaignede	10	Wilkinson [5 PENs]
9	Galthie	9	Dawson (c)
8	Pelous (c)	8	Dallaglio
7	Magne	7	Back
6	Benazzi	6	Hill
5	Brouzet	5	Shaw
4	Matiu	4	Archer
3	Tournaire	3	Vickery
2	Dal Maso	2	Greening
1	Califano	1	Leonard

Comments: Richard Dourthe kicked three second-half penalties for the hosts, but his efforts were eclipsed by fifteen points from the boot of Jonny Wilkinson.

IRELAND 44 SCOTLAND 22; at Lansdowne Road; 19th of February 2000

15	Dempsey	15	Metcalfe [TRY]
14	Horgan [TRY]	14	Longstaff
13	O'Driscoll [TRY]	13	Mayer
12	Mullins	12	Shiel
11	Hickie	11	Logan [TRY, PEN, 2 CONs]
10	O'Gara [2 PENs, 2 CONs]	10	Townsend
9	Stringer	9	Redpath (c)
8	Foley	8	Simpson
7	Dawson	7	Pountney
6	Easterby	6	Leslie
5	O'Kelly [TRY]	5	Grimes
4	Galwey	4	Murray
3	Hayes	3	Stewart
2	Wood (c) [TRY]	2	Bulloch
1	Clohessy	1	Smith

Comments: Humphreys came off the bench and added 14 points, including a try and a penalty for Ireland, and the substitute Graham scored a try for the Scots.

WALES 47 ITALY 16; at the Millennium Stadium, 19th of February 2000

15	Howarth [TRY]	15	Pini
14	Thomas	14	Stoica
13	Bateman [TRY]	13	Rivaro
12	Taylor	12	Martin
11	Williams [TRY]	11	Dallan .
10	Jenkins. N [7 PENs, 3 CONs]	10	Dominguez [2 PENs, DG, CON]
9	Howley	9	Troncon (c)
8	Quinnell. S [TRY]	8	Visser [TRY]
7	Sinkinson	7	Bergamasco
6	Lewis	6	Checchinato
5	Wyatt	5	Gritti
4	Quinnell. C	4	Lanzi
3	Young (c)	3	Paoletti
2	Jenkins. G	2	Moscardi
1	Rogers	1	Cuttitta

Comments: Neil Jenkins provided the home team with 27 points as Wales managed a win at their new venue, after the false start against France.

ENGLAND 46 WALES 12; at Twickenham; 4th of March 2000

15	Perry	15	Howarth
14	Healey	14	Thomas
13	Tindall	13	Bateman
12	Catt	12	Taylor
11	Cohen [TRY]	11	Williams
10	Wilkinson [5 PENs, 3 CONs]	10	Jenkins. N [3 PENs, DG]
9	Dawson (c)	9	Howley
8	Dallaglio [TRY]	8	Quinnell. S
7	Back [TRY]	7	Sinkinson
6	Hill [TRY]	6	Charvis
5	Shaw	5	Wyatt
4	Archer	4	Quinnell. C
3	Vickery	3	Young (c)
2	Greening [TRY]	2	Jenkins. G
1	Leonard	1	Rogers

Comments: England's back row forwards achieved the milestone of each grabbing a try in the same match. The hosts also won the try count five to nil.

IRELAND 60 ITALY 13; at Lansdowne Road; 4th of March 2000

15	Dempsey [TRY]	15	Pini
14	Horgan [2 TRIES]	14	Francesio
13	O'Driscoll [TRY]	13	Stoica
12	Mullins	12	Martin
11	Hickie	11	Dallan
10	O'Gara [6 PENs, 6 CONs]	10	Dominguez [2 PENs, CON]
9	Stringer	9	Troncon (c)
8	Foley	8	de Rossi [TRY]
7	Dawson [TRY]	7	Bergamasco
6	Easterby	6	Visser
5	O'Kelly	5	Gritti
4	Galwey	4	Checchinato
3	Hayes	3	Paoletti
2	Wood (c) [TRY]	2	Moscardi
1	Clohessy	1	Cuttitta

Comments: Ireland stormed into a 33-0 interval lead. Horgan crossed the try-line twice while Ronan O'Gara helped himself to 30 points with his successful kicks.

SCOTLAND 16 FRANCE 28; at Murrayfield; 4th of March 2000

15	Paterson [2 PENs, CON]	15	Castaignede [TRY]
14	Metcalfe	14	Ntamack
13	McLaren	13	Venditti
12	Leslie. J (c)	12	Lombard
11	Logan [PEN]	11	Dominici
10	Townsend	10	Merceron [3 PENs, 2 CONs]
9	Nicol [TRY]	9	Laussucq
8	Reid	8	Pelous (c)
7	Pountney	7	Magne [2 TRIES]
6	Leslie. M	6	Chabal
5	Weir	5	Brouzet
4	Murray	4	Daude
3	Stewart	3	Tournaire
2	Brotherstone	2	Dal Maso
1	Smith	1	Califano

Comments: Olivier Magne bagged a pair of tries while Gerald Merceron weighed in with 13 points to secure France's second successive triumph in Edinburgh.

ITALY 12 ENGLAND 59; at Rome; 18th of March 2000

15	Pilat	15	Perry
14	Stoica [TRY]	14	Healey [3 TRIES]
13	Zisti	13	Tindall
12	Martin [TRY]	12	Catt
11	Dallan	11	Cohen [2 TRIES]
10	Dominguez [CON]	10	Wilkinson [2 PENs, 4 CONs]
9	Troncon (c)	9	Dawson (c) [2 TRIES]
8	de Rossi	8	Dallaglio
7	Bergamasco	7	Back [TRY]
6	Cristofoletto	6	Hill
5	Gritti	5	Shaw
4	Checchinato	4	Archer
3	Paoletti	3	Garforth
2	Moscardi	2	Greening
1	Lo Cicero	1	Leonard

Comments: England were now 1 step away from another Grand Slam, courtesy of a hat-trick of tries from Austin Healey. The substitute Alex King also seized a try.

WALES 26 SCOTLAND 18; at the Millennium Stadium; 18th of March 2000

15 Cardey	15 Paterson
14 Thomas	14 Moir
13 Bateman	13 Townsend [TRY]
12 Taylor	12 Leslie. J (c)
11 Williams [2 TRIES]	11 Metcalfe
10 Jones [4 PENs, 2 CONs]	10 Hodge [2 PENs, CON]
9 Moon	9 Nicol
8 Lewis	8 Reid
7 Charvis	7 Pountney
6 Budgett	6 Leslie. M [TRY]
5 Moore	5 Grimes
4 Gough	4 Murray
3 Young (c)	3 Stewart
2 Jenkins	2 Brotherstone
1 Rogers	1 Smith

Comments: A combination of two tries from Shane Williams and sixteen points from Stephen Jones condemned Scotland to a third away defeat in their 2000 campaign.

FRANCE 25 IRELAND 27; at Stade de France; 19th of March 2000

15 Ntamack	15 Dempsey
14 Bernat-Salles	14 Maggs
13 Desbrosse	13 O'Driscoll [3 TRIES]
12 Glas	12 Henderson
11 Bory	11 Hickie
10 Merceron [6 PENs, CON]	10 O'Gara [2 CONs]
9 Laussucq [TRY]	9 Stringer
8 Lievremont	8 Foley
7 Benazzi	7 Dawson
6 Costes	6 Easterby
5 Pelous (c)	5 O'Kelly
4 Brouzet	4 Galwey
3 Tournaire	3 Hayes
2 Dal Maso	2 Wood (c)
1 Califano	1 Clohessy

Comments: Not even Merceron's total of 20 points could outshine Brian O'Driscoll's hat-trick of tries. Humphreys came off the bench and kicked 8 more points.

FRANCE 42 ITALY 31; at Stade de France; 1st of April 2000

15	Castaignede [TRY]		15	Pini
14	Bernat-Salles		14	Mazzucato [TRY]
13	Dourthe [3 PENs, 4 CONs]		13	Martin [TRY]
12	Ntamack		12	Zisti
11	Bory		11	Stoica
10	Penaud [2 TRIES]		10	Dominguez [DG, 4 CONs]
9	Hueber		9	Troncon (c) [2 TRIES]
8	Lievremont		8	de Rossi
7	Magne		7	Bergamasco
6	Mallier		6	Cristofoletto [SENT OFF]
5	Pelous (c) [TRY]		5	Gritti
4	Brouzet		4	Checchinato
3	Tournaire		3	Paoletti
2	Dal Maso		2	Moscardi
1	Califano		1	Lo Cicero

Comments: France had lost to all the other nations in their previous home matches and only just overcame Italy. Benazzi also came off the bench to grab a try.

IRELAND 19 WALES 23; at Lansdowne Road; 1st of April 2000

15	Dempsey		15	Williams. R
14	Horgan [TRY]		14	Thomas
13	O'Driscoll		13	Bateman
12	Henderson		12	Gibbs
11	Hickie		11	Williams. S
10	O'Gara [4 PENs, CON]		10	Jones [TRY, PEN, 2 CONs]
9	Stringer		9	Moon
8	Foley		8	Lewis
7	Dawson		7	Charvis
6	Easterby		6	Budgett [TRY]
5	O'Kelly		5	Moore
4	Galwey		4	Gough
3	Hayes		3	Young (c)
2	Wood (c)		2	Jenkins
1	Clohessy		1	Rogers

Comments: For the ninth time in ten years, the home team were unable to win this fixture. Neil Jenkins came on as a substitute and kicked two penalties.

SCOTLAND 19 ENGLAND 13; at Murrayfield; 2nd of April 2000

15	Paterson		15	Perry
14	Moir		14	Healey
13	Townsend		13	Tindall
12	McLaren		12	Catt
11	Metcalfe. G		11	Cohen
10	Hodge [TRY, 4 PENs, CON]		10	Wilkinson [2 PENs, CON]
9	Nicol (c)		9	Dawson (c)
8	Leslie		8	Dallaglio [TRY]
7	Pountney		7	Back
6	White		6	Hill
5	Metcalfe. R		5	Shaw
4	Murray		4	Archer
3	Stewart		3	Vickery
2	Brotherstone		2	Greening
1	Smith		1	Leonard

Comments: It was 1990 revisited as England's Grand Slam goal was foiled in Edinburgh. Duncan Hodge was the hero (or the villain), depending on your nationality.

2000 FINAL TABLE

		Points For	Points Against	Total Points
1ST	ENGLAND	183	70	8
2ND	FRANCE	140	92	6
3RD	IRELAND	168	133	6
4TH	WALES	111	135	6
5TH	SCOTLAND	95	145	2
6TH	ITALY	106	228	2

Comments: Having failed to beat France or Scotland once during the 1990s, Ireland beat them both in the same tournament.

2001

ITALY 22 IRELAND 41; at Rome; 3rd of February 2001

15	Stoica		15	Dempsey
14	Pilat [TRY, PEN]		14	Horgan [TRY]
13	Martin		13	Mullins
12	Raineri		12	Henderson [3 TRIES]
11	Dallan		11	Howe
10	Pez [2 CONs]		10	O'Gara [TRY, 4 PENs, 2 CONs]
9	Troncon [SENT OFF]		9	Stringer
8	Dal Maso		8	Foley
7	Bergamasco [TRY]		7	Wallace
6	Caione		6	Quinlan
5	Checchinato [TRY]		5	O'Kelly
4	Visser		4	Galwey
3	Muraro		3	Hayes
2	Moscardi (c)		2	Wood (c)
1	Lo Cicero		1	Clohessy

Comments: Rob Henderson grabbed a hat-trick of tries and Ronan O'Gara helped himself to 21 points as Ireland made light work of Italy.

WALES 15 ENGLAND 44; at the Millennium Stadium; 3rd of February 2001

15	Jones		15	Balshaw
14	Thomas		14	Cohen [TRY]
13	Taylor		13	Greenwood [3 TRIES]
12	Gibbs		12	Catt
11	James		11	Luger
10	Jenkins [PEN, CON]		10	Wilkinson [2 PENs, 4 CONs]
9	Howley [TRY]		9	Dawson [2 TRIES]
8	Quinnell [TRY]		8	Dallaglio
7	Williams		7	Back
6	Charvis		6	Hill
5	Wyatt		5	Grewcock
4	Gough		4	Johnson (c)
3	Young (c)		3	Vickery
2	McBryde		2	West
1	Morris		1	Leonard

Comments: Although the hosts crossed the try-line in each half, they were outgunned by England, for whom Will Greenwood collected a hat-trick of tries.

FRANCE 16 SCOTLAND 6; at Stade de France; 4th of February 2001

15	Garbajosa	15	Paterson
14	Bernat-Salles [TRY]	14	Murray. C
13	Dourthe	13	McLaren
12	Comba	12	Leslie. J
11	Bory	11	Logan [2 PENs]
10	Lamaison [3 PENs, CON]	10	Townsend
9	Galthie	9	Nicol (c)
8	Juillet	8	Petrie
7	Magne	7	Pountney
6	Moni	6	Leslie. M
5	Pelous (c)	5	Metcalfe
4	Auradou	4	Murray. S
3	de Villiers	3	Stewart
2	Ibanez	2	Bulloch
1	Marconnet	1	Smith

Comments: This match was tied 6-6 at the interval, but a home win was sealed by a try for Philippe Bernat-Salles who then scored tries in all five matches.

IRELAND 22 FRANCE 15; at Lansdowne Road; 17th of February 2001

15	Dempsey	15	Garbajosa
14	Hickie	14	Bernat-Salles [TRY]
13	O'Driscoll [TRY]	13	Dourthe
12	Henderson	12	Comba
11	Howe	11	Bory
10	O'Gara [5 PENs, CON]	10	Lamaison [PEN, CON]
9	Stringer	9	Carbonneau
8	Foley	8	Juillet
7	Wallace	7	Magne
6	Quinlan	6	Moni
5	O'Kelly	5	Pelous (c) [TRY]
4	Galwey	4	Auradou
3	Hayes	3	de Villiers
2	Wood (c)	2	Ibanez
1	Clohessy	1	Marconnet

Comments: This time the Irish held on to a half-time lead against the French. O'Driscoll tormented Les Bleus avec another try, whilst O'Gara kicked 17 points.

ENGLAND 80 ITALY 23; at Twickenham; 17th of February 2001

15	Balshaw [2 TRIES]		15	Scanavacca [3 PENs, 2 CONs]
14	Healey [2 TRIES]		14	Martin
13	Greenwood [TRY]		13	Stoica
12	Catt		12	Pozzebon
11	Cohen [TRY]		11	Dallan [TRY]
10	Wilkinson [TRY, 4 PENs, 9 CONs]		10	Raineri
9	Dawson		9	Queirolo
8	Dallaglio [TRY]		8	Checchinato [TRY]
7	Back		7	Bergamasco
6	Hill		6	Caione
5	Grewcock		5	Visser
4	Johnson (c)		4	Gritti
3	Vickery		3	Muraro
2	West		2	Moscardi (c)
1	Leonard		1	Lo Cicero

Comments: Italy 'only' trailed 33-23 at the interval. Wilkinson contributed a staggering 35 points. Regan and Worsley came off the bench to score a try each.

SCOTLAND 28 WALES 28; at Murrayfield; 17th of February 2001

15	Paterson [TRY]		15	Williams. R
14	Murray. C		14	Jones
13	McLaren [TRY]		13	Taylor [TRY]
12	Leslie. J		12	Gibbs
11	Logan [3 PENs, CON]		11	James
10	Hodge [CON]		10	Jenkins [4 PENs, 3 DGs, CON]
9	Nicol (c)		9	Howley
8	Petrie		8	Quinnell
7	Pountney		7	Williams. M
6	Leslie. M		6	Charvis
5	Metcalfe		5	Moore
4	Murray. S		4	Gough
3	Stewart		3	Young (c)
2	Bulloch		2	McBryde
1	Smith [TRY]		1	Morris

Comments: Neil Jenkins landed a hat-trick of drop goals amidst his total of 23 points as the two teams produced an increasingly rare drawn encounter.

ITALY 19 FRANCE 30; at Rome; 3rd of March 2001

15	Stoica	15	Sadourny [TRY]
14	Perziano [TRY]	14	Bernat-Salles [TRY]
13	Pozzebon	13	Bonetti [TRY]
12	Dallan. M	12	Lombard
11	Dallan. D	11	Dominici
10	Dominguez [4 PENs, CON]	10	Lamaison [3 PENs, 3 CONs]
9	Troncon	9	Galthie
8	Checchinato	8	Juillet
7	Bergamasco	7	Magne
6	Persico	6	Moni
5	Gritti	5	Pelous (c)
4	Visser	4	Auradou
3	Paoletti	3	de Villiers
2	Moscardi (c)	2	Ibanez
1	Lo Cicero	1	Califano

Comments: Sebastien Bonetti recorded a try on his debut, but the 'punchbag' of Italy limited their guests to a mere 30 points, 15 of which came from Lamaison.

ENGLAND 43 SCOTLAND 3; at Twickenham; 3rd of March 2001

15	Balshaw [2 TRIES]	15	Paterson
14	Healey	14	Murray. C
13	Greenwood [TRY]	13	Bulloch. A
12	Catt	12	Leslie. J
11	Cohen	11	Logan
10	Wilkinson [PEN, 5 CONs]	10	Hodge [PEN]
9	Dawson	9	Nicol (c)
8	Dallaglio [2 TRIES]	8	Taylor
7	Back	7	Pountney
6	Hill [TRY]	6	Leslie. M
5	Grewcock	5	Metcalfe
4	Johnson (c)	4	Murray. S
3	Vickery	3	Stewart
2	West	2	Bulloch. G
1	Leonard	1	Smith

Comments: On their last outing, Scotland ended a sequence of 66 games in which the away team reached double figures. This time they were whipped 6 tries to 0.

FRANCE 35 WALES 43; at Stade de France; 17th of March 2001

15	Sadourny		15	Williams. R
14	Bernat-Salles [TRY]		14	Thomas
13	Bonetti [TRY]		13	Taylor
12	Lombard		12	Gibbs
11	Dominici		11	James [TRY]
10	Merceron [4 PENs, CON]		10	Jenkins [TRY, 3 PENs, 2 DGs, 4 CONs]
9	Galthie		9	Howley [TRY]
8	Juillet		8	Quinnell [TRY]
7	Magne		7	Williams. M
6	Moni		6	Charvis
5	Pelous (c)		5	Moore
4	Auradou		4	Gough
3	de Villiers		3	Young (c)
2	Ibanez		2	McBryde
1	Califano		1	Morris

Comments: Lamaison came on as substitute to kick 11 points, but they were in vain. Jenkins weighed in with an impressive 28 points to produce an amazing win.

SCOTLAND 23 ITALY 19; at Murrayfield; 17th of March 2001

15	Paterson		15	Stoica
14	Craig		14	Perziano
13	Townsend		13	Pozzebon
12	Leslie. J		12	Dallan
11	Logan		11	Martin
10	Hodge [5 PENs, DG]		10	Dominguez [4 PENs, CON]
9	Redpath		9	Frati
8	Taylor		8	Checchinato
7	Pountney (c)		7	Bergamasco [TRY]
6	Leslie. M		6	Persico
5	Grimes		5	Gritti
4	Murray		4	Visser
3	Stewart		3	Curti
2	Bulloch		2	Moscardi (c)
1	Smith [TRY]		1	Lo Cicero

Comments: The Scots narrowly avoided back-to-back defeats against Italy, thanks to a second-half try from Tom Smith. The Italians had led 10-6 at half-time.

ENGLAND 48 FRANCE 19; at Twickenham; 7th of April 2001

15	Balshaw [TRY]	15	Sadourny
14	Healey	14	Bernat-Salles [TRY]
13	Greenwood [TRY]	13	Glas
12	Catt [TRY]	12	Garbajosa
11	Cohen	11	Dominici
10	Wilkinson [2 PENs, 6 CONs]	10	Merceron [3 PENs, DG, CON]
9	Dawson	9	Galthie
8	Dallaglio	8	Pelous (c)
7	Back	7	Magne
6	Hill [TRY]	6	Milheres
5	Borthwick	5	Benazzi
4	Johnson (c)	4	Nallet
3	White	3	de Villiers
2	Greening [TRY]	2	Ibanez
1	Leonard	1	Marconnet

Comments: Perry came on as a substitute and added a try. Red-hot England had now amassed 215 points from 4 stunning triumphs. Steve Borthwick made his debut.

ITALY 23 WALES 33; at Rome; 8th of April 2001

15	Stoica	15	Williams. R
14	Perziano	14	Thomas
13	Pozzebon	13	Taylor
12	Raineri	12	Gibbs [2 TRIES]
11	Dallan	11	James
10	Dominguez [5 PENs, DG]	10	Jenkins [4 PENs, 3 CONs]
9	Mazzantini	9	Cooper [TRY]
8	Checchinato [TRY]	8	Quinnell
7	Bergamasco	7	Williams. M
6	Persico	6	Charvis
5	Gritti	5	Moore
4	Visser	4	Gough
3	Curti	3	Young (c)
2	Moscardi (c)	2	McBryde
1	Lo Cicero	1	Morris

Comments: Wales were now unbeaten in their last four Six Nations away matches courtesy of a debut try from Gareth Cooper and a pair of tries from Scott Gibbs.

SCOTLAND 32 IRELAND 10; at Murrayfield; 22nd of September 2001

15	Metcalfe	15	Dempsey [TRY]
14	Steel	14	Murphy
13	McLaren	13	O'Driscoll
12	Leslie [TRY]	12	Horgan
11	Paterson [2 PENs, 2 CONs]	11	Hickie
10	Townsend [CON]	10	O'Gara [PEN]
9	Redpath	9	Easterby
8	Taylor	8	Foley
7	Pountney (c) [TRY]	7	Dawson
6	Simpson	6	Easterby
5	Murray	5	O'Kelly
4	White	4	Davidson
3	Stewart	3	Hayes
2	Bulloch	2	Wood (c)
1	Smith [TRY]	1	Clohessy

Comments: This match was re-arranged due to the Foot And Mouth crisis. Henderson came off the bench to add another try while Humphreys came on to kick 2 points.

WALES 6 IRELAND 36; at the Millennium Stadium; 13th of October 2001

15	Morgan	15	Dempsey
14	James	14	Horgan [TRY]
13	Davies	13	O'Driscoll [TRY]
12	Bateman	12	Maggs
11	Williams	11	Hickie [TRY]
10	Jones [2 PENs]	10	Humphreys [5 PENs, 2 CONs]
9	Howley	9	Stringer
8	Lewis	8	Foley
7	Sinkinson	7	Wallace
6	Charvis	6	Miller
5	Moore	5	O'Kelly
4	Wyatt	4	Galwey
3	Young (c)	3	Hayes
2	McBryde	2	Wood (c)
1	Thomas	1	Clohessy

Comments: David Humphreys kicked 19 points as Ireland made another successful foray into Wales. Ronan O'Gara came on as a substitute and kicked a conversion.

IRELAND 20 ENGLAND 14; at Lansdowne Road; 20th of October 2001

15	Dempsey		15	Balshaw
14	Horgan		14	Luger
13	O'Driscoll		13	Greenwood
12	Maggs		12	Catt
11	Hickie		11	Robinson
10	Humphreys [3 PENs]		10	Wilkinson [3 PENs]
9	Stringer		9	Dawson (c)
8	Foley		8	Hill
7	Wallace		7	Back
6	Miller		6	Corry
5	O'Kelly		5	Grewcock
4	Galwey		4	Shaw
3	Hayes		3	White
2	Wood (c) [TRY]		2	Greening
1	Clohessy		1	Leonard

Comments: Healey came off the bench to score a try but England fell at the final Grand Slam hurdle again. O'Gara also came on and kicked two vital penalties.

2001 FINAL TABLE

		Points For	Points Against	Total Points
1ST	ENGLAND	229	80	8
2ND	IRELAND	129	89	8
3RD	SCOTLAND	92	116	5
4TH	WALES	125	166	5
5TH	FRANCE	115	138	4
6TH	ITALY	106	207	0

Comments: Ireland ruined England's Grand Slam hopes but the latter amassed a phenomenal total of 229 points and 29 tries.

2002

FRANCE 33 ITALY 12; at Stade de France; 2nd of February 2002

15	Jeanjean	15	Vaccari
14	Rougerie	14	Pedrazzi
13	Marsh	13	Martin
12	Traille [TRY]	12	Stoica
11	Bory	11	Dallan
10	Merceron [7 PENs, CON]	10	Dominguez [4 PENs]
9	Michalak	9	Troncon
8	Hall	8	Phillips
7	Magne (c)	7	Bergamasco
6	Betsen [TRY]	6	Bortolami
5	Privat	5	Dellape
4	Auradou	4	Checchinato
3	de Villiers	3	Muraro
2	Bru	2	Moscardi (c)
1	Crenca	1	Lo Cicero

Comments: Italy only trailed 19-12 at the halfway stage, but Merceron punished them with 23 points from his boot while the hosts also scored a try in each half.

SCOTLAND 3 ENGLAND 29; at Murrayfield; 2nd of February 2002

15	Metcalfe	15	Robinson [2 TRIES]
14	Laney	14	Healey
13	McLaren	13	Greenwood
12	Townsend	12	Tindall [TRY]
11	Paterson	11	Cohen [TRY]
10	Hodge [PEN]	10	Wilkinson [PEN, 2 CONs]
9	Redpath	9	Bracken
8	Taylor	8	Worsley
7	Pountney (c)	7	Back
6	White	6	Hill
5	Grimes	5	Kay
4	Murray	4	Johnson (c)
3	Stewart	3	White
2	Bulloch	2	Thompson
1	Smith	1	Rowntree

Comments: Jason Robinson helped himself to a pair of tries on the debut of Steve Thompson. Charlie Hodgson came on as a substitute and also kicked a conversion.

IRELAND 54 WALES 10; at Lansdowne Road; 3rd of February 2002

15	Dempsey	15	Morgan. K
14	Murphy [2 TRIES]	14	James
13	O'Driscoll	13	Robinson
12	Maggs	12	Harris
11	Hickie [TRY]	11	Morgan. C
10	Humphreys [6 PENs, 2 CONs]	10	Jones [TRY, PEN, CON]
9	Stringer	9	Howley
8	Foley	8	Quinnell. S (c)
7	Wallace	7	Williams
6	Easterby	6	Budgett
5	O'Connell [TRY]	5	Wyatt
4	Galwey (c)	4	Quinnell. C
3	Hayes	3	Anthony
2	Sheahan	2	McBryde
1	Clohessy	1	John

Comments: Paul O'Connell and the substitute Keith Gleeson achieved debut tries while Ronan O'Gara also came off the bench to record a try and a conversion.

ITALY 12 SCOTLAND 29; at Rome; 16th of February 2002

15	Vaccari	15	Laney [TRY, 5 PENs, 2 CONs]
14	Pedrazzi	14	Metcalfe
13	Bergamasco. Mi	13	McLaren
12	Stoica	12	Henderson
11	Dallan	11	Paterson
10	Dominguez [4 PENs]	10	Townsend [TRY]
9	Troncon	9	Redpath (c)
8	Phillips	8	Taylor
7	Bergamasco. Ma	7	Mower
6	Bortolami	6	White
5	Dellape	5	Grimes
4	Checchinato	4	Murray
3	Pucciarello	3	Stewart
2	Moscardi (c)	2	Bulloch
1	de Carli	1	Smith

Comments: All of Italy's points again came from Diego Dominguez but they had no answer to Scottish Kiwi Brendan Laney who accumulated 24 points of his own.

ENGLAND 45 IRELAND 11; at Twickenham; 16th of February 2002

15	Robinson		15	Dempsey
14	Healey		14	Murphy
13	Greenwood [2 TRIES]		13	O'Driscoll
12	Tindall		12	Maggs
11	Cohen [TRY]		11	Hickie
10	Wilkinson [TRY, PEN, 6 CONs]		10	Humphreys [2 PENs]
9	Bracken		9	Stringer
8	Worsley [TRY]		8	Foley
7	Back		7	Wallace
6	Hill		6	Miller
5	Kay [TRY]		5	O'Kelly
4	Johnson (c)		4	Galwey (c)
3	Vickery		3	Hayes
2	Thompson		2	Sheahan
1	Rowntree		1	Clohessy

Comments: Jonny Wilkinson converted all six tries, including a double from Will Greenwood. Ronan O'Gara came on as a substitute and grabbed a consolation try.

WALES 33 FRANCE 37; at the Millennium Stadium; 16th of February 2002

15	Morgan. K [TRY]		15	Brusque
14	James		14	Rougerie [TRY]
13	Shanklin		13	Marsh [2 TRIES]
12	Marinos		12	Traille [PEN]
11	Morgan. C		11	Garbajosa
10	Jones [4 PENs, 3 CONs]		10	Merceron [4 PENs, DG, 2 CONs]
9	Howley		9	Mignoni
8	Quinnell. S (c)		8	Hall
7	Williams		7	Harinordoquy
6	Budgett [TRY]		6	Betsen
5	Moore		5	Brouzet
4	Quinnell. C [TRY]		4	Privat
3	Anthony		3	de Villiers
2	McBryde		2	Ibanez (c)
1	John		1	Crenca

Comments: Wales shared in the 6 tries but they fell foul of the boot of Merceron who amassed 19 points. Tony Marsh, a French Kiwi, also weighed in with 2 tries.

FRANCE 20 ENGLAND 15; at Stade de France; 2nd of March 2002

15	Brusque	15	Robinson [TRY]
14	Rougerie	14	Healey
13	Marsh	13	Greenwood
12	Traille	12	Tindall
11	Bory	11	Cohen [TRY]
10	Merceron [TRY, 2 PENs, 2 CONs]	10	Wilkinson [PEN, CON]
9	Galthie	9	Grayson
8	Harinordoquy [TRY]	8	Worsley
7	Magne	7	Back
6	Betsen	6	Hill
5	Brouzet	5	Kay
4	Auradou	4	Johnson (c)
3	de Villiers	3	Vickery
2	Ibanez (c)	2	Thompson
1	Crenca	1	Rowntree

Comments: Imanol Harinordoquy recorded a try in his second international. Although England fought back in the second half, they came up short in this encounter.

WALES 44 ITALY 20; at the Millennium Stadium; 2nd of March 2002

15	Morgan. K	15	Peens [PEN, CON]
14	James [TRY]	14	Pedrazzi
13	Shanklin	13	Bergamasco. Mi
12	Marinos [TRY]	12	Stoica
11	Morgan. C [TRY]	11	Mazzucato
10	Jones [3 PENs, 5 CONs]	10	Pez [PEN, CON]
9	Howley	9	Troncon
8	Quinnell (c) [TRY]	8	Checchinato [TRY]
7	Williams	7	Bergamasco. Ma
6	Budgett	6	Persico
5	Moore	5	Bortolami
4	Gough	4	Giacheri
3	Anthony	3	Perugini
2	McBryde	2	Moscardi (c)
1	Thomas	1	de Carli

Comments: Although the substitute Mazzariol recorded a try, Italy were no match for the hosts, for whom Rhys Williams came off the bench to score another try.

IRELAND 43 SCOTLAND 22; at Lansdowne Road; 2nd of March 2002

15	Dempsey		15	Laney [5 PENs, CON]
14	Horgan [TRY]		14	Metcalfe
13	O'Driscoll [3 TRIES]		13	McLaren
12	Maggs		12	Henderson
11	Hickie		11	Paterson
10	Humphreys [4 PENs, 2 CONs]		10	Townsend
9	Stringer		9	Redpath (c)
8	Foley		8	Taylor
7	Wallace		7	Pountney
6	Miller		6	White
5	O'Kelly		5	Grimes
4	Galwey (c)		4	Murray
3	Hayes		3	Stewart
2	Sheahan		2	Bulloch
1	Clohessy		1	Smith

Comments: O'Driscoll recorded another hat-trick of tries. The replacements Easterby and Leslie added tries for their teams while O'Gara kicked a conversion.

IRELAND 32 ITALY 17; at Lansdowne Road; 23rd of March 2002

15	Dempsey		15	Peens [DG]
14	Kelly [2 TRIES]		14	Mazzucato
13	O'Driscoll		13	Stoica
12	Horgan		12	Raineri
11	Hickie [TRY]		11	Dallan
10	Humphreys (c) [4 PENs]		10	Dominguez [2 CONs]
9	Stringer		9	Troncon
8	Foley		8	Phillips
7	Wallace		7	Bergamasco [TRY]
6	Easterby		6	Persico
5	O'Kelly		5	Giacheri
4	Longwell		4	Bortolami
3	Hayes		3	Perugini
2	Byrne		2	Moscardi (c)
1	Clohessy		1	de Carli [TRY]

Comments: John Kelly bagged a brace of tries on his debut while O'Gara came off the bench to kick a penalty and a conversion. Ireland led 19-0 at half-time.

ENGLAND 50 WALES 10; at Twickenham; 23rd of March 2002

	England		Wales
15	Healey	15	Morgan. K
14	Luger [2 TRIES]	14	James
13	Greenwood [TRY]	13	Thomas. G
12	Tindall	12	Marinos
11	Cohen	11	Morgan. C
10	Wilkinson [TRY, 4 PENs, DG, 5 CONs]	10	Harris [TRY, PEN, CON]
9	Bracken	9	Howley
8	Hill	8	Quinnell (c)
7	Back (c)	7	Williams
6	Moody	6	Budgett
5	Kay	5	Wyatt
4	Grewcock	4	Moore
3	White	3	Anthony
2	Thompson	2	McBryde
1	Rowntree	1	Thomas. I

Comments: Tim Stimpson came on as a replacement and added a try as England won the Triple Crown in emphatic style, helped by Wilkinson's haul of thirty points.

SCOTLAND 10 FRANCE 22; at Murrayfield; 23rd of March 2002

	Scotland		France
15	Laney [PEN, CON]	15	Brusque
14	Metcalfe	14	Rougerie
13	McLaren	13	Marsh [2 TRIES]
12	Leslie. J	12	Traille
11	Paterson	11	Bory
10	Townsend	10	Merceron [PEN, 2 CONs]
9	Redpath (c) [TRY]	9	Galthie (c) [TRY]
8	Taylor	8	Harinordoquy
7	Pountney	7	Magne
6	Leslie. M	6	Betsen
5	White	5	Brouzet
4	Murray	4	Pelous
3	Stewart	3	Poux
2	Bulloch	2	Ibanez
1	Smith	1	Crenca

Comments: Tony Marsh contributed another pair of tries as France recorded their third consecutive win in Edinburgh and were now one step away from a Grand Slam.

FRANCE 44 IRELAND 5; at Stade de France; 6th of April 2002

15	Brusque [2 TRIES]	15	Dempsey
14	Rougerie [TRY]	14	Horgan
13	Marsh	13	O'Driscoll
12	Traille	12	Henderson
11	Bory	11	Hickie
10	Merceron [5 PENs, 2 CONs]	10	Humphreys
9	Galthie (c)	9	Stringer
8	Harinordoquy	8	Foley
7	Magne	7	Wallace
6	Betsen [2 TRIES]	6	Easterby
5	Brouzet	5	O'Kelly
4	Pelous	4	Longwell
3	de Villiers	3	Hayes
2	Ibanez	2	Wood (c) [TRY]
1	Crenca	1	Clohessy

Comments: Serge Betsen and Nicolas Brusque shared four tries in this non-contest. The hosts led 28-5 at the interval en route to another Grand Chelem.

WALES 22 SCOTLAND 27; at the Millennium Stadium; 6th of April 2002

15	Morgan. K	15	Laney [4 PENs, CON]
14	Williams. R [TRY]	14	Logan
13	Taylor	13	McLaren
12	Marinos	12	Leslie. J
11	Morgan. C	11	Paterson
10	Jones [5 PENs, CON]	10	Townsend
9	Howley	9	Redpath (c)
8	Charvis (c)	8	Taylor
7	Williams. M	7	Pountney
6	Budgett	6	Leslie. M
5	Moore	5	White
4	Gough	4	Murray
3	Anthony	3	Stewart
2	Williams. B	2	Bulloch [2 TRIES]
1	Thomas	1	Smith

Comments: Gordon Bulloch earned the rare accolade of a pair of tries from a hooker while the substitute Duncan Hodge added a penalty to ensure an away victory.

ITALY 9 ENGLAND 45; at Rome; 7th of April 2002

15	Peens		15	Robinson [TRY]
14	Mazzucato		14	Luger
13	Stoica		13	Greenwood [2 TRIES]
12	Raineri		12	Tindall
11	Dallan		11	Cohen [TRY]
10	Dominguez [3 PENs]		10	Wilkinson [PEN, 5 CONs]
9	Troncon		9	Bracken
8	Phillips		8	Hill
7	Bergamasco		7	Back (c)
6	Persico		6	Moody
5	Giacheri		5	Kay
4	Bortolami		4	Grewcock
3	Pucciarello		3	White
2	Moscardi (c)		2	Thompson
1	de Carli		1	Rowntree

Comments: The substitutes Dallaglio and Healey also scored tries. All England's 6 tries were converted, including 1 from the scrum-half replacement Matt Dawson.

2002 FINAL TABLE

		Points For	Points Against	Total Points
1ST	FRANCE	156	75	10
2ND	ENGLAND	184	53	8
3RD	IRELAND	145	138	6
4TH	SCOTLAND	91	128	4
5TH	WALES	119	188	2
6TH	ITALY	70	183	0

Comments: For the seventh successive year, England lost only one match. Their conquerors, France, won the Grand Slam.

2003

ITALY 30 WALES 22; at Rome; 15th of February 2003

15	Vaccari		15	Williams. R
14	Bergamasco		14	Jones
13	Stoica		13	Shanklin [TRY]
12	Raineri		12	Davies. L
11	Dallan		11	Thomas. G
10	Dominguez [PEN, 2 DGs, 3 CONs]		10	Harris [PEN, 2 CONs]
9	Troncon (c)		9	Peel [TRY]
8	Phillips [TRY]		8	Charvis (c)
7	Persico		7	Williams. M
6	de Rossi		6	Owen
5	Bortolami		5	Williams. S [TRY]
4	Bezzi		4	Sidoli
3	Martinez		3	Evans
2	Festuccia [TRY]		2	Davies. M
1	de Carli [TRY]		1	Thomas. I

Comments: The hosts recorded their first Six Nations win over Wales. Carlo Festuccia scored a try on his debut as both teams contributed three tries each.

ENGLAND 25 FRANCE 17; at Twickenham; 15th of February 2003

15	Robinson [TRY]		15	Poitrenaud [TRY]
14	Luger		14	Rougerie
13	Greenwood		13	Garbajosa
12	Hodgson		12	Traille [TRY]
11	Cohen		11	Clerc
10	Wilkinson [5 PENs, DG, CON]		10	Merceron [CON]
9	Gomersall		9	Galthie (c)
8	Hill		8	Harinordoquy
7	Back		7	Magne [TRY]
6	Moody		6	Betsen
5	Kay		5	Pelous
4	Johnson (c)		4	Brouzet
3	White		3	Califano
2	Thompson		2	Ibanez
1	Leonard		1	Crenca

Comments: The reigning champions outscored England three tries to one but they succumbed to the superior goalkicking of Jonny Wilkinson.

SCOTLAND 6 IRELAND 36; at Murrayfield; 16th of February 2003

15	Metcalfe		15	Dempsey
14	Logan		14	Horgan
13	Craig		13	O'Driscoll (c)
12	Laney		12	Maggs
11	Paterson		11	Hickie [TRY]
10	Ross [2 PENs]		10	Humphreys [TRY, 5 PENs, 3 CONs]
9	Redpath (c)		9	Stringer
8	Taylor		8	Foley
7	Mower		7	Gleeson
6	Leslie		6	Costello
5	Grimes		5	O'Kelly
4	Murray		4	Longwell
3	Douglas		3	Hayes
2	Bulloch		2	Byrne
1	Smith		1	Corrigan

Comments: Ireland registered their first win in Edinburgh since 1985 with Humphreys accumulating 26 points and Murphy coming off the bench to register a try.

ITALY 13 IRELAND 37; at Rome; 22nd of February 2003

15	Vaccari		15	Murphy [TRY]
14	Bergamasco		14	Kelly [TRY]
13	Stoica		13	O'Driscoll (c) [TRY]
12	Raineri		12	Maggs
11	Dallan [TRY]		11	Hickie
10	Dominguez [PEN]		10	Humphreys [TRY, 2 PENs, 3 CONs]
9	Troncon (c)		9	Stringer [TRY]
8	Phillips		8	Foley
7	Persico		7	Gleeson
6	de Rossi		6	Costello
5	Bortolami		5	O'Kelly
4	Bezzi		4	Longwell
3	Martinez		3	Hayes
2	Festuccia		2	Byrne
1	de Carli		1	Clohessy

Comments: Humphreys could 'only' muster 17 points this time but Ireland still scored 5 tries. Ramiro Pez came on as a substitute and kicked 5 points for Italy.

WALES 9 ENGLAND 26; at the Millennium Stadium; 22nd of February 2003

15	Morgan		15	Robinson
14	Williams. R		14	Luger
13	Taylor		13	Greenwood [TRY]
12	Shanklin		12	Hodgson
11	Thomas. Gar		11	Cohen
10	Sweeney [3 PENs]		10	Wilkinson [2 PENs, 2 DGs, 2 CONs]
9	Cooper		9	Bracken
8	Thomas. Gav		8	Dallaglio
7	Williams. M		7	Back
6	Jones		6	Hill
5	Williams. S		5	Kay
4	Sidoli		4	Johnson (c)
3	Evans		3	Morris
2	Humphreys (c)		2	Thompson
1	Thomas. I		1	Rowntree

Comments: Both of England's tries came after the interval when they were restricted to a 9-6 lead. Joe Worsley came off the bench to record one of the 2 tries.

FRANCE 38 SCOTLAND 3; at Stade de France; 23rd of February 2003

15	Poitrenaud [TRY]		15	Metcalfe
14	Rougerie [TRY]		14	Paterson [PEN]
13	Garbajosa		13	Townsend
12	Traille [TRY]		12	Utterson
11	Clerc		11	Logan
10	Gelez [4 PENs, 3 CONs]		10	Laney
9	Galthie (c)		9	Redpath (c)
8	Harinordoquy		8	Taylor
7	Magne		7	Mower
6	Betsen		6	Leslie
5	Brouzet		5	Grimes
4	Pelous [TRY]		4	Murray
3	Marconnet		3	Douglas
2	Ibanez		2	Bulloch
1	Crenca		1	Smith

Comments: Les Bleus made light work of the Scottish challenge with a four-try display. Francois Gelez also chipped in with eighteen points from his goal kicks.

IRELAND 15 FRANCE 12; at Lansdowne Road; 8th of March 2003

15	Murphy [DG]		15	Poitrenaud
14	Kelly		14	Rougerie
13	O'Driscoll (c)		13	Garbajosa
12	Maggs		12	Traille
11	Hickie		11	Clerc
10	Humphreys [4 PENs]		10	Gelez [4 PENs]
9	Stringer		9	Yachvili
8	Foley		8	Harinordoquy
7	Gleeson		7	Magne
6	Costello		6	Betsen
5	O'Kelly		5	Brouzet
4	Longwell		4	Pelous (c)
3	Hayes		3	Marconnet
2	Byrne		2	Ibanez
1	Horan		1	Crenca

Comments: Leicester's Geordan Murphy chose an opportune time to land his only international drop goal as it proved the difference between the two teams.

SCOTLAND 30 WALES 22; at Murrayfield; 8th of March 2003

15	Metcalfe		15	Morgan
14	Paterson [TRY, 3 PENs, 3 CONs]		14	Williams. R [TRY]
13	McLaren		13	Taylor [TRY]
12	Utterson		12	Shanklin
11	Logan		11	Thomas. Gar
10	Townsend		10	Jones. S [PEN, 2 CONs]
9	Redpath (c)		9	Cooper [TRY]
8	Taylor [TRY]		8	Thomas. Gav
7	Mower		7	Williams. M (c)
6	White		6	Jones. D
5	Grimes		5	Williams. S
4	Murray		4	Sidoli
3	Douglas [TRY]		3	Evans
2	Bulloch		2	Williams. G
1	Smith		1	Thomas. I

Comments: Chris Paterson provided the home team with twenty points which condemned Wales to another defeat in what would be a woeful whitewash year for them.

ENGLAND 40 ITALY 5; at Twickenham; 9th of March 2003

15	Lewsey [2 TRIES]	15	Bergamasco [TRY]
14	Simpson-Daniel [TRY]	14	Mazzucato
13	Greenwood	13	Vaccari
12	Tindall [TRY]	12	Raineri
11	Luger [TRY]	11	Dallan
10	Wilkinson (c) [4 CONs]	10	Pez
9	Dawson [CON]	9	Troncon (c)
8	Dallaglio	8	Phillips
7	Hill	7	Persico
6	Worsley	6	de Rossi
5	Kay	5	Giacheri
4	Grewcock	4	Bezzi
3	Morris	3	Martinez
2	Thompson [TRY]	2	Festuccia
1	Rowntree	1	de Carli

Comments: This match was over by half-time with the rampant English leading 33-0. Josh Lewsey grabbed a couple of tries in this comfortable victory.

WALES 24 IRELAND 25; at the Millennium Stadium; 22nd of March 2003

15	Williams. R	15	Murphy
14	Jones. M	14	Bishop
13	Taylor	13	O'Driscoll (c)
12	Shanklin	12	Maggs
11	Thomas. G [TRY]	11	Hickie
10	Jones. S [TRY, DG, 3 CONs]	10	Humphreys [4 PENs]
9	Cooper	9	Stringer
8	Jones. D	8	Foley
7	Williams. M [TRY]	7	Gleeson [2 TRIES]
6	Charvis	6	Quinlan
5	Llewellyn	5	O'Kelly
4	Sidoli	4	Cullen
3	Jenkins	3	Hayes
2	Humphreys (c)	2	Byrne
1	Thomas. I	1	Horan

Comments: Keith Gleeson scored two tries, but the drama came at the end when Ronan O'Gara came off the bench and slotted home a last-ditch drop goal.

ENGLAND 40 SCOTLAND 9; at Twickenham; 22nd of March 2003

	England		Scotland
15	Lewsey [TRY]	15	Metcalfe
14	Robinson [2 TRIES]	14	Paterson [3 PENs]
13	Greenwood	13	McLaren
12	Tindall	12	Craig
11	Cohen [TRY]	11	Logan
10	Wilkinson [4 PENs, 3 CONs]	10	Townsend
9	Dawson	9	Redpath (c)
8	Dallaglio	8	Taylor
7	Back	7	Mower
6	Hill	6	White
5	Kay	5	Hines
4	Johnson (c)	4	Murray
3	Leonard	3	Douglas
2	Thompson	2	Bulloch
1	Rowntree	1	Smith

Comments: Lethal England converted all four of their tries, two of which came from Jason Robinson. Paul Grayson came on as a substitute and added a conversion.

ITALY 27 FRANCE 53; at Rome; 23rd of March 2003

	Italy		France
15	Bergamasco [TRY]	15	Poitrenaud
14	Mazzucato	14	Rougerie [2 TRIES]
13	Vaccari	13	Casteignede [TRY]
12	Raineri	12	Traille [2 TRIES]
11	Dallan	11	Garbajosa
10	Pez [TRY, PEN, 2 CONs]	10	Michalak [TRY]
9	Troncon (c)	9	Yashvili [2 PENs, 6 CONs]
8	Phillips [TRY]	8	Harinordoquy
7	Persico [TRY]	7	Magne
6	de Rossi	6	Betsen [TRY]
5	Giacheri	5	Brouzet
4	Bezzi	4	Pelous (c)
3	Martinez	3	Marconnet
2	Festuccia	2	Ibanez
1	Lo Cicero	1	Crenca

Comments: Italy scored four tries and still lost heavily. Aurelien Rougerie and Damien Traille each helped themselves to a pair of tries.

FRANCE 33 WALES 5; at Stade de France; 29th of March 2003

15	Poitrenaud		15	Williams. R
14	Rougerie		14	Morgan
13	Castaignede [TRY]		13	Taylor
12	Traille		12	Harris
11	Garbajosa		11	Thomas. G [TRY]
10	Michalak [TRY]		10	Jones. S
9	Yachvili [4 PENs, 3 CONs]		9	Peel
8	Harinordoquy		8	Jones. D
7	Magne		7	Williams. M (c)
6	Betsen		6	Charvis
5	Brouzet		5	Llewellyn
4	Pelous (c)		4	Sidoli
3	Marconnet		3	Jenkins
2	Ibanez		2	Davies
1	Crenca		1	Thomas. I

Comments: Dimitri Yachvili kicked eighteen points in addition to the home team's three tries, one of which was scored by the flying replacement Vincent Clerc.

SCOTLAND 33 ITALY 25; at Murrayfield; 29th of March 2003

15	Metcalfe		15	Bergamasco [TRY]
14	Paterson [TRY, 3 PENs, 2 CONs]		14	Vaccari
13	McLaren [TRY]		13	Masi
12	Craig		12	Raineri
11	Logan [TRY]		11	Dallan
10	Townsend		10	Pez [TRY, 2 PENs, 2 CONs]
9	Redpath (c)		9	Troncon (c)
8	Taylor		8	Phillips
7	Mower		7	Persico
6	White [TRY]		6	de Rossi
5	Hines		5	Giacheri
4	Murray		4	Bezzi
3	Douglas		3	Martinez
2	Bulloch		2	Festuccia
1	Smith		1	Lo Cicero

Comments: Scott Palmer came on as a replacement and provided Italy with a try, but Paterson weighed in with 18 points for the hosts as Italy lost narrowly.

IRELAND 6 ENGLAND 42; at Lansdowne Road; 30th of March 2003

15	Murphy		15	Lewsey
14	Bishop		14	Robinson
13	O'Driscoll (c)		13	Greenwood [2 TRIES]
12	Maggs		12	Tindall [TRY]
11	Hickie		11	Cohen
10	Humphreys [PEN, DG]		10	Wilkinson [PEN, 2 DGs, 3 CONs]
9	Stringer		9	Dawson
8	Foley		8	Dallaglio [TRY]
7	Gleeson		7	Back
6	Costello		6	Hill
5	O'Kelly		5	Kay
4	Longwell		4	Johnson (c)
3	Hayes		3	Leonard
2	Byrne		2	Thompson
1	Horan		1	Rowntree

Comments: The substitutes Luger and Grayson added a try and conversion respectively as England ensured that they didn't fluff their Grand Slam lines this time.

2003 FINAL TABLE

		Points For	Points Against	Total Points
1ST	ENGLAND	173	46	10
2ND	IRELAND	119	97	8
3RD	FRANCE	153	75	6
4TH	SCOTLAND	81	161	4
5TH	ITALY	100	185	2
6TH	WALES	82	144	0

Comments: England won the Grand Slam at the eighth time of asking. The once-mighty Wales lost all five of their matches.

2004

FRANCE 35 IRELAND 17; at Stade de France; 14th of February 2004

15	Brusque	15	Dempsey
14	Clerc [TRY]	14	Horgan
13	Jauzion [TRY]	13	D'Arcy
12	Traille	12	Maggs
11	Dominic	11	Howe [TRY]
10	Michalak [3 PENs, 3 CONs]	10	O'Gara [PEN, 2 CONs]
9	Elissalde [TRY]	9	Stringer
8	Harinordoquy	8	Foley [TRY]
7	Magne	7	Gleeson
6	Betsen	6	Easterby
5	Pape [TRY]	5	O'Connell (c)
4	Pelous (c)	4	O'Kelly
3	de Villiers	3	Hayes
2	Servat	2	Byrne
1	Marconnet	1	Corrigan

Comments: It wasn't quite the St. Valentine's Day massacre, but a try from debutant Pascal Pape helped France to another routine home win over the Irish.

WALES 23 SCOTLAND 10; at the Millennium Stadium; 14th of February 2004

15	Thomas	15	Hinshelwood
14	Williams. R [2 TRIES]	14	Danielli
13	Parker	13	Philip
12	Harris	12	Laney
11	Williams. S	11	Henderson
10	Jones. S [2 PENs, CON]	10	Paterson (c) [DG, CON]
9	Cooper	9	Cusiter
8	Jones. D	8	Taylor [TRY]
7	Williams. M	7	Hogg
6	Charvis (c)	6	Mather
5	Llewellyn	5	Grimes
4	Cockbain	4	Murray
3	Rhys Jones [TRY]	3	Douglas
2	Davies	2	Bulloch
1	Jones. A	1	Smith

Comments: The Welsh returned to winning ways after seven successive Six Nations defeats. The Scots may have been confused by all the Williamses and Joneses!

ITALY 9 ENGLAND 50; at Rome; 15th of February 2004

15	Masi	15	Balshaw [TRY]
14	Mazzucato	14	Lewsey [TRY]
13	Stoica	13	Greenwood
12	Dallan. M	12	Robinson [3 TRIES]
11	Dallan. D	11	Cohen
10	Wakarua [2 PENs, DG]	10	Grayson [TRY, 3 PENs, 3 CONs]
9	Griffen	9	Gomersall
8	Parisse	8	Dallaglio (c)
7	Persico	7	Hill
6	de Rossi (c)	6	Worsley
5	Bortolami	5	Kay
4	Dellape	4	Grewcock
3	Castrogiovanni	3	Vickery
2	Ongaro	2	Thompson
1	Lo Cicero	1	Woodman

Comments: Chris Jones came off the bench to add to the tries feast, but the headlines were made by Jason Robinson's hat-trick of tries for the world champions.

FRANCE 25 ITALY 0; at Stade de France; 21st of February 2004

15	Brusque	15	de Marigny
14	Clerc	14	Bergamasco
13	Jauzion	13	Stoica
12	Traille [PEN]	12	Barbini
11	Dominici	11	Dallan
10	Petrelongue	10	Wakarua
9	Elissalde [PEN, 2 CONs]	9	Griffen
8	Harinordoquy [2 TRIES]	8	Parisse
7	Magne	7	Persico
6	Betsen	6	de Rossi (c)
5	Pape	5	Bortolami
4	Pelous (c)	4	Dellape
3	de Villiers	3	Castrogiovanni
2	Servat	2	Ongaro
1	Marconnet	1	Lo Cicero

Comments: Elhorga came on as a substitute and his try added to Harinordoquy's double. This was the first Six Nations match in which Italy failed to score.

SCOTLAND 13 ENGLAND 35; at Murrayfield; 21st of February 2004

15	Hinshelwood		15	Balshaw [TRY]
14	Danielli [TRY]		14	Lewsey [TRY]
13	Philip		13	Greenwood
12	Laney		12	Robinson
11	Webster		11	Cohen [TRY]
10	Paterson (c) [2 PENs, CON]		10	Grayson [3 PENs, 3 CONs]
9	Cusiter		9	Gomersall
8	Taylor		8	Dallaglio (c)
7	Mather		7	Hill
6	White		6	Jones
5	Grimes		5	Kay
4	Murray		4	Grewcock [TRY]
3	Douglas		3	Vickery
2	Bulloch		2	Thompson
1	Smith		1	Woodman

Comments: This was England's ninth successive victory in the Six Nations, but the wheels would soon come off their golden age of European and world domination.

IRELAND 36 WALES 15; at Lansdowne Road; 22nd of February 2004

15	Dempsey		15	Thomas. G
14	Horgan		14	Williams. R
13	O'Driscoll (c) [2 TRIES]		13	Parker
12	D'Arcy		12	Harris
11	Howe		11	Williams. S
10	O'Gara [TRY, 3 CONs]		10	Jones. S [PEN, CON]
9	Stringer		9	Cooper
8	Foley [TRY]		8	Jones. D
7	Gleeson		7	Williams. M (c)
6	Easterby		6	Thomas. J
5	O'Connell		5	Sidoli
4	O'Callaghan		4	Cockbain
3	Hayes		3	Rhys Jones
2	Byrne [2 TRIES]		2	McBryde
1	Corrigan		1	Thomas. I

Comments: Substitute Tom Shanklin bagged a pair of tries, but Wales were soundly beaten with Shane Byrne and Brian O'Driscoll scoring try doubles for Ireland.

ITALY 20 SCOTLAND 14; at Rome; 6th of March 2004

15	Canale		15	Hinshelwood
14	Mazzucato		14	Danielli
13	Stoica		13	Philip
12	Dallan. M		12	Laney
11	Dallan. D		11	Webster [TRY]
10	de Marigny [5 PENs]		10	Paterson (c) [3 PENs]
9	Griffen		9	Cusiter
8	Parisse		8	Taylor
7	Persico		7	Hogg
6	de Rossi (c)		6	White
5	Bortolami		5	Grimes
4	Dellape		4	Murray
3	Castrogiovanni		3	Douglas
2	Ongaro [TRY]		2	Bulloch
1	Lo Cicero		1	Jacobsen

Comments: This match was tied 9-9 at the halfway stage, but Fabio Ongaro's second half try and 2 more penalties from Roland de Marigny ensured a rare home win.

ENGLAND 13 IRELAND 19; at Twickenham; 6th of March 2004

15	Balshaw		15	Dempsey [TRY]
14	Lewsey		14	Horgan
13	Greenwood		13	O'Driscoll (c)
12	Robinson		12	D'Arcy
11	Cohen		11	Howe
10	Grayson [2 PENs, CON]		10	O'Gara [4 PENs, CON]
9	Dawson [TRY]		9	Stringer
8	Dallaglio (c)		8	Foley
7	Hill		7	Gleeson
6	Worsley		6	Easterby
5	Kay		5	O'Connell
4	Borthwick		4	O'Kelly
3	Vickery		3	Hayes
2	Thompson		2	Byrne
1	Woodman		1	Corrigan

Comments: England's run of fourteen successive home wins in the Five/Six Nations was ended. Girvan Dempsey grabbed the crucial try for the visitors.

WALES 22 FRANCE 29; at the Millennium Stadium; 7th of March 2004

15	Thomas. G	15	Brusque
14	Williams. R	14	Clerc
13	Taylor	13	Jauzion
12	Harris	12	Traille
11	Williams. S	11	Dominici
10	Jones. S [5 PENs, CON]	10	Michalak
9	Cooper	9	Elissalde [TRY, 5 PENs, 2 CONs]
8	Jones. D	8	Lievremont
7	Charvis (c)	7	Harinordoquy [TRY]
6	Thomas. J	6	Betsen
5	Owen	5	Pape
4	Cockbain	4	Pelous (c)
3	Jenkins	3	de Villiers
2	Davies	2	Servat
1	Thomas. I	1	Marconnet

Comments: Martyn Williams came off the bench to grab a try for Wales, but Jean-Baptiste Elissalde dominated the proceedings with his haul of 24 points.

IRELAND 19 ITALY 3; at Lansdowne Road; 20th of March 2004

15	Dempsey	15	Canale
14	Horgan [TRY]	14	Mazzucato
13	O'Driscoll (c) [TRY]	13	Stoica
12	D'Arcy	12	Barbini
11	Murphy	11	Dallan
10	O'Gara [2 CONs]	10	de Marigny [PEN]
9	Stringer	9	Griffen
8	Foley	8	Palmer
7	Gleeson	7	Persico
6	Easterby	6	de Rossi (c)
5	O'Callaghan	5	Bortolami
4	O'Kelly [TRY]	4	Checchinato
3	Hayes	3	Castrogiovanni
2	Byrne	2	Ongaro
1	Corrigan	1	Lo Cicero

Comments: This was another predictable home win for Ireland over Italy. Malcolm O'Kelly's try was the only thing that was not predicted in the final reckoning.

ENGLAND 31 WALES 21; at Twickenham; 20th of March 2004

15	Robinson		15	Thomas. G [TRY]
14	Lewsey		14	Williams. R
13	Greenwood		13	Taylor [TRY]
12	Tindall		12	Shanklin
11	Cohen [2 TRIES]		11	Williams. S
10	Barkley [4 PENs, 2 CONs]		10	Jones. S [3 PENs, CON]
9	Dawson		9	Cooper
8	Dallaglio (c)		8	Jones. Da
7	Hill		7	Charvis (c)
6	Jones		6	Thomas. J
5	Kay		5	Owen
4	Grewcock		4	Cockbain
3	Vickery		3	Jenkins
2	Thompson		2	McBryde
1	Woodman		1	Jones. Du

Comments: Ben Cohen's 2 tries were the difference between the two teams. England were also grateful to Joe Worsley who came on as a replacement and added a try.

SCOTLAND 0 FRANCE 31; at Murrayfield; 21st of March 2004

15	Lee		15	Brusque
14	Danielli		14	Elhorga
13	Philip		13	Jauzion [2 TRIES]
12	Henderson		12	Traille
11	Webster		11	Dominici
10	Paterson (c)		10	Michalak
9	Cusiter		9	Elissalde [4 PENs, 2 CONs]
8	Taylor		8	Lievremont
7	Mather		7	Magne [TRY]
6	White		6	Betsen
5	Grimes		5	Pape
4	Murray		4	Pelous (c)
3	Douglas		3	de Villiers
2	Bulloch		2	Servat
1	Jacobsen		1	Marconnet

Comments: Yannick Jauzion crossed the try-line twice as a humiliated Scotland failed to score at home in the Five/Six Nations for the first time since 1978.

WALES 44 ITALY 10; at the Millennium Stadium; 27th of March 2004

15	Thomas. G [TRY]	15	Canale
14	Williams. R [2 TRIES]	14	Mazzucato
13	Taylor	13	Masi [TRY]
12	Harris	12	Stoica
11	Williams. S [2 TRIES]	11	Dallan
10	Jones. S [2 PENs, 4 CONs]	10	de Marigny [PEN]
9	Cooper	9	Griffen
8	Jones. Da	8	de Rossi (c)
7	Williams. M	7	Persico
6	Charvis (c)	6	Bortolami
5	Owen	5	dal Fava
4	Llewellyn	4	Dellape
3	Jenkins	3	Castrogiovanni
2	McBryde	2	Ongaro
1	Jones. Du	1	Lo Cicero

Comments: Wales finished their campaign with 6 tries. Shanklin and Waharua scored a try and a conversion respectively for their teams, having been on the bench.

IRELAND 37 SCOTLAND 16; at Lansdowne Road; 27th of March 2004

15	Dempsey	15	Paterson (c) [2 PENs, CON]
14	Horgan	14	Danielli
13	O'Driscoll (c)	13	Philip
12	D'Arcy [2 TRIES]	12	Henderson
11	Murphy [TRY]	11	Webster
10	O'Gara [2 PENs, 3 CONs]	10	Parks [DG]
9	Stringer [TRY]	9	Cusiter
8	Foley	8	Taylor
7	Wallace [TRY]	7	Hogg [TRY]
6	Easterby	6	White
5	O'Connell	5	Grimes
4	O'Kelly	4	Murray
3	Hayes	3	Douglas
2	Byrne	2	Bulloch
1	Corrigan	1	Jacobsen

Comments: Gordon D'Arcy collected a couple of tries as Ireland won their first Triple Crown after a nineteen-year drought. Further success was on the horizon.

FRANCE 24 ENGLAND 21; at Stade de France; 28th of March 2004

15	Brusque	15	Robinson
14	Elhorga	14	Lewsey [TRY]
13	Jauzion	13	Greenwood
12	Traille	12	Tindall
11	Dominici	11	Cohen [TRY]
10	Michalak	10	Barkley [3 PENs, CON]
9	Yachvili [TRY, 4 PENs, CON]	9	Dawson
8	Harinordoquy [TRY]	8	Dallaglio (c)
7	Magne	7	Hill
6	Betsen	6	Worsley
5	Pape	5	Kay
4	Pelous (c)	4	Grewcock
3	de Villiers	3	Vickery
2	Servat	2	Thompson
1	Marconnet	1	Woodman

Comments: France's two tries came in the first-half to give them a 21-3 lead, but England replied with two second-half tries, only to lose narrowly.

2004 FINAL TABLE

		Points For	Points Against	Total Points
1ST	FRANCE	144	60	10
2ND	IRELAND	128	82	8
3RD	ENGLAND	150	86	6
4TH	WALES	125	116	4
5TH	ITALY	42	152	2
6TH	SCOTLAND	53	146	0

Comments: Scotland went from Grand Slam in 1984 to 1 point in 1994 and whitewash in 2004. France took another Grand Slam.

2005

FRANCE 16 SCOTLAND 9; at Stade de France; 5th of February 2005

15	Elhorga		15	Paterson [3 PENs]
14	Rougerie		14	Danielli
13	Liebenberg		13	Craig
12	Traille [TRY]		12	Southwell
11	Dominici		11	Lamont
10	Delaigue [2 PENS, DG]		10	Parks
9	Mignoni		9	Cusiter
8	Tabacco		8	Hogg
7	Chabal		7	Petrie
6	Bonnaire		6	White
5	Thion		5	Murray
4	Pelous (c)		4	Grimes
3	de Villiers		3	Kerr
2	Servat		2	Bulloch (c)
1	Marconnet		1	Smith

Comments: Chris Paterson kicked Scotland into a 6-0 interval lead. However France fought back with a Traille try! This was converted by the substitute Michalak.

WALES 11 ENGLAND 9; at the Millennium Stadium; 5th of February 2005

15	Thomas (c)		15	Robinson (c)
14	Luscombe		14	Cueto
13	Shanklin		13	Tait
12	Henson [PEN]		12	Noon
11	Williams. S [TRY]		11	Lewsey
10	Jones. S [PEN]		10	Hodgson [3 PENs]
9	Peel		9	Dawson
8	Owen		8	Worsley
7	Williams. M		7	Hazell
6	Jones. D		6	Jones
5	Sidoli		5	Kay
4	Cockbain		4	Grewcock
3	Rhys Jones		3	White
2	Davies		2	Thompson
1	Jenkins		1	Rowntree

Comments: Gavin Henson landed a memorable long-range penalty as unfancied Wales recorded their first win over the next-door neighbours since 1999.

ITALY 17 IRELAND 28; at Rome; 6th of February 2005

15	de Marigny [3 PENs]		15	Murphy [TRY]
14	Bergamasco. Mi		14	Horgan
13	Canale		13	O'Driscoll (c)
12	Masi		12	D'Arcy
11	Nitoglia		11	Hickie [TRY]
10	Orquera [PEN]		10	O'Gara [3 PENs, 2 CONs]
9	Troncon		9	Stringer [TRY]
8	Parisse		8	Foley
7	Bergamasco. Ma		7	Leamy
6	Persico		6	Easterby
5	Bortolami (c)		5	O'Connell
4	Dellape		4	O'Kelly
3	Castrogiovanni [TRY]		3	Hayes
2	Ongaro		2	Byrne
1	Lo Cicero		1	Corrigan

Comments: Ireland recorded another win over Italy with three tries to one, but their rusty performance was less than had been expected of them.

ITALY 8 WALES 38; at Rome; 12th of February 2005

15	de Marigny [PEN]		15	Thomas. G (c)
14	Bergamasco. Mi		14	Luscombe
13	Possebon		13	Shanklin [TRY]
12	Masi		12	Henson
11	Nitoglia		11	Williams. S [TRY]
10	Orquera [TRY]		10	Jones [4 CONs]
9	Troncon		9	Peel
8	Parisse		8	Owen
7	Persico		7	Williams. M [TRY]
6	Bergamasco. Ma		6	Thomas. J [TRY]
5	Bortolami (c)		5	Sidoli [TRY]
4	Dellape		4	Cockbain [TRY]
3	Castrogiovanni		3	Rhys Jones
2	Ongaro		2	Davies
1	Lo Cicero		1	Jenkins

Comments: Both Martyn Williams and the elusive Shane Williams were amongst the try-scorers as Wales registered nineteen points in each half of this triumph.

SCOTLAND 13 IRELAND 40; at Murrayfield; 12th of February 2005

15	Paterson [PEN]		15	Murphy
14	Danielli		14	Horgan
13	Craig		13	D'Arcy
12	Southwell [TRY]		12	Maggs
11	Lamont		11	Hickie [TRY]
10	Parks		10	O'Gara [3 PENs, 2 CONs]
9	Cusiter		9	Stringer
8	Taylor		8	Foley
7	Petrie [TRY]		7	O'Connor
6	White		6	Easterby
5	Murray		5	O'Connell (c) [TRY]
4	Grimes		4	O'Kelly [TRY]
3	Kerr		3	Hayes [TRY]
2	Bulloch (c)		2	Byrne
1	Smith		1	Corrigan

Comments: This was Scotland's seventh successive defeat in the Six Nations. Duffy and Humphreys came off the bench and added a try and conversion respectively.

ENGLAND 17 FRANCE 18; at Twickenham; 13th of February 2005

15	Robinson (c)		15	Elhorga
14	Cueto		14	Marlu
13	Noon		13	Liebenberg
12	Barkley [TRY]		12	Traille
11	Lewsey [TRY]		11	Dominici
10	Hodgson [PEN, 2 CONs]		10	Delaigue
9	Ellis		9	Yachvili [6 PENs]
8	Corry		8	Bonnaire
7	Moody		7	Chabal
6	Worsley		6	Betsen
5	Kay		5	Thion
4	Grewcock		4	Pelous (c)
3	Vickery		3	Mas
2	Thompson		2	Bruno
1	Rowntree		1	Marconnet

Comments: This was England's fourth defeat in their last five matches in the Six Nations. Their goalkicking let them down as Yachvili showed them how it's done.

SCOTLAND 18 ITALY 10; at Murrayfield; 26th of February 2005

15	Paterson [6 PENs]	15	de Marigny [PEN, CON]
14	Webster	14	Bergamasco
13	Craig	13	Masi [TRY]
12	Southwell	12	Stoica
11	Lamont	11	Nitoglia
10	Parks	10	Onquera
9	Cusiter	9	Troncon
8	Taylor	8	Parisse
7	Hogg	7	Dal Maso
6	Petrie	6	Persico
5	Murray	5	Bortolami (c)
4	Grimes	4	Dellape
3	Kerr	3	Castrogiovanni
2	Bulloch (c)	2	Ongaro
1	Smith	1	Lo Cicero

Comments: The Scots were grateful to the accurate goal kicks of Paterson for finally securing a win. Defeated Italy at least managed to cross the try-line.

FRANCE 18 WALES 24; at Stade de France; 26th of February 2005

15	Laharrague	15	Thomas (c)
14	Rougerie [TRY]	14	Morgan
13	Jauzion	13	Shanklin
12	Traille	12	Henson
11	Dominici	11	Williams. S
10	Delaigue	10	Jones. S [3 PENs, DG, CON]
9	Yachvili [TRY, PEN, CON]	9	Peel
8	Bonnaire	8	Owen
7	Nyanga	7	Williams. M [2 TRIES]
6	Betsen	6	Jones. R
5	Thion	5	Sidoli
4	Pelous (c)	4	Cockbain
3	Mas	3	Rhys Jones
2	Bruno	2	Davies
1	Marconnet	1	Jenkins

Comments: France deservedly led 15-6 at half-time. Thereafter Wales fought back for a famous victory. Michalak came off the bench to add a penalty for France.

IRELAND 19 ENGLAND 13; at Lansdowne Road; 27th of February 2005

15	Murphy		15	Robinson (c)
14	Dempsey		14	Cueto
13	O'Driscoll (c) [TRY]		13	Noon
12	Horgan		12	Barkley
11	Hickie		11	Lewsey
10	O'Gara [2 PENs, 2 DGs, CON]		10	Hodgson [PEN, DG, CON]
9	Stringer		9	Ellis
8	Foley		8	Corry [TRY]
7	O'Connor		7	Moody
6	Easterby		6	Worsley
5	O'Connell		5	Kay
4	O'Kelly		4	Grewcock
3	Hayes		3	Stevens
2	Byrne		2	Thompson
1	Corrigan		1	Rowntree

Comments: Remarkably England were staring now at a potential whitewash. A combination of O'Gara's accurate kicks and O'Driscoll's try helped to seal a home win.

IRELAND 19 FRANCE 26; at Lansdowne Road; 12th of March 2005

15	Murphy		15	Laharrague
14	Dempsey		14	Heymans
13	O'Driscoll (c) [TRY]		13	Jauzion
12	Maggs		12	Baby [TRY]
11	Hickie		11	Dominici [2 TRIES]
10	O'Gara [4 PENs, CON]		10	Michalak [DG]
9	Stringer		9	Yachvili [2 PENs, CON]
8	Foley		8	Bonnaire
7	O'Connor		7	Nyanga
6	Easterby		6	Betsen
5	O'Connell		5	Thion
4	O'Kelly		4	Pelous (c)
3	Hayes		3	Mas
2	Byrne		2	Bruno
1	Corrigan		1	Marconnet

Comments: Benoit Baby scored a try on his debut while Christophe Dominici weighed in with two others to wreck Ireland's Grand Slam ambitions.

ENGLAND 39 ITALY 7; at Twickenham; 12th of March 2005

	England			Italy
15	Balshaw [TRY]		15	Peens [CON]
14	Cueto [3 TRIES]		14	Pedrazzi
13	Noon		13	Masi
12	Barkley		12	Barbini
11	Lewsey		11	Nitoglia
10	Hodgson [PEN, 2 CONs]		10	Orquera
9	Ellis		9	Troncon [TRY]
8	Corry (c)		8	Parisse
7	Moody		7	Dal Maso
6	Worsley		6	Persico
5	Kay		5	Bortolami (c)
4	Grewcock		4	del Fava
3	Stevens		3	Perugini
2	Thompson [TRY]		2	Ongaro
1	Rowntree		1	Lo Cicero

Comments: Cueto's hat-trick comprised half of England's tries. Goode came off the bench to add a conversion while fellow substitute Andy Hazell added a try.

SCOTLAND 22 WALES 46; at Murrayfield; 13th of March 2005

	Scotland			Wales
15	Paterson [TRY, PEN, 2 CONs]		15	Morgan [2 TRIES]
14	Lamont. R [TRY]		14	Williams. R [2 TRIES]
13	Craig [TRY]		13	Shanklin
12	Southwell		12	Henson
11	Lamont. S		11	Williams. S [TRY]
10	Parks		10	Jones. S [2 PENs, 5 CONs]
9	Cusiter		9	Peel
8	Hogg		8	Owen (c)
7	Petrie		7	Williams. M
6	Taylor		6	Jones. R [TRY]
5	Murray		5	Sidoli
4	Grimes		4	Cockbain
3	Kerr		3	Rhys Jones
2	Bulloch (c)		2	Davies
1	Smith		1	Jenkins

Comments: The home team produced three second-half tries, but Wales had already delivered five tries in a first-half exhibition of mouthwatering running rugby.

ITALY 13 FRANCE 56; at Rome; 19th of March 2005

15	Peens [2 PENs, CON]	15	Laharrague [TRY]
14	Robertson [TRY]	14	Heymans
13	Masi	13	Jauzion [TRY]
12	Picone	12	Marty [2 TRIES]
11	Nitoglia	11	Dominici
10	Orquera	10	Delaigue
9	Troncon	9	Yachvili [3 PENs, 4 CONs]
8	Parisse	8	Bonnaire
7	Dal Maso	7	Nyanga [TRY]
6	Persico	6	Betsen
5	Bortolami (c)	5	Thion
4	Dellape	4	Pelous (c)
3	Perugini	3	Mas
2	Ongaro	2	Bruno
1	Lo Cicero	1	Marconnet

Comments: David Marty registered 2 tries on his debut for France. The substitutes Lamboley and Mignoni also bagged a try each while Michalak kicked four points.

WALES 32 IRELAND 20; at the Millennium Stadium; 19th of March 2005

15	Morgan [TRY]	15	Murphy [TRY]
14	Taylor	14	Dempsey
13	Shanklin	13	O'Driscoll (c)
12	Henson [PEN, DG]	12	Maggs
11	Williams. S	11	Hickie
10	Jones. S [4 PENs, 2 CONs]	10	O'Gara [2 PENs]
9	Peel	9	Stringer
8	Owen (c)	8	Foley
7	Williams. M	7	O'Connor
6	Jones. R	6	Easterby
5	Sidoli	5	O'Connell
4	Cockbain	4	O'Kelly
3	Rhys Jones	3	Hayes
2	Davies	2	Byrne
1	Jenkins [TRY]	1	Corrigan

Comments: Wales scored 16 points in each half to clinch the Grand Slam. Horan came off the bench to add a try for Ireland and Humphreys kicked two conversions.

ENGLAND 43 SCOTLAND 22; at Twickenham; 19th of March 2005

	England		Scotland
15	Balshaw	15	Paterson [PEN, 2 CONs]
14	Cueto [TRY]	14	Lamont. R
13	Noon [3 TRIES]	13	Craig [TRY]
12	Barkley	12	Southwell
11	Lewsey [TRY]	11	Lamont. S [TRY]
10	Hodgson [4 CONs]	10	Ross
9	Ellis [TRY]	9	Blair
8	Corry (c)	8	Taylor [TRY]
7	Moody	7	Hogg
6	Worsley [TRY]	6	White
5	Kay	5	Murray
4	Grewcock	4	Hines
3	Bell	3	Kerr
2	Thompson	2	Bulloch (c)
1	Stevens	1	Smith

Comments: Jamie Noon contributed a hat-trick of tries in this ten-tries Calcutta Cup extravaganza between two teams who were merely tournament also-rans.

2005 FINAL TABLE

		Points For	Points Against	Total Points
1ST	WALES	151	77	10
2ND	FRANCE	134	82	8
3RD	IRELAND	126	101	6
4TH	ENGLAND	121	77	4
5TH	SCOTLAND	84	155	2
6TH	ITALY	55	179	0

Comments: Whilst the World Champions slipped backwards, Wales emerged from nowhere to relive the glories of the 'seventies.

2006

IRELAND 26 ITALY 16; at Lansdowne Road; 4th of February 2006

15	Murphy	15	Stoica
14	Horgan	14	Canavosio
13	O'Driscoll (c)	13	Canale
12	D'Arcy	12	Bergamasco. Mi [TRY]
11	Bowe [TRY]	11	Nitoglia
10	O'Gara [4 PENs, 2 CONs]	10	Pez [2 PENs, CON]
9	Stringer	9	Griffen [PEN]
8	Leamy	8	Parisse
7	Wallace	7	Bergamasco. Ma
6	Easterby	6	Sole
5	O'Connell	5	Bortolami (c)
4	O'Kelly	4	Dellape
3	Hayes	3	Nieto
2	Flannery [TRY]	2	Ongaro
1	Horan	1	Perugini

Comments: Italy held Ireland 10-10 at the the halfway stage, but the hosts just about managed to get over the finishing line for two tournament points.

ENGLAND 47 WALES 13; at Twickenham; 4th of February 2006

15	Lewsey	15	Thomas (c)
14	Cueto [TRY]	14	Jones. M
13	Noon	13	Luscombe
12	Tindall [TRY]	12	Watkins
11	Cohen	11	Williams. S
10	Hodgson [3 PENs, 2 CONs]	10	Jones. S [2 PENs, CON]
9	Ellis	9	Peel
8	Corry (c)	8	Owen
7	Moody [TRY]	7	Williams. M [TRY]
6	Worsley	6	Charvis
5	Grewcock	5	Sidoli
4	Borthwick	4	Gough
3	Stevens	3	Rhys Jones
2	Thompson	2	Rhys Thomas
1	Sheridan	1	Jones. D

Comments: Dallaglio, Dawson, and Voyce all emerged from the bench to contribute tries to this thrashing while fellow substitute Andy Goode kicked 2 conversions.

SCOTLAND 20 FRANCE 16; at Murrayfield; 5th of February 2006

15	Southwell		15	Brusque
14	Paterson [2 PENs, 2 CONs]		14	Heymans
13	Di Rollo		13	Fritz
12	Henderson		12	Valbon
11	Lamont [2 TRIES]		11	Dominici
10	Parks		10	Michalak
9	Blair		9	Elissalde [2 PENs]
8	Taylor		8	Bonnaire [TRY]
7	Hogg		7	Martin
6	White (c)		6	Nyanga
5	Murray		5	Thion
4	Kellock		4	Pelous (c)
3	Douglas		3	de Villiers
2	Hall		2	Szarzewski
1	Kerr		1	Marconnet

Comments: Bruno, France's replacement hooker, scored a try, but a try in each half from Lamont helped Scotland record their first win against France since 1999.

FRANCE 43 IRELAND 31; at Stade de France; 11th of February 2006

15	Dominici		15	Murphy
14	Rougerie [TRY]		14	Horgan
13	Fritz		13	O'Driscoll (c)
12	Marty [2 TRIES]		12	D'Arcy [TRY]
11	Heymans [2 TRIES]		11	Bowe
10	Michalak		10	O'Gara [TRY, PEN, 4 CONs]
9	Elissalde [PEN, 5 CONs]		9	Stringer
8	Bonnaire		8	Leamy
7	Magne [TRY]		7	Wallace
6	Nyanga		6	Easterby
5	Thion		5	O'Connell
4	Pelous (c)		4	O'Kelly
3	de Villiers		3	Hayes
2	Ibanez		2	Flannery
1	Milloud		1	Corrigan

Comments: The hosts were out of sight thanks to try doubles for Heymans and Marty before substitutes O'Callaghan and Trimble scored tries in an Irish revival.

ITALY 16 ENGLAND 31; at Rome; 11th of February 2006

15	Stoica		15	Voyce
14	Canavosio		14	Cueto [TRY]
13	Canale		13	Noon
12	Bergamasco. Mi [TRY]		12	Tindall [TRY]
11	Nitoglia		11	Cohen
10	Pez [PEN, 2 DGs, CON]		10	Hodgson [TRY, PEN, 4 CONs]
9	Griffen		9	Ellis
8	Parisse		8	Corry (c)
7	Bergamasco. Ma		7	Moody
6	Sole		6	Worsley
5	Bortolami (c)		5	Grewcock
4	Dellape		4	Borthwick
3	Nieto		3	Stevens
2	Ongaro		2	Thompson
1	Perugini		1	Sheridan

Comments: Again Italy's challenge evaporated after the interval when they only trailed 7-6. The substitute Simpson-Daniel contributed a try to England's cause.

WALES 28* SCOTLAND 18; at the Millennium Stadium; 12th of February 2006

15	Thomas [2 TRIES]		15	Southwell [TRY]
14	Jones. M		14	Paterson [TRY, 2 PENs, CON]
13	Luscombe		13	MacDougall
12	Watkins		12	Henderson
11	Williams. S		11	Lamont
10	Jones. S [4 CONs]		10	Parks
9	Peel		9	Blair
8	Owen		8	Taylor
7	Williams. M		7	Hogg
6	Charvis (c)		6	White (c)
5	Sidoli [TRY]		5	Murray [SENT OFF]
4	Gough		4	Kellock
3	Rhys Jones		3	Douglas
2	Rhys Thomas		2	Lawson
1	Jones. D		1	Kerr

Comments: Played under a covered roof, this match will be remembered for a pair of tries for Gareth Thomas and for Scott Murray's sending-off for the visitors.

*Wales's points included a penalty try.

FRANCE 37 ITALY 12; at Stade de France; 25th of February 2006

15	Castaignede	15	Stoica
14	Rougerie [TRY]	14	Canavosio
13	Fritz	13	Canale
12	Traille	12	Bergamasco. Mi
11	Dominici	11	Nitoglia
10	Michalak [TRY]	10	Pez [3 PENs, DG]
9	Elissalde [PEN]	9	Griffen
8	Lievremont [TRY]	8	Parisse
7	Magne	7	Bergamasco. Ma
6	Nyanga [TRY]	6	Sole
5	Thion	5	Bortolami (c)
4	Pelous (c)	4	del Fava
3	de Villiers [TRY]	3	Nieto
2	Ibanez	2	Ongaro
1	Milloud	1	Perugini

Comments: Italy led 12-8 at half-time but again they wilted in the second half. Yachvili came on as a replacement and kicked a penalty and 3 conversions.

SCOTLAND 18 ENGLAND 12; at Murrayfield; 25th of February 2006

15	Southwell	15	Lewsey
14	Paterson [5 PENs]	14	Cueto
13	Di Rollo	13	Noon
12	Henderson	12	Tindall
11	Lamont	11	Cohen
10	Parks [DG]	10	Hodgson [4 PENs]
9	Blair	9	Ellis
8	Taylor	8	Corry (c)
7	Hogg	7	Moody
6	White (c)	6	Worsley
5	Kellock	5	Grewcock
4	MacLeod	4	Borthwick
3	Douglas	3	White
2	Hall	2	Thompson
1	Kerr	1	Sheridan

Comments: This try-less Calcutta Cup encounter was dominated by the accurate boot of Chris Paterson. Dan Parks also weighed in with an important drop goal.

IRELAND 31 WALES 5; at Lansdowne Road; 26th of February 2006

15	Murphy		15	Byrne
14	Horgan [TRY]		14	Jones. M [TRY]
13	O'Driscoll (c)		13	Luscombe
12	D'Arcy		12	Watkins
11	Trimble		11	James
10	O'Gara [4 PENs, 2 CONs]		10	Jones. S
9	Stringer [TRY]		9	Peel
8	Leamy		8	Owen (c)
7	Wallace [TRY]		7	Williams
6	Easterby		6	Charvis
5	O'Kelly		5	Sidoli
4	O'Callaghan		4	Gough
3	Hayes		3	Rhys Jones
2	Flannery		2	Rhys Thomas
1	Horan		1	Jones. D

Comments: For the second successive home match, Ronan O'Gara kicked sixteen points. This issue was decided by two second-half tries by the hosts.

WALES 18 ITALY 18; at the Millenium Stadium; 11th of March 2006

15	Byrne		15	Galon [TRY]
14	Jones. M [TRY]		14	Canavosio [TRY]
13	Luscombe		13	Canale
12	Watkins		12	Bergamasco
11	Williams. S		11	Nitoglia
10	Jones. S [TRY, 2 PENs, CON]		10	Pez [2 PENs, CON]
9	Peel		9	Griffen
8	Owen (c)		8	Sole
7	Williams. M		7	Zaffiri
6	Charvis		6	Parisse
5	Sidoli		5	Bortolami (c)
4	Gough		4	Dellape
3	Rhys Jones		3	Nieto
2	Rhys Thomas		2	Festuccia
1	Jones. D		1	Perugini

Comments: The Italians managed to keep up with the Joneses (all 4 of them) as they drew 15-15 at the interval and at full-time they won a share of the points.

IRELAND 15 SCOTLAND 9; at Lansdowne Road; 11th of March 2006

15	Murphy		15	Southwell
14	Horgan		14	Paterson [3 PENs]
13	O'Driscoll (c)		13	Di Rollo
12	D'Arcy		12	Henderson
11	Trimble		11	Lamont
10	O'Gara [5 PENs]		10	Parks
9	Stringer		9	Blair
8	Leamy		8	Taylor
7	Wallace		7	Hogg
6	Easterby		6	White (c)
5	O'Connell		5	Murray
4	O'Kelly		4	Hines
3	Hayes		3	Douglas
2	Flannery		2	Hall
1	Horan		1	Kerr

Comments: In this dour struggle, Scotland lost a try-less encounter by six points, two weeks after having won a try-less contest by the same margin.

FRANCE 31 ENGLAND 6; at Stade de France; 12th of March 2006

15	Castaignede		15	Lewsey
14	Rougerie		14	Cueto
13	Fritz [TRY]		13	Noon
12	Traille [TRY]		12	Tindall
11	Dominici [TRY]		11	Cohen
10	Michalak		10	Hodgson [PEN]
9	Yachvili [4 PENs, 2 CONs]		9	Dawson
8	Lievremont		8	Corry (c)
7	Magne		7	Moody
6	Nyanga		6	Worsley
5	Thion		5	Grewcock
4	Pelous (c)		4	Borthwick
3	de Villiers		3	White
2	Ibanez		2	Thompson
1	Marconnet		1	Stevens

Comments: Dimitri Yachvili added to France's three tries with sixteen points. Andy Goode added a penalty for England, having been a substitute in this defeat.

ITALY 10 SCOTLAND 13; at Rome; 18th of March 2006

15	Stoica		15	Southwell
14	Canavosio		14	Paterson [TRY, PEN, CON]
13	Canale		13	Di Rollo
12	Bergamasco [TRY]		12	Henderson
11	Nitoglia		11	Lamont
10	Pez [PEN, CON]		10	Ross [DG]
9	Griffen		9	Cusiter
8	Sole		8	Taylor
7	Zaffiri		7	Hogg
6	Parisse		6	White (c)
5	Bortolami (c)		5	Murray
4	Dellape		4	Hines
3	Castrogiovanni		3	Douglas
2	Ongaro		2	Hall
1	Perugini		1	Kerr

Comments: Mirco Bergamasco added to his tries against Ireland and England, but Paterson scored one of his own in the first-half as he rescued Scotland again.

WALES 16 FRANCE 21; at the Millennium Stadium; 18th of March 2006

15	Byrne		15	Castaignede
14	James		14	Rougerie
13	Luscombe [TRY]		13	Fritz [TRY]
12	Watkins		12	Traille
11	Williams. S		11	Dominici
10	Jones. S [2 PENs, CON]		10	Michalak
9	Phillips		9	Yachvili [2 PENs]
8	Popham		8	Lievremont
7	Williams. M		7	Bonnaire
6	Owen (c)		6	Nyanga
5	Sidoli		5	Thion
4	Gough		4	Pelous (c)
3	Rhys Jones		3	de Villiers
2	Rhys Thomas		2	Ibanez
1	Jones. D		1	Marconnet

Comments: Henson came off the bench to hit a penalty, but France were assisted by a try from Szarzewski and five points kicked by Elissalde, another substitute.

ENGLAND 24 IRELAND 28; at Twickenham; 18th of March 2006

15	Voyce	15	Murphy
14	Cueto	14	Horgan [2 TRIES]
13	Noon [TRY]	13	O'Driscoll (c)
12	Abbott	12	D'Arcy
11	Cohen	11	Trimble
10	Goode	10	O'Gara [3 PENs, 2 CONs]
9	Ellis [4 PENs, CON]	9	Stringer
8	Corry (c)	8	Leamy [TRY]
7	Moody	7	Wallace
6	Worsley	6	Easterby
5	Shaw	5	O'Connell
4	Borthwick [TRY]	4	O'Kelly
3	White	3	Hayes
2	Mears	2	Flannery
1	Sheridan	1	Horan

Comments: Jamie Noon scored a try in the opening seconds and Shane Horgan crossed the try-line in the dying seconds as Ireland pulled off an amazing victory.

2006 FINAL TABLE

		Points For	Points Against	Total Points
1ST	FRANCE	148	85	8
2ND	IRELAND	131	97	8
3RD	SCOTLAND	78	81	6
4TH	ENGLAND	120	106	4
5TH	WALES	80	135	3
6TH	ITALY	72	125	1

Comments: Ireland grabbed their second Triple Crown in three years, but France pipped them to the Championship first spot.

2007

ITALY 3 FRANCE 39; at Rome; 3rd of February 2007

15	de Marigny	15	Poitrenaud
14	Dallan	14	Heymans [TRY]
13	Canale	13	Jauzion [TRY]
12	Bergamasco. Mi	12	Fritz
11	Masi	11	Dominici [TRY]
10	Scanavacca	10	Skrela [PEN, 4 CONs]
9	Griffen	9	Mignoni
8	Parisse	8	Chabal [2 TRIES]
7	Bergamasco. Ma	7	Bonnaire
6	Sole	6	Betsen
5	Bortolami (c)	5	Thion
4	Dellape	4	Nallet
3	Nieto	3	de Villiers
2	Ongaro	2	Ibanez (c)
1	Perugini	1	Milloud

Comments: The bearded wonder Sebastien Chabal bagged a couple of tries while the substitutes Pez and Beauxis kicked a penalty for Italy and France respectively.

ENGLAND 42 SCOTLAND 20; at Twickenham; 3rd of February 2007

15	Morgan	15	Southwell
14	Lewsey	14	Lamont
13	Tindall	13	di Rollo
12	Farrell	12	Henderson
11	Robinson [2 TRIES]	11	Paterson (c) [2 PENs, 2 CONs]
10	Wilkinson [TRY, 5 PENs, DG, 2 CONs]	10	Parks
9	Ellis	9	Cusiter
8	Corry	8	Callam
7	Lund [TRY]	7	Brown
6	Worsley	6	Taylor [TRY]
5	Grewcock	5	Kellock
4	Deacon	4	Hamilton
3	Vickery (c)	3	Murray
2	Chuter	2	Hall
1	Freshwater	1	Kerr

Comments: A returning Wilkinson savaged Scotland with 27 points while Jason Robinson ran in 2 tries. Rob Dewey came off the bench to grab a consolation try.

WALES 9 IRELAND 19; at the Millennium Stadium; 4th of February 2007

15	Morgan	15	Dempsey
14	Luscombe	14	Trimble
13	Robinson	13	O'Driscoll (c) [TRY]
12	Hook	12	D'Arcy
11	Czekaj	11	Hickie
10	Jones. S (c) [3 PENs]	10	O'Gara [TRY, 2 CONs]
9	Peel	9	Stringer
8	Jones. R	8	Leamy
7	Williams	7	Wallace
6	Popham	6	Easterby
5	Wyn Jones	5	O'Connell
4	Gough	4	O'Callaghan
3	Horsman	3	Hayes
2	Rhys Thomas	2	Best [TRY]
1	Jenkins	1	Horan

Comments: Wales dominated much of this match but a clinical Ireland still crossed the try-line 3 times. The hosts had to rely on Stephen Jones to kick 9 points.

ENGLAND 20 ITALY 7; at Twickenham; 10th of February 2007

15	Balshaw	15	de Marigny
14	Lewsey	14	Robertson
13	Tindall	13	Canale
12	Farrell	12	Bergamasco
11	Robinson [TRY]	11	Dallan
10	Wilkinson [5 PENs]	10	Scanavacca [TRY, CON]
9	Ellis	9	Troncon
8	Corry	8	Parisse
7	Lund	7	Zaffiri
6	Easter	6	Sole
5	Grewcock	5	Bortolami (c)
4	Deacon	4	Dellape
3	Vickery (c)	3	Castrogiovanni
2	Chuter	2	Festuccia
1	Freshwater	1	Lo Cicero

Comments: Jason Robinson scored a first-half try but England were much less convincing than they had been a week ago. Jonny Wilkinson kicked the other points.

SCOTLAND 21 WALES 9; at Murrayfield; 10th of February 2007

15	Southwell		15	Morgan
14	Lamont		14	Jones. M
13	Di Rollo		13	Robinson
12	Dewey		12	Hook
11	Paterson (c) [7 PENs]		11	Czekaj
10	Godman		10	Jones. S (c) [3 PENs]
9	Cusiter		9	Peel
8	Callam		8	Jones. R
7	Brown		7	Williams
6	Taylor		6	Popham
5	Murray. S		5	Wyn Jones
4	Hamilton		4	Sidoli
3	Murray. E		3	Rhys Jones
2	Hall		2	Rhys Thomas
1	Kerr		1	Jones. D

Comments: Chris Paterson outscored Stephen Jones 3 penalties to 2 in the first-half and then 4 penalties to 1 in the second-half of this try-less engagement.

IRELAND 17 FRANCE 20; at Croke Park; 11th of February 2007

15	Dempsey		15	Poitrenaud
14	Murphy		14	Clerc [TRY]
13	D'Arcy		13	Marty
12	Horgan		12	Jauzion
11	Hickie		11	Dominici
10	O'Gara [TRY, 4 PENs]		10	Skrela [2 PENs, CON]
9	Boss		9	Mignoni
8	Leamy		8	Chabal
7	Wallace		7	Harinordoquy
6	Easterby		6	Betsen
5	O'Connell (c)		5	Pape
4	O'Callaghan		4	Nallet
3	Hayes		3	de Villiers
2	Best		2	Ibanez (c) [TRY]
1	Horan		1	Marconnet

Comments: Ireland conceded a late try to Clerc, converted by the substitute Beauxis as France won the first rugby match at the GAA's mecca of Croke Park.

SCOTLAND 17 ITALY 37; at Murrayfield; 24th of February 2007

15	Southwell	15	de Marigny
14	Lamont	14	Robertson [TRY]
13	Di Rollo	13	Canale
12	Dewey [TRY]	12	Bergamasco. Mi
11	Paterson (c) [TRY, PEN, 2 CONs]	11	Masi
10	Godman	10	Scanavacca [TRY, 3 PENs, 4 CONs]
9	Cusiter	9	Troncon [TRY]
8	Callam	8	Parisse
7	Brown	7	Bergamasco. Ma [TRY]
6	Taylor	6	Zanni
5	Murray. S	5	Bortolami (c)
4	Hines	4	Dellape
3	Murray. E	3	Castrogiovanni
2	Hall	2	Festuccia
1	Kerr	1	Lo Cicero

Comments: 22 points from Andrea Scanavacca helped Italy to their first away success in the Six Nations at the twentieth time of asking.

IRELAND 43 ENGLAND 13; at Croke Park; 24th of February 2007

15	Dempsey [TRY]	15	Morgan
14	Horgan [TRY]	14	Lewsey
13	O'Driscoll (c)	13	Tindall
12	D'Arcy	12	Farrell
11	Hickie	11	Strettle [TRY]
10	O'Gara [5 PENs, 3 CONs]	10	Wilkinson [2 PENs, CON]
9	Stringer	9	Ellis
8	Leamy	8	Corry
7	Wallace [TRY]	7	Lund
6	Easterby	6	Worsley
5	O'Connell	5	Grewcock
4	O'Callaghan	4	Deacon
3	Hayes	3	Vickery (c)
2	Best	2	Chuter
1	Horan	1	Freshwater

Comments: Ronan O'Gara kicked 21 points in this humbling of the once-mighty England while the Ulster replacements Boss and Wallace added a try and conversion.

FRANCE 32 WALES 21; at Stade de France; 24th of February 2007

15	Poitrenaud		15	Byrne
14	Clerc		14	Jones. M
13	Marty		13	Shanklin [TRY]
12	Jauzion		12	Hook
11	Dominici [TRY]		11	Williams. S
10	Skrela [5 PENs, 2 CONs]		10	Jones. S (c) [3 CONs]
9	Mignoni		9	Peel
8	Vermeulen		8	Jones. R
7	Bonnaire		7	Williams. M
6	Betsen		6	Popham [TRY]
5	Thion		5	Wyn Jones
4	Nallet [TRY]		4	Gough
3	Mas		3	Horsman
2	Ibanez (c)		2	Rees
1	Milloud		1	Jenkins

Comments: Wales won 3-2 on tries in this evening match but Skrela hit 19 points. The substitutes Robinson and Beauxis scored a try and penalty for their teams.

SCOTLAND 18 IRELAND 19; at Murrayfield; 10th of March 2007

15	Southwell		15	Dempsey
14	Lamont		14	Horgan
13	Di Rollo		13	O'Driscoll (c)
12	Dewey		12	D'Arcy
11	Paterson (c) [6 PENs]		11	Hickie
10	Parks		10	O'Gara [TRY, 4 PENs, CON]
9	Cusiter		9	Stringer
8	Callam		8	Leamy
7	Brown		7	Wallace
6	Taylor		6	Easterby
5	Murray. S		5	O'Connell
4	Hines		4	O'Callaghan
3	Murray. E		3	Hayes
2	Hall		2	Best. R
1	Kerr		1	Best. S

Comments: Chris Paterson amassed 18 points but Ronan O'Gara went one better, as the consistent Irish won the Triple Crown for the third time in four seasons.

ITALY 23 WALES 20; at Rome; 10th of March 2007

	ITALY			WALES
15	de Marigny		15	Morgan
14	Robertson [TRY]		14	Jones. M
13	Canale		13	Shanklin
12	Bergamasco. Mi		12	Hook [2 PENs, CON]
11	Pratichetti		11	Williams. S [TRY]
10	Pez [3 PENs, 2 CONs]		10	Jones. S (c) [CON]
9	Troncon		9	Peel
8	Parisse		8	Jones. R
7	Bergamasco. Ma [TRY]		7	Williams. M
6	Zanni		6	Popham
5	Bortolami (c)		5	Wyn Jones
4	Dellape		4	Gough
3	Nieto		3	Horsman
2	Festuccia		2	Rees [TRY]
1	Lo Cicero		1	Jenkins

Comments: Wales may have shared in the four tries but they joined Scotland in their embarrassment at losing to the Six Nations novices of Italy.

ENGLAND 26 FRANCE 18; at Twickenham; 11th of March 2007

	ENGLAND			FRANCE
15	Lewsey		15	Poitrenaud
14	Strettle		14	Clerc
13	Tindall [TRY]		13	Marty
12	Catt (c)		12	Jauzion
11	Robinson		11	Dominici
10	Flood [TRY, 3 PENs, CON]		10	Skrela [3 PENs]
9	Ellis		9	Yachvili [3 PENs]
8	Easter		8	Chabal
7	Rees		7	Bonnaire
6	Worsley		6	Betsen
5	Palmer		5	Thion
4	Corry		4	Nallet
3	White		3	de Villiers
2	Chuter		2	Ibanez (c)
1	Payne		1	Milloud

Comments: England came from behind with the aid of 16 points from Toby Flood. Shane Geraghty came off the bench to hit a penalty and a conversion for the hosts.

ITALY 24 IRELAND 51; at Rome; 17th of March 2007

	Italy		Ireland
15	de Marigny [TRY]	15	Dempsey [2 TRIES]
14	Robertson	14	Horgan [TRY]
13	Galon	13	O'Driscoll. B (c)
12	Bergamasco	12	D'Arcy [TRY]
11	Pratichetti	11	Hickie [2 TRIES]
10	Pez [2 PENs, 2 DGs]	10	O'Gara [TRY, PEN, 4 CONs]
9	Troncon	9	Stringer
8	Parisse	8	Leamy
7	Zaffiri	7	Wallace
6	Zanni	6	Easterby [TRY]
5	Bortolami (c) [TRY]	5	O'Driscoll. M
4	Dellape	4	O'Callaghan
3	Nieto	3	Hayes
2	Festuccia	2	Best
1	Perugini	1	Horan

Comments: Ireland finally got to play on St. Patrick's Day and they celebrated with 8 tries. Scanavacca came off the bench to add a late conversion for Italy.

FRANCE 46 SCOTLAND 19; at Stade de France; 17th of March 2007

	France		Scotland
15	Poitrenaud	15	Paterson (c) [2 CONs]
14	Clerc	14	Lamont [TRY]
13	Marty [TRY]	13	Dewey
12	Jauzion [TRY]	12	Henderson
11	Heymans [TRY]	11	Walker [TRY]
10	Beauxis [2 PENs, 5 CONs]	10	Parks
9	Mignoni	9	Lawson
8	Harinordoquy [TRY]	8	Beattie
7	Bonnaire	7	Hogg
6	Betsen	6	Taylor
5	Thion	5	Murray. S
4	Nallet	4	Hines
3	de Villiers	3	Murray. E [TRY]
2	Ibanez (c)	2	Ford
1	Milloud [TRY]	1	Kerr

Comments: Although Scotland managed 3 tries, the French scored twice as many, with the substitute Elvis Vermeulen scoring a Championship-winning try at the end.

WALES 27 ENGLAND 18; at the Millennium Stadium; 17th of March 2007

15	Morgan	15	Cueto
14	Jones. M	14	Strettle
13	Shanklin	13	Tait
12	Thomas (c)	12	Catt (c)
11	Williams. S	11	Robinson [TRY]
10	Hook [TRY, 4 PENs, DG, CON]	10	Flood [PEN, DG, CON]
9	Peel	9	Ellis [TRY]
8	Jones. R	8	Worsley
7	Williams. M	7	Rees
6	Popham	6	Haskell
5	Wyn Jones	5	Palmer
4	Gough	4	Corry
3	Horsman [TRY]	3	White
2	Rees	2	Chuter
1	Jenkins	1	Payne

Comments: James Hook spared Wales a whitewash humiliation with a 22-points performance. This was England's fourth successive away defeat in the Six Nations.

2007 FINAL TABLE

		Points For	Points Against	Total Points
1ST	FRANCE	155	86	8
2ND	IRELAND	149	84	8
3RD	ENGLAND	119	115	6
4TH	ITALY	94	147	4
5TH	WALES	86	113	2
6TH	SCOTLAND	95	153	2

Comments: Italy scaled the new heights of two wins, while France fended off the Triple Crown-winning Irish for first place.

2008

IRELAND 16 ITALY 11; at Croke Park; 2nd of February 2008

15	Dempsey [TRY]	15	Bortolussi [2 PENs]
14	Trimble	14	Robertson
13	O'Driscoll (c)	13	Canale
12	D'Arcy	12	Bergamasco. Mi
11	Murphy	11	Canavosio
10	O'Gara [3 PENs, CON]	10	Masi (c)
9	Reddan	9	Travagli
8	Leamy	8	Parisse
7	Wallace	7	Bergamasco. Ma
6	Easterby	6	Sole
5	O'Kelly	5	del Fava
4	O'Callaghan	4	Dellape
3	Hayes	3	Castrogiovanni [TRY]
2	Best	2	Ghiraldini
1	Horan	1	Lo Cicero

Comments: Girvan Dempsey scored a first-half try but Ireland were still suffering a hangover from their poor World Cup. Italy narrowly failed to overcome them.

ENGLAND 19 WALES 26; at Twickenham; 2nd of February 2008

15	Balshaw	15	Byrne [TRY]
14	Sackey	14	Jones. M
13	Tindall	13	Parker
12	Flood [TRY]	12	Henson
11	Strettle	11	Williams. S
10	Wilkinson [3 PENs, DG, CON]	10	Hook [4 PENs, 2 CONs]
9	Gomersall	9	Phillips [TRY]
8	Narraway	8	Jones. R (c)
7	Moody	7	Williams. M
6	Haskell	6	Thomas
5	Shaw	5	Wyn Jones
4	Borthwick	4	Gough
3	Vickery (c)	3	Rhys Jones
2	Regan	2	Bennett
1	Sheridan	1	Jones. D

Comments: Wales recorded their first win at Twickenham since 1988 with two second-half tries which helped overturn the 16-6 interval deficit.

SCOTLAND 6 FRANCE 27; at Murrayfield; 3rd of February 2008

15	Lamont		15	Heymans
14	Walker		14	Clerc [2 TRIES]
13	de Luca		13	Marty
12	Henderson		12	Traille [2 PENs]
11	Webster		11	Malzieu [TRY]
10	Parks [PEN, DG]		10	Trinh-Duc
9	Blair		9	Elissalde [2 CONs]
8	Callam		8	Vermeulen
7	Barclay		7	Ouedraogo
6	White (c)		6	Dusautoir
5	Hamilton		5	Nallet (c)
4	Hines		4	Jacquet
3	Murray		3	Brugnaut
2	Ford		2	Servat
1	Jacobsen		1	Faure

Comments: Julien Malzieu scored a debut try in addition to a pair of tries from the pacey Vincent Clerc while David Skrela came off the bench to add 2 points.

WALES 30 SCOTLAND 15; at the Millennium Stadium; 9th of February 2008

15	Byrne		15	Southwell
14	Roberts		14	Walker
13	Shanklin		13	de Luca
12	Henson		12	Henderson
11	Williams. S [2 TRIES]		11	Paterson [5 PENs]
10	Hook [TRY, PEN, 2 CONs]		10	Parks
9	Phillips		9	Blair
8	Jones. R (c)		8	Brown
7	Williams. M		7	Barclay
6	Thomas		6	White (c)
5	Evans		5	Hamilton
4	Gough		4	Hines
3	Rhys Jones		3	Murray
2	Bennett		2	Ford
1	Jones. D		1	Jacobsen

Comments: Jamie Roberts made his debut as Wales won the try count three to nil. Stephen Jones came on as a substitute and landed two penalties and a conversion.

FRANCE 26 IRELAND 21*; at Stade de France; 9th of February 2008

15	Heymans [TRY]		15	Dempsey
14	Rougerie		14	Murphy
13	Marty		13	O'Driscoll (c)
12	Traille		12	Trimble
11	Clerc [3 TRIES]		11	Kearney
10	Skrela		10	O'Gara [3 PENs, CON]
9	Elissalde [3 CONs]		9	Reddan
8	Bonnaire		8	Heaslip
7	Ouedraogo		7	Wallace [TRY]
6	Dusautoir		6	Leamy
5	Mela		5	O'Kelly
4	Nallet (c)		4	O'Callaghan
3	Mas		3	Hayes
2	Szarzewski		2	Jackman
1	Faure		1	Horan

Comments: Vincent Clerc destroyed Ireland again with a hat-trick of tries, but again Ireland produced a late flourish when France made too many substitutions.

*Ireland's points included a penalty try.

ITALY 19 ENGLAND 23; at Rome; 10th of February 2008

15	Bortolussi [4 PENs, CON]		15	Balshaw
14	Robertson		14	Sackey [TRY]
13	Canale		13	Noon
12	Bergamasco. Mi		12	Flood [TRY]
11	Galon		11	Vainikolo
10	Masi		10	Wilkinson [3 PENs, 2 CONs]
9	Travagli		9	Gomersall
8	Parisse (c)		8	Easter
7	Bergamasco. Ma		7	Lipman
6	Sole		6	Haskell
5	del Fava		5	Borthwick (c)
4	Dellape		4	Shaw
3	Castrogiovanni		3	Stevens
2	Ghiraldini		2	Regan
1	Lo Cicero		1	Payne

Comments: The replacement Simon Picone scored his only international try in the second half as Italy came close to a victory, having trailed 20-6 at half-time.

WALES 47 ITALY 8; at the Millennium Stadium; 23rd of February 2008

15	Byrne [2 TRIES]		15	Marcato [PEN]
14	Jones. M		14	Sgarbi
13	Shanklin [TRY]		13	Canale
12	Henson		12	Bergamasco. Mi
11	Williams. S [2 TRIES]		11	Galon
10	Jones. S [4 PENs, 3 CONs]		10	Masi
9	Peel		9	Picone
8	Jones. R (c)		8	Parisse (c)
7	Williams. M		7	Bergamasco. Ma
6	Thomas. J		6	Sole
5	Evans		5	del Fava
4	Gough		4	Dellape
3	Thomas. R		3	Castrogiovanni [TRY]
2	Rees		2	Ghiraldini
1	Jenkins		1	Perugini

Comments: Martin Castrogiovanni scored his second try of the campaign but Wales overwhelmed Italy in the second half. Hook came off the bench to kick 4 points.

IRELAND 34 SCOTLAND 13; at Croke Park; 23rd of February 2008

15	Murphy		15	Southwell
14	Bowe [2 TRIES]		14	Lamont
13	O'Driscoll. B (c)		13	Webster [TRY]
12	Trimble		12	Henderson
11	Kearney [TRY]		11	Walker
10	O'Gara [PEN, 3 CONs]		10	Paterson [2 PENs, CON]
9	Reddan		9	Blair (c)
8	Heaslip		8	Brown
7	Wallace [TRY]		7	Hogg
6	Leamy		6	Strokosch
5	O'Driscoll. M		5	MacLeod
4	O'Callaghan		4	Hines
3	Hayes		3	Murray
2	Jackman		2	Ford
1	Horan [TRY]		1	Jacobsen

Comments: Tommy Bowe crossed the try-line twice as Ireland kept alive their hopes of a Triple Crown. This was Scotland's sixth successive Six Nations defeat.

FRANCE 13 ENGLAND 24; at Stade de France; 23rd of February 2008

15	Heymans		15	Balshaw
14	Rougerie		14	Sackey [TRY]
13	Marty		13	Noon
12	Traille [CON]		12	Flood
11	Clerc		11	Vainikolo
10	Trinh-Duc		10	Wilkinson [3 PENs, DG, CON]
9	Parra [PEN]		9	Wigglesworth [TRY]
8	Picamoles		8	Easter
7	Dusautoir		7	Lipman
6	Bonnaire		6	Haskell
5	Nallet (c) [TRY]		5	Borthwick
4	Pape		4	Shaw
3	Mas		3	Vickery (c)
2	Szarzewski		2	Regan
1	Faure		1	Sheridan

Comments: England grabbed a try in each half to win away to France for the second time in 6 months. Yachvili came on as a French substitute and hit a penalty.

IRELAND 12 WALES 16; at Croke Park; 8th of March 2008

15	Kearney		15	Byrne
14	Horgan		14	Jones. M
13	O'Driscoll (c)		13	Shanklin
12	Trimble		12	Henson
11	Bowe		11	Williams. S [TRY]
10	O'Gara [4 PENs]		10	Jones. S [2 PENs, CON]
9	Reddan		9	Phillips
8	Heaslip		8	Jones. R (c)
7	Wallace		7	Williams. M
6	Leamy		6	Thomas
5	O'Connell		5	Wyn Jones
4	O'Callaghan		4	Gough
3	Hayes		3	Rhys Jones
2	Best		2	Rees
1	Horan		1	Jenkins

Comments: Shane Williams provided the only try of the match after the interval. James Hook came off the bench to kick a penalty as Wales won the Triple Crown.

SCOTLAND 15 ENGLAND 9; at Murrayfield; 8th of March 2008

	Scotland		England
15	Southwell	15	Balshaw
14	Lamont	14	Sackey
13	Webster	13	Noon
12	Morrison	12	Flood
11	Walker	11	Vainikolo
10	Paterson [4 PENs]	10	Wilkinson [3 PENs]
9	Blair (c)	9	Wigglesworth
8	Taylor	8	Easter
7	Hogg	7	Lipman
6	Strokosch	6	Croft
5	MacLeod	5	Borthwick
4	Hines	4	Shaw
3	Murray	3	Vickery (c)
2	Ford	2	Mears
1	Jacobsen	1	Sheridan

Comments: It was 2006 all over again as Chris Paterson kicked Scotland to victory with the help of a drop goal from the replacement Dan Parks.

FRANCE 25 ITALY 13; at Stade de France; 9th of March 2008

	France		Italy
15	Floch [TRY]	15	Marcato [2 PENs, CON]
14	Rougerie [TRY]	14	Robertson
13	David	13	Canale
12	Jauzion [TRY]	12	Bergamasco
11	Malzieu	11	Galon
10	Trinh-Duc	10	Masi
9	Yachvili [2 PENs, 2 CONs]	9	Picone
8	Picamoles	8	Parisse (c)
7	Diarra	7	Zanni
6	Ouedraogo	6	Sole
5	Thion	5	Bortolami
4	Nallet (c)	4	del Fava
3	Mas	3	Castrogiovanni [TRY]
2	Szarzewski	2	Ghiraldini
1	Barcella	1	Lo Cicero

Comments: Five players won their first French caps as France executed another routine win over Italy, though Martin Castrogiovanni scored another try.

ITALY 23* SCOTLAND 20; at Rome; 15th of March 2008

15	Marcato [2 PENs, DG, 2 CONs]		15	Southwell
14	Robertson		14	Danielli
13	Canale [TRY]		13	Webster
12	Bergamasco		12	Morrison
11	Galon		11	Paterson [PEN, 2 CONs]
10	Masi		10	Parks [PEN]
9	Picone		9	Blair (c) [TRY]
8	Parisse (c)		8	Taylor
7	Zanni		7	Hogg [TRY]
6	Sole		6	Strokosch
5	Bortolami		5	MacLeod
4	del Fava		4	Hines
3	Castrogiovanni		3	Murray
2	Ghiraldini		2	Thomson
1	Lo Cicero		1	Jacobsen

Comments: The Italians came back from 17-10 behind at the halfway stage to register back-to-back Six Nations wins against Scotland.

*Italy's points included a penalty try.

ENGLAND 33 IRELAND 10; at Twickenham; 15th of March 2008

15	Balshaw		15	Murphy
14	Sackey [TRY]		14	Bowe
13	Noon [TRY]		13	Trimble
12	Flood		12	Horgan
11	Vainikolo		11	Kearney [TRY]
10	Cipriani [4 PENs, 3 CONs]		10	O'Gara (c) [PEN, CON]
9	Wigglesworth		9	Reddan
8	Easter		8	Heaslip
7	Lipman		7	Wallace
6	Croft		6	Leamy
5	Borthwick		5	O'Connell
4	Shaw		4	O'Callaghan
3	Vickery (c)		3	Hayes
2	Mears		2	Best
1	Sheridan		1	Horan

Comments: Danny Cipriani ran the show as England ended an awful sequence of 4 matches without a win against Ireland. Tait came off the bench and added a try.

WALES 29 FRANCE 12; at the Millennium Stadium; 15th of March 2008

15	Byrne		15	Floch
14	Jones. M		14	Clerc
13	Shanklin		13	Jauzion
12	Henson		12	Traille
11	Williams. S [TRY]		11	Malzieu
10	Hook [3 PENs]		10	Skrela
9	Phillips		9	Elissalde [3 PENs]
8	Jones. R (c)		8	Bonnaire
7	Williams. M [TRY]		7	Ouedraogo
6	Thomas		6	Dusautoir
5	Wyn Jones		5	Thion
4	Gough		4	Nallet (c)
3	Rhys Jones		3	Mas
2	Bennett		2	Szarzewski
1	Jenkins		1	Barcella

Comments: Substitute Stephen Jones kicked 2 penalties and 2 conversions while Yachvili came off the bench to land a penalty as Wales cruised to the Grand Slam.

2008 FINAL TABLE

		Points For	Points Against	Total Points
1ST	WALES	148	66	10
2ND	ENGLAND	108	83	6
3RD	FRANCE	103	93	6
4TH	IRELAND	93	99	4
5TH	SCOTLAND	69	123	2
6TH	ITALY	74	131	2

Comments: Wales ran rings around everybody else for the second time in four seasons. Italy managed to beat Scotland again.

2009

ENGLAND 36 ITALY 11; at Twickenham; 7th of February 2009

15	Armitage. D	15	Masi
14	Sackey	14	Robertson
13	Noon	13	Canale
12	Flutey [TRY]	12	Garcia
11	Cueto [TRY]	11	Bergamasco. Mi [TRY]
10	Goode [TRY, PEN, 4 CONs]	10	Marcato
9	Ellis [2 TRIES]	9	Bergamasco. Ma
8	Easter	8	Parisse (c)
7	Armitage. S	7	Zanni
6	Haskell	6	Sole
5	Kennedy	5	Bortolami
4	Borthwick (c)	4	Dellape
3	Vickery	3	Castrogiovanni
2	Mears	2	Ongaro
1	Sheridan	1	Perugini

Comments: Andy Goode provided 16 points while Harry Ellis weighed in with a try in each half. Luke McLean came off the bench to kick two penalties for Italy.

IRELAND 30 FRANCE 21; at Croke Park; 7th of February 2009

15	Kearney	15	Poitrenaud
14	Bowe	14	Medard [TRY]
13	O'Driscoll (c) [TRY]	13	Fritz
12	Wallace. P	12	Jauzion
11	Fitzgerald	11	Malzieu
10	O'Gara [3 PENs, 3 CONs]	10	Beauxis [PEN, 2 DGs, CON]
9	O'Leary	9	Tillous-Bordes
8	Heaslip [TRY]	8	Harinordoquy [TRY]
7	Wallace. D	7	Ouedraogo
6	Ferris	6	Dusautoir
5	O'Connell	5	Chabal
4	O'Callaghan	4	Nallet (c)
3	Hayes	3	Lecouls
2	Flannery	2	Szarzewski
1	Horan	1	Faure

Comments: Jamie Heaslip and Brian O'Driscoll scored tries either side of half-time but it took a try from substitute Gordon D'Arcy to seal a superb home win.

SCOTLAND 13 WALES 26; at Murrayfield; 8th of February 2009

15	Southwell	15	Byrne
14	Webster	14	Halfpenny [TRY]
13	Cairns	13	Shanklin [TRY]
12	Morrison	12	Roberts
11	Lamont	11	Williams. S [TRY]
10	Godman	10	Jones. S [2 PENs]
9	Blair (c)	9	Phillips
8	Taylor	8	Powell
7	Barclay	7	Williams. M (c)
6	Hogg	6	Jones. D
5	Hamilton	5	Wyn Jones [TRY]
4	White	4	Gough
3	Cross	3	Rhys Jones
2	Ford	2	Rees
1	Jacobsen	1	Jenkins

Comments: The substitute Max Evans grabbed a late consolation try for the Scots while fellow substitute Chris Paterson kicked two penalties and a conversion.

FRANCE 22 SCOTLAND 13; at Stade de France; 14th of February 2009

15	Poitrenaud	15	Southwell
14	Medard	14	Danielli
13	Jauzion	13	Evans. M
12	Baby	12	Morrison
11	Heymans	11	Evans. T [TRY]
10	Beauxis [5 PENs, CON]	10	Godman [2 PENs]
9	Tillous-Bordes	9	Blair (c)
8	Harinordoquy	8	Taylor
7	Ouedraogo [TRY]	7	Barclay
6	Dusautoir	6	Strokosch
5	Millo-Chluski	5	Hamilton
4	Nallet (c)	4	White
3	Mas	3	Dickinson
2	Szarzewski	2	Ford
1	Barcella	1	Jacobsen

Comments: Beauxis registered 17 points and this time it was Thom Evans who crossed the try-line for a late consolation, converted by the substitute Paterson.

WALES 23 ENGLAND 15; at the Millennium Stadium; 14th of February 2009

15	Byrne		15	Armitage [TRY]
14	Halfpenny [TRY, PEN]		14	Sackey [TRY]
13	Shanklin		13	Tindall
12	Roberts		12	Flutey
11	Jones. M		11	Cueto
10	Jones. S [5 PENs]		10	Goode [DG]
9	Phillips		9	Ellis
8	Powell		8	Easter
7	Williams		7	Worsley
6	Jones. R (c)		6	Haskell
5	Wyn Jones		5	Kennedy
4	Gough		4	Borthwick (c)
3	Rhys Jones		3	Vickery
2	Rees		2	Mears
1	Jenkins		1	Sheridan

Comments: Sackey and Armitage recorded a try in each half, but Stephen Jones's 5 penalties proved decisive. Toby Flood came off the bench to kick a conversion.

ITALY 9 IRELAND 38; at Rome; 15th of February 2009

15	Masi		15	Kearney [CON]
14	Robertson		14	Bowe [TRY]
13	Canale		13	O'Driscoll (c) [TRY]
12	Bergamasco. Mi		12	Wallace. P
11	Pratichetti		11	Fitzgerald [2 TRIES]
10	McLean [3 PENs]		10	O'Gara [PEN, 4 CONs]
9	Griffen		9	O'Leary
8	Parisse (c)		8	Heaslip
7	Bergamasco. Ma		7	Wallace. D [TRY]
6	Zanni		6	Ferris
5	Reato		5	O'Connell
4	Dellape		4	O'Callaghan
3	Castrogiovanni		3	Hayes
2	Ongaro		2	Flannery
1	Perugini		1	Horan

Comments: Italy originally led 6-0 before Ireland got into their stride. The Irish were assisted by a pair of tries for Luke Fitzgerald as they earned 2 points.

FRANCE 21 WALES 16; at Stade de France; 27th of February 2009

15	Medard		15	Byrne [TRY]
14	Malzieu		14	Halfpenny
13	Bastareaud		13	Shanklin
12	Jauzion		12	Roberts
11	Heymans [TRY]		11	Williams. S
10	Baby		10	Jones. S [2 PENs, CON]
9	Parra [3 PENs, CON]		9	Phillips
8	Harinordoquy		8	Powell
7	Ouedraogo		7	Williams. M
6	Dusautoir [TRY]		6	Jones. R (c)
5	Chabal		5	Wyn Jones
4	Nallet (c)		4	Gough
3	Marconnet		3	Rhys Thomas
2	Szarzewski		2	Rees
1	Barcella		1	Jenkins

Comments: France hit back after trailing 13-3 with tries for Dusautoir and Heymans in this Friday night fixture. Hook came off the bench and kicked a penalty.

SCOTLAND 26 ITALY 6; at Murrayfield; 28th of February 2009

15	Southwell		15	Marcato
14	Danielli [TRY]		14	Bergamasco. Mi
13	Evans. M		13	Canale
12	Morrison		12	Garcia
11	Evans. T		11	Pratichetti
10	Godman [PEN, CON]		10	McLean [PEN]
9	Blair (c)		9	Griffen
8	Taylor		8	Parisse (c) [DG]
7	Barclay		7	Bergamasco. Ma
6	Strokosch		6	Zanni
5	Kellock		5	Bortolami
4	White		4	Dellape
3	Murray		3	Castrogiovanni
2	Ford		2	Ghiraldini
1	Jacobsen		1	Perugini

Comments: Simon Danielli and the replacement Scott Gray scored a try in each half, while Paterson emerged from the bench to kick 3 penalties and a conversion.

IRELAND 14 ENGLAND 13; at Croke Park; 28th of February 2009

15	Kearney		15	Armitage [TRY, PEN]
14	Bowe		14	Sackey
13	O'Driscoll (c) [TRY, DG]		13	Tindall
12	Wallace. P		12	Flutey
11	Fitzgerald		11	Cueto
10	O'Gara [2 PENs]		10	Flood [PEN]
9	O'Leary		9	Ellis
8	Heaslip		8	Easter
7	Wallace. D		7	Worsley
6	Ferris		6	Haskell
5	O'Connell		5	Kennedy
4	O'Callaghan		4	Borthwick (c)
3	Hayes		3	Vickery
2	Flannery		2	Mears
1	Horan		1	Sheridan

Comments: A late try for Delon Armitage converted by the substitute Andy Goode flattered England. Brian O'Driscoll scored eight crucial points for the Irish.

ITALY 15 WALES 20; at Rome; 14th of March 2009

15	Marcato [5 PENs]		15	Byrne
14	Rubini		14	Jones. M
13	Canale		13	Roberts
12	Bergamasco. Mi		12	Henson
11	Pratichetti		11	Williams. S [TRY]
10	McLean		10	Hook [2 PENs, 2 CONs]
9	Griffen		9	Phillips
8	Parisse (c)		8	Powell
7	Bergamasco. Ma		7	Jones. D
6	Zanni		6	Thomas. J
5	Bortolami		5	Wyn Jones (c)
4	Dellape		4	Charteris
3	Nieto		3	Thomas. R
2	Ghiraldini		2	Bennett
1	Perugini		1	Yapp

Comments: Andrea Marcato kicked Italy into a 15-13 lead, but a late converted try from the substitute Tom Shanklin spared Wales a second successive away defeat.

SCOTLAND 15 IRELAND 22; at Murrayfield; 14th of March 2009

15	Paterson [5 PENs]	15	Kearney
14	Danielli	14	Bowe
13	Evans. M	13	O'Driscoll (c)
12	Morrison	12	D'Arcy
11	Evans. T	11	Fitzgerald
10	Godman	10	O'Gara [4 PENs, DG, CON]
9	Blair (c)	9	Stringer
8	Taylor	8	Leamy
7	Barclay	7	Wallace
6	Strokosch	6	Ferris
5	Hamilton	5	O'Connell
4	White	4	O'Callaghan
3	Murray	3	Hayes
2	Ford	2	Best
1	Dickinson	1	Horan

Comments: Scotland led 12-6 shortly before the interval but they had no answer after the fleet-footed replacement Jamie Heaslip scored the decisive try.

ENGLAND 34 FRANCE 10; at Twickenham; 15th of March 2009

15	Armitage [TRY]	15	Medard
14	Cueto [TRY]	14	Malzieu [TRY]
13	Tindall	13	Bastareaud
12	Flutey [2 TRIES]	12	Jauzion
11	Monye	11	Heymans
10	Flood [PEN, 3 CONs]	10	Trinh-Duc
9	Ellis	9	Parra
8	Easter	8	Harinordoquy
7	Worsley [TRY]	7	Chabal
6	Croft	6	Dusautoir
5	Shaw	5	Thion
4	Borthwick (c)	4	Nallet (c)
3	Vickery	3	Marconnet
2	Mears	2	Szarzewski [TRY]
1	Sheridan	1	Faure

Comments: By the start of the second-half England had blown France away to the tune of 34-0. Riki Flutey had already grabbed a couple of tries in this rout.

ITALY 8 FRANCE 50; at Rome; 21st of March 2009

15	Marcato [PEN]		15	Traille
14	Rubini		14	Medard [2 TRIES]
13	Canale		13	Fritz
12	Bergamasco. Mi		12	Jauzion
11	Pratichetti		11	Heymans [TRY]
10	McLean		10	Trinh-Duc [TRY]
9	Griffen		9	Parra [3 PENs, 3 CONs]
8	Parisse (c) [TRY]		8	Harinordoquy
7	Bergamasco. Ma		7	Bonnaire
6	Zanni		6	Dusautoir
5	Bortolami		5	Chabal [TRY]
4	Dellape		4	Nallet (c)
3	Nieto		3	Marconnet
2	Ghiraldini		2	Szarzewski
1	Perugini		1	Barcella

Comments: Les Bleus signed off with a 7 tries to 1 demolition, scoring 25 points in each half. Domingo and Malzieu came off the bench to add two further tries.

ENGLAND 26 SCOTLAND 12; at Twickenham; 21st of March 2009

15	Armitage		15	Paterson [3 PENs]
14	Cueto		14	Danielli
13	Tindall		13	Evans. M
12	Flutey [TRY]		12	Morrison
11	Monye [TRY]		11	Evans. T
10	Flood [2 PENs, CON]		10	Godman [PEN]
9	Ellis		9	Blair (c)
8	Easter		8	Taylor
7	Worsley		7	Gray
6	Croft		6	Strokosch
5	Shaw		5	Hamilton
4	Borthwick (c)		4	White
3	Vickery		3	Murray
2	Mears		2	Ford
1	Sheridan		1	Dickinson

Comments: Monye and Flutey grabbed 2 first-half tries and this triumph was sealed with a late try from the substitute Tait and a drop goal from substitute Care.

WALES 15 IRELAND 17; at the Millennium Stadium; 21st of March 2009

15	Byrne	15	Kearney
14	Jones. M	14	Bowe [TRY]
13	Shanklin	13	O'Driscoll (c) [TRY]
12	Henson	12	D'Arcy
11	Williams. S	11	Fitzgerald
10	Jones. S [4 PENs, DG]	10	O'Gara [DG, 2 CONs]
9	Phillips	9	O'Leary
8	Jones. R (c)	8	Heaslip
7	Williams. M	7	Wallace
6	Jones. D	6	Ferris
5	Wyn Jones	5	O'Connell
4	Gough	4	O'Callaghan
3	Rhys Jones	3	Hayes
2	Rees	2	Flannery
1	Jenkins	1	Horan

Comments: Two tries in quick succession after the interval transformed this match, but it still took a late drop goal from O'Gara to ensure a narrow victory.

2009 FINAL TABLE

		Points For	Points Against	Total Points
1ST	IRELAND	121	73	10
2ND	ENGLAND	124	70	6
3RD	FRANCE	124	101	6
4TH	WALES	100	81	6
5TH	SCOTLAND	79	102	2
6TH	ITALY	49	170	0

Comments: After an abysmal 1990s, Ireland capped a fine decade of resurgence with a long-overdue Grand Slam.

1970: France and Wales share the Championship
1971: Wales (GRAND SLAM)
1972: The Championship was not completed
1973: All 5 countries shared the Championship
1974: Ireland (champions)
1975: Wales (champions)
1976: Wales (GRAND SLAM)
1977: France (GRAND SLAM); Wales (Triple Crown)
1978: Wales (GRAND SLAM)
1979: Wales (Triple Crown)
1980: England (GRAND SLAM)
1981: France (GRAND SLAM)
1982: Ireland (Triple Crown)
1983: France and Ireland share the Championship
1984: Scotland (GRAND SLAM)
1985: Ireland (Triple Crown)
1986: France and Scotland share the Championship
1987: France (GRAND SLAM)
1988: Wales (Triple Crown) share the Championship with France

1989: France (champions)
1990: Scotland (GRAND SLAM)
1991: England (GRAND SLAM)
1992: England (GRAND SLAM)
1993: France (champions)
1994: Wales (champions)
1995: England (GRAND SLAM)
1996: England (Triple Crown)
1997: France (GRAND SLAM); England (Triple Crown)
1998: France (GRAND SLAM); England (Triple Crown)
1999: Scotland (champions)
2000: England (champions)
2001: England (champions)
2002: France (GRAND SLAM); England (Triple Crown)
2003: England (GRAND SLAM)
2004: France (GRAND SLAM); Ireland (Triple Crown)
2005: Wales (GRAND SLAM)
2006: Ireland (Triple Crown)
2007: Ireland (Triple Crown)
2008: Wales (GRAND SLAM)
2009: Ireland (GRAND SLAM)

THE BOOK TRADE

If you are a publisher, you ought to be aware of the following standard, customised rejection letter that comprises the response from Gardners Books to any new title. To all would-be authors, when publishers promise you that your book will be available on Amazon and Waterstones, this means nothing. Unless your book is selected for stock by Britain's leading books wholesaler, you will NOT achieve substantial sales. Here follows verbatim their pathetic, standard customised rejection letter which is most probably issued to all self-publishers and small publishers. Welcome to the book trade, children!

Thank you for your letter recently received regarding the above title. Unfortunately, I am writing to confirm that, on this occasion, we have decided not to take it into stock. We are currently holding approximately 600,000 titles and we need to ensure that we are responding to our customers' demands when we consider taking on additional lines.

We do, however, have a team of Regional Account Managers who are in constant contact with our customers and if it becomes obvious that there is a clear requirement for your publication, we will contact you immediately.

In the meantime, we operate a Special Order Service whereby our customers can order any book in print from us, provided that the ISBN is listed on Nielsen Bookdata. Confirmed orders will be sent to the listed publisher via Nielsen Teleordering. Once ordered, the book will be added and listed on our stock file as being available. We monitor this activity very closely and if sales through this channel suggest that we should reconsider our decision then, again, we will be in contact, with you.

We wish you every success with your publication.
Yours sincerely
New Publishers Buying Team
Gardners Books Ltd.

Note the absence of anyone's name from Gardners to take responsibilty for the decision.

Note how flattering it is when they can stock 600,000 titles but not yours as well.

Note that Gardners' "customers" are book retailers. Unless there are advance orders for your book and you need to be a celebrity to achieve that, then there will be no "customers' demands".

WELCOME TO THE CELEBRITY-DRIVEN BOOK TRADE!!!!!

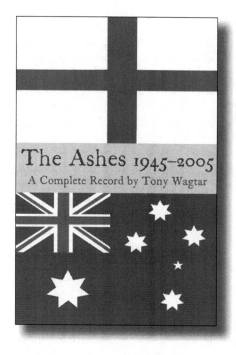

IF YOU FEEL THAT YOU HAVE A BOOK IN YOU AND YOU
WANT YOUR PROJECT TO BE TAKEN SERIOUSLY AND NOT
SIMPLY IGNORED BY THE CELEBRITY-CHASING MAINSTREAM
PUBLISHERS, THEN FEEL FREE TO SUBMIT A SAMPLE TO:
gw930@hotmail.co.uk

Any comments or complaints about this book can also be directed to this
same address!